Organizational Identity and Memory

Organizational Identity and Memory analyzes the relationship between organizational identity and organizational memory, in particular history and commemoration. The goal is to further our understanding of the role of this relationship in processes critical to today's organizations: the evolution of organizational identity, the creation and use of organizational memory, organizational learning and change, and employee identification with organizations.

The literature on organizational memory and organizational identity has developed independently and at times in separate disciplines. Scholars have debated whether organizational identity is mutable or enduring. In this debate, organizational history, a form of organizational memory, has been a key factor, but neither side of the debate has pursued in depth the well-developed multidisciplinary literature on collective memory to understand this relationship and its impact on organizational identity. Organizational memory defined as commemoration and history has been connected to different forms of identity, both national and organizational, but this relationship and its impact on organizational memory processes has received limited attention.

Organizational Identity and Memory takes a multidisciplinary approach to explore and articulate the dynamic relationship between organizational identity and memory, drawing on work from anthropology, history, organizational studies, and sociology. A multidisciplinary theoretical framework for future research on organizational identity and memory is presented. Implications for managers are discussed with engaging insights from organizational research and practices in creating corporate museums, galleries, visitor centers, and other displays of this relationship.

Andrea Casey is an Associate Professor of Human and Organizational Learning at The George Washington University Graduate School of Education & Human Development, USA.

Routledge Studies in Management, Organizations and Society

This series presents innovative work grounded in new realities, addressing issues crucial to an understanding of the contemporary world. This is the world of organized societies, where boundaries between formal and informal, public and private, local and global organizations have been displaced or have vanished, along with other 19th-century dichotomies and oppositions. Management, apart from becoming a specialized profession for a growing number of people, is an everyday activity for most members of modern societies.

Similarly, at the level of inquiry, culture and technology, as well as literature and economics, can no longer be conceived as isolated intellectual fields; conventional canons and established mainstreams are contested. **Management, Organizations and Society** addresses these contemporary dynamics of transformation in a manner that transcends disciplinary boundaries, with books that will appeal to researchers, students and practitioners alike.

For a full list of titles in this series, please visit www.routledge.com

Organizational Identity and Memory

A Multidisciplinary Approach

Andrea Casey

Routledge
Taylor & Francis Group

LONDON AND NEW YORK

First published 2019 by Routledge

2 Park Square, Milton Park, Abingdon, Oxon, OX14 4RN
605 Third Avenue, New York, NY 10017

Routledge is an imprint of the Taylor & Francis Group, an informa business

First issued in paperback 2020

Library of Congress Cataloging-in-Publication Data
A catalog record for this book has been requested

ISBN: 978-1-138-94794-8 (hbk)
ISBN: 978-0-367-73229-5 (pbk)

Typeset in Sabon
by Apex CoVantage, LLC

To my dear family, who provided love, support, and understanding throughout this extended writing process.

Contents

Acknowledgments

I would like to acknowledge and thank the many people in my life who provided assistance and inspiration as I developed and completed this book.

My students provided inspiration and encouragement and offered interesting and challenging questions. They also understood the ongoing need to extend deadlines and the guilt that often comes with these extensions, as well as the exhilaration of meeting other deadlines. My George Washington University (GW) colleagues were also role models for me in finding time for writing and teaching.

I also extend a warm "thank you" to Anne Huff, who has been a mentor, friend, and inspiration for more than 25 years. Her expertise in managerial cognition and strategy were invaluable in my early years as a student and then new scholar, but I most appreciate her wise counsel related to scholarly writing that she offered in editing my first book chapter in 1997 and the generative manner in which she guides students and faculty in this process through her books on scholarly writing and research. I am also grateful for her hosting me for part of my 2014 sabbatical when I developed the proposal for this book. I also thank my friends and colleagues at the University of Minho for hosting part of that sabbatical. I value their thoughtful questions and suggestions as well as their curiosity about my work.

I am most grateful to Cindy Orticio, who provided expert editing and guidance on writing throughout the development of this book and many other writing projects. I am indebted to her for her help with these projects and also her work with the doctoral students in the GW Executive Leadership Doctoral Program. She is the ultimate professional in every way.

And thank you to Tara Patterson from the Virginia Science and Technology Campus Library and Dorinne Banks from the Gelman Library at GW. Their knowledge of the library resources and information systems and their willingness to secure documents, articles, and books with friendly good humor are most appreciated.

I am indebted to the many scholars and authors from across the social sciences disciplines whose work has informed this book on collective memory and identity and to those I did not discover who in turn influenced those who are cited and the direction of the field. The relationships across disciplines and the construction of knowledge is such an important part of our lives and our work together.

Thank you to Routledge for their generous extensions and patience.

And a heartfelt "thank you" to my dear family (my loving husband, Dan, my brilliant daughters, Elisabeth and Erin, my wise and curious son-in law, Josh, my funny and surprising grandchildren, Nathan and Samantha, and Josh's loving parents, Faith and Bruce), to whom this book is dedicated, for their ongoing support of my professional endeavors.

Introduction

Organizational identity and memory are critical concepts for theory, research, and practice in organizations. Identity and memory are "two of the most frequently used terms in public and private discourse, though their status as key words is relatively recent" (Gillis, 1994, p. 3). Gillis noted that "the parallel lives of these two terms alert us to the fact that the notion of identity depends on the idea of memory, and vice versa" (Gillis, 1994, p. 3). What is remembered is defined by identity, and remembering sustains identity. Whether defined as a noun or as a verb, these concepts and their relationships are usually considered to be socially constructed and embedded or influenced by gender, power, class, and other contextual features. Through their great popularity, both concepts may be losing any precise definitions or meaning and becoming clichés (Gillis, 1994).

From a theory and research perspective, each of these concepts—i.e., organizational identity and organizational memory and, in particular, collective memory and national identity—has been studied independently, yet they are frequently recognized as interwoven concepts, with one influencing the other. Further understanding of this relationship can significantly expand our understanding of each of these concepts to improve theorizing and empirical studies of the concept. For example, much of the debate related to organizational identity since 1985 has revolved around the degree to which identity changes or endures over time. A greater understanding of the processes of commemoration as a type of collective memory and the role of history in these processes could support our theorizing regarding how the labels for organizational identity claims may stay the same while the meaning of these claims changes over time with different groups in an organization, through the process of commemoration of past events—i.e., how and why these events are selected as important and how the stories of the events are told. From an organizational memory perspective, understanding the relationship would help in our theorizing about what and how events from an organization's past are recalled, particularly as organizations strategize their future. Research has revealed that these events and how they are commemorated are linked to the organizational identity or identity of a collective. This identity may evolve over time and therefore influence which events are considered significant and how they might be commemorated.

From a practice perspective, the relationship between organizational identity and memory is critical. How an organization frames its decisions related to future actions is impacted by this relationship, and these decisions and related actions can strongly influence the attraction of an organization to potential employees as well as the identification and retention of current employees. In addition, organizations use their history to attract consumers and other stakeholders. Which events organizations decide to use to reflect who they are and who they have been—i.e., their memory—is influenced by the relationship with organizational identity. For example, in planned organizational change initiatives, how the past is recalled or how past change initiatives were implemented can influence how current and future changes are perceived. The past and its relationship to organizational identity influence these perceptions.

The purpose of this book is to explore, analyze, and frame the relationship between organizational identity and memory, in particular history and commemoration, thus providing a robust theoretical and empirical foundation for further exploration of the relationship in organizational studies. This books draws both from the work in organizational studies and from the work in other social sciences, such as anthropology, history, and sociology, to inform this relationship. Olick, Vinitzky-Seroussi, and Levy (2011) addressed the multidisciplinary foundations of collective memory and the trajectory of this theory and research across disciplines and concepts such as cultural memory, social memory, and collective memory. In an anthology of works on collective memory, Olick et al. (2011) framed the anthology as "social memory studies" and asserted that, in doing so, this term "does not raise confusions about its object of reference" (p. 40). There could be many variations in how *collective* is defined, and yet they asserted that the label of social memory studies "remains presuppositionally open to a variety of phenomena while pointing out that all remembering is in some sense social" (Olick et al., 2011, p. 41). They acknowledged that the major disciplinary roots of collective memory are found in sociology, history, psychology, and anthropology (p. 41). Many of these texts have sections or chapters on the relationship between collective memory and identity (Olick et al., 2011). There are also texts that focus on collective identity concepts such as national identity (Gillis, 1994; Kelman, 1997, 2001) and their relationship to aspects of collective memory such as history and commemoration.

This book draws from this well-established foundation of theory and research on collective memory as well as its relationship to identity and to a lesser extent the work on national identity. In doing so, this book is unique in three essential ways. First, its primary goal is to explore the relationship between organizational identity and memory and the impact of this relationship on the scholarship in organizational studies and on organizational processes and practice. Second, to achieve this goal, it provides a multidisciplinary approach to understanding the related concepts such as collective memory and identity and their relationships, thereby drawing from a wide range of social science theory and research. The social sciences highlighted in this book concentrate on the collective level of analysis, i.e., anthropology, history, organizational studies, and sociology. Finally, it not only discusses the implications of these ideas for theory and future research in organizational studies through the presentation of a multidisciplinary theoretical framework, but it also specifically speaks to how this relationship impacts organizational actions in practice.

The Value of a Multidisciplinary Perspective

The concepts of organizational identity and memory have been theorized and researched from multidisciplinary perspectives. Building on this research to understand the nature of the relationship between organizational identity and memory thus entails a multidisciplinary perspective. The steadily rising interest in collective memory and related concepts across the social science disciplines (Espinoza, Piper, & Fernandez, 2014; Loveday, 2014; Olick et al., 2011; Radstone, 2000) has offered the opportunity for social memory research to expand beyond a static focus in disciplines such as psychology (Haas & Levasseur, 2013, p. 61).

Beginning in the 1980s, a memory boom surfaced across the social sciences of psychology, sociology, anthropology, and organizational studies, with an emphasis on the social aspects of memory. Theorists across the social sciences speculated on the causes of this boom. In anthropology, for example, it has been attributed to "decolonization," with an emphasis on pluralism and surfacing the multiple voices and memories of collectives that emerge (Berliner, 2005; Haas & Levasseur, 2013; Haukanes & Trnka, 2013) as countries are destroyed and then restructured and communities emerge or re-emerge in the process. The focus in memory studies has been on the collective and on the social aspects rather than the dominance of the individual and psychological perspectives (Hewer & Roberts, 2012). An example is the change of focus from the "Cartesian notion of the individual as a discrete and separate entity towards a position that contends that individual minds are the product of culture and history" (Hewer & Roberts, 2012, p. 169). There is also a postmodern turn toward understanding the relationship between the collective memory of these communities and their identity, whether national, cultural, or ethnic (Berliner, 2005; Hall, 1996). The dominance of North American social psychological perspectives has been reduced (Feindt, Krawatzek, Mehler, Pestel, & Trimcev, 2014) as the disciplines have acknowledged the critical debates in societies and the broad processes of change.

A multidisciplinary approach has also been apparent in the organizational identity and memory literature, making it more appropriate to take a multidisciplinary approach in examining the relationship between the two. At its roots, organizational studies is a multidisciplinary field. It builds from disciplines such as sociology, psychology (Whetten, Felin, & King, 2009), economics, and anthropology, among others. In considering organizational memory, many researchers have asserted the importance of multidisciplinary theorizing and empirical work in the exploration of organizational memory. Most work on organizational memory since the seminal work of Walsh and Ungson (1991) has either taken a managerial functionalist approach (Anteby & Molnar, 2012; Rowlinson, Booth, Clark, Delahaye, & Procter, 2010) or drawn extensively from psychological theories of individual memory (Sorensen, 2014). In addition, given that memory is defined by the past, more recently, organizational memory studies and organizational studies more broadly have included history as a concept as well as a field of study, using the many perspectives in that discipline to enhance theorizing about organizational memory. Sociological theory on collective memory and processes such as memorializing and history (Halbwachs, 1980; Schwartz, 2000, 2005) have more recently served as a theoretical foundation for exploring the collective processes of history and commemoration (Casey, 1997; Hatch & Schultz, 2017; Ocasio, Mauskapf, & Steele, 2016). A multidisciplinary approach has also served well in exploring the role of power in recollection of past events and commemoration (Nissley & Casey, 2002; Sorensen, 2014).

The foundation for the theory and research on organizational identity is human development and psychology, drawing from Erickson's (1968, 1980) developmental psychology and theory on identity and social psychology, such as Brewer's (2003) theory of optimal distinctiveness. The social actor perspective (Albert & Whetten, 1985) of organizational identity was framed in sociology and institutional theory. As the theorizing on organizational identity has developed, it has continued to draw from social identity theories. Some of the theorizing about organizational identity from a social constructionist perspective (Ravasi & Schultz, 2006) connected it to concepts such as organizational culture and history, which intersected with the sociological literature. As interest in the relationship between identity and history or memory has increased, organizational researchers have been increasingly drawing on sociology and history. This book continues to expand our understanding of the relationship between organizational identity and memory through work in disciplines such as sociology, anthropology, and history in addition to organizational studies.

The multidisciplinary perspective is also critical from a practice perspective. As organizations and their environments become increasingly complex, they need to address issues by building on knowledge across disciplines.

This book has chosen a narrow selection of the social sciences: anthropology, history, organizational studies, and sociology. These disciplines address the collective nature of the concepts and support theorizing and related empirical work. Organizational memory and organizational identity are by definition collective concepts in organizational theory. Sociology and anthropology also take a collective-level perspective on these concepts in that they focus on collective memory or social or cultural memory and the identity of groups, nations, or societies. History as a discipline is silent on the issue of level of analysis to a large degree but instead investigates some facets of collective memory including commemoration processes and memory of specific events or time periods or individuals and their lives during these time periods. Although there is extensive work in psychology on individual-level memory, most of the research on social memory is developed in social psychology, where memory as a social process surfaces. The relevant social psychology literature is stored in databases in the other social sciences, including organizational studies, and was captured, in part, in these disciplinary database searches. This book could have been expanded to other disciplines that would also inform these complexities, including economics and political science. The premise of this book, however, is that a multidisciplinary approach with a focus on the collective versus the individual expands and enhances our understanding versus a simply economic or managerial approach to these issues.

Literature Search Methods

Within the selected multidisciplinary fields, literature searches were conducted from the fall of 2014 to mid-2017, focusing primarily on peer-reviewed scholarly articles appearing in a range of databases, including ABI/Inform Complete Plus with a focus on business administration, Business Source Complete, Sociological Abstracts, Anthropology Plus, and Historical Abstracts. The literature was searched using terms that reflected the collective level of analysis and not individual memory and identity. Many different combinations of searches and search terms were used, with results delimited to those with the terms in the abstracts and key words of peer-reviewed articles in English. Efforts to narrow the search of these concepts to substantive works could have missed important contributions to the positions taken in this text. Books and other sources such as monographs and research reports were discovered by reviewing references in the peer-reviewed articles selected across the disciplines and occasionally through disciplinary databases. This book is not a comprehensive literature review of multidisciplinary work on collective memory and identity but rather is a text that has focused on the relationship between these two constructs and identity and in doing so offers selected works from organizational studies, anthropology, history, and sociology that inform our understanding of this relationship.

Specific search terms were used for different sources. For example, the search terms used in business databases were "organizational memory" and "organizational identity," while the search terms used in the other social sciences databases were "identity" and "collective memory." Searches were not done on the key words of history, commemoration, stories, narratives, social memory, and similar terms, but some of this work surfaced when searching for memory and collective memory. Work that defines memory in terms of organizational knowledge appeared in searches for organizational memory. While knowledge is acknowledged as a type of organizational memory, organizational knowledge was not the focus of the book.

Originally, information systems was proposed as a separate discipline to inform our knowledge of this relationship. Searches were conducted using a variety of search terms and databases, including ACM Digital Library, and then within specific journals such as *European Journal of Information Systems*, *Information Systems Research Journal*, and *MIS Quarterly*. Few peer-reviewed articles surfaced that focused on the relationship between the two concepts. A summary of that literature was created, and the relevant references and key contributions are included within the organizational studies discipline rather than highlighting information systems as a separate discipline.

Introduction to Key Concepts

The Organization

Part of the challenge in theorizing about organizational-level concepts such as organizational identity and memory is defining the concept of *organization* and deciding why, or if, it is unique from other social collectives such as nations, social movements, or markets (King, Felin, & Whetten, 2010, p. 290). Many organizational studies scholars (Brickson, 2013; King et al., 2010; Whetten et al., 2009) have asserted that the theories we import (Brickson, 2013, p. 226) into organizational studies may help us define and address what constitutes an organization or the *"noun-like, enduring, and distinctive* qualities of organizations as actors" (King et al., 2010, p. 291, emphasis in original). Organizations are more than "aggregations of individuals or instantiations of their environment" (King et al., 2010, p. 292). While some scholars (Whetten et al., 2009) have cautioned about theory borrowing—either vertically, crossing levels of analysis or abstraction, or horizontally, across social contexts—as these practices raise construct validity concerns (Whetten et al., 2009; Walsh & Ungson, 1991), other scholars have called for defining the verb form *organizing* (Heath & Sitkin, 2001, as cited in Brickson, 2013, p. 226) as a "process enabling organizational action," versus defining the noun *organization*.

King et al. (2010) asserted the importance of theorizing and understanding the unique social space that organizations, as a noun, occupy in societies and advocated for a "distinctively *organizational* analytical perspective" (p. 290). They offered two assumptions about organizations viewed from this perspective: external attribution and intentionality (p. 290). External attribution assumptions hold "that organizations must be attributed as capable of acting by other actors, especially by their primary stakeholders and audiences" (p. 292). Societies grant them this status, and there is intentionality in their decisions and behavior (King et al., 2010). King et al. (2010), in referencing Morgeson and Hofmann (1999), asserted that concepts can be borrowed across levels if the functionality is the same, even if the structures may differ. They proposed that the identity of a community is different from that of an organization in that communities derive their identities from the collective identity of their members, and "organizations imprint their identity on members" (p. 298) and provide sensegiving and sensemaking opportunities (Gioia & Chittipeddi, 1991).

Seminal Work: Organizational Identity

In organizational identity research, the seminal definition of organizational identity offered by Albert and Whetten is grounded in institutional theory and organizational identity:

> We propose, by way of a preliminary definition, that an adequate statement of organizational identity satisfies the following criteria:
>
> 1. The answer points to features that are somehow seen as the essence of the organization: *the criterion of claimed central character*.
> 2. The answer points to features that distinguish the organization from others with which it may be compared: *the criterion of claimed distinctiveness*.
> 3. The answer points to features that exhibit some degree of sameness or continuity over time: *the criterion of claimed temporal continuity*.
>
> For the purposes of defining organizational identity as a scientific concept, we treat the criteria of central character, distinctiveness and temporal continuity as each necessary and as a set sufficient.
>
> (Albert & Whetten, 1985, p. 265)

The *social actor* conceptualization of organizational identity draws from institutional theory (Scott & Meyer, 1994). As Whetten and Mackey (2002) noted, the differences in definitions of organizational identity often stem from different definitions of the "we," thus setting the stage for defining and theorizing about identity *in* organizations versus the identity *of* an organization (Whetten & Mackey, 2002). The social actor perspective of organizational identity (King & Whetten, 2008) defines organizational identity as "an organization's coherent self-definition (roughly: 'who we are as an organization') invoked as a common frame of reference by 'member-agents' in the course of acting or speaking on behalf of the organization" (p. 194) and is "empirically tethered to an organization's distinguishing features and attributes" (p. 194). "According to the CED [central, enduring, distinctive] definition, an organization's identifying features address both needs by locating an organizational actor within a particular social group with legitimate standing and by distinguishing that organization from other members of that group" (King & Whetten, 2008, p. 196). Defining organizations in this way "acknowledges the unique social status afforded organizations in 'modern society'—invested with roughly the same rights and responsibilities as individuals" (King & Whetten, 2008, p. 195).

In contrast to the original social actor perspective, most theory and research on organizational identity since 1985 has taken a *social constructionist* perspective, where *organization* or *organizing* is defined in reference to an aggregation of individual actors, and organizational identity is defined as how organizational members or groups of members answer the question, "Who are we as an organization?" This work on organizational identity often builds on the seminal definition, with the idea that it consists of characteristics of an organization that make the organization unique or distinct from others like it in its social category and that are core to the organization. Because the perspective builds on a social constructionist approach, it takes exception with the idea that these characteristics endure over time and instead assumes that they emerge or are reconstructed to meet the needs of internal and external environments. The answer to the question, "Who are we as an organization?" is constructed through individuals and can take the form of processes or characteristics of the individuals in the collective (Kreiner, Hollensbe, Sheep, Smith, & Kataria, 2015).

Much of this work relies on psychological theories of identity, such as that of Breakwell (2010), and often links to *organizational identification*, or the degree to which an individual organizational member identifies with the organization. For example, Kreiner et al. (2015) asserted that organizational members construct organizational identity, and they defined organizational identity work as "the cognitive, discursive and behavioral processes in which individuals engage to create, present, sustain, share, and/or adapt organizational identity" (p. 985). The emphasis is on individual agency in this construction. Frequently in this work, the term *organization* isn't defined directly. These scholars often note they take a social constructionist approach and then define organizational identity in terms of how organizational members perceive the answer to the question "Who are we as an organization?" or define it as a process. Kreiner et al. (2015) noted that their findings related to organizational identity and identity work built on dialectical tensions, and these tensions held the promise of expanding "our understanding of a specific theory of organization" (p. 1004), but they provided no definition. Both the social actor perspective and the social constructionist perspective reference memory, history, tradition, and legacy in different terms, yet the role of memory is underdeveloped.

Seminal Work: Organizational Memory

Organizational memory scholarship also addresses the issue of defining the concept of *organization*. The seminal work by Walsh and Ungson (1991) highlighted this point and noted that researchers have asserted that "memory can reside in supraindividual collectives" because it can function as a repository of knowledge (p. 58), yet they also acknowledged the ambiguity that this results in. They offered that organizational memory is used as a metaphor in some of the work and in doing so risks anthropomorphizing the concept. They raised the question of construct validity even if it functions in much the same way as in individuals. Walsh and Ungson theorized from three assumptions about organizations. First, "organizations functionally resemble information processing systems that process information from the environment" (p. 60). Second, organizations are a "network of intersubjectively shared meanings that are sustained through the development and use of a common language and everyday social interactions" (p. 60). Their third assumption built on the views of Daft and Weick (1984), who proposed that "organizations have cognitive systems and memories" (Daft & Weick, 1984, p. 285), and, despite employee turnover, "organizations preserve knowledge, behaviors, mental maps, norms and values over time" (Daft & Weick, 1984, p. 285).

Literature Since the Seminal Work

The literature on organizational identity and memory has developed independently and at times in separate disciplines. Definitions of organizational identity have been framed from Albert and Whetten's (1985) seminal definition and in doing so assert that organizational identity involves those features of an organization that are core and enduring or temporally continuous and that distinguish an organization from others in a similar category (Corley et al., 2006). The social constructionist perspective on organizational identity defines organizational identity as "shared emergent beliefs" or "identity understandings" (Ravasi & Schultz, 2006, p. 436) about what is core and distinct about the organization. Organizational identity is articulated as organizational members' answers to the question: "Who are we as an organization?"

Scholars continue to debate the degree to which organizational identity is mutable or enduring. In this debate, organizational history, a form of organizational memory, has been proposed as a factor in the definition of identity—i.e., its enduringness—but neither side of the debate has drawn extensively on the well-developed literature on collective memory or social memory to understand this relationship and its impact on organizational identity. Depending on how organizational identity is defined, both perspectives have speculated on how the forms of organizational memory such as history, legacy, commemoration, and founders influence identity. Organizational identity has been linked to organizational change, strategy, mergers and acquisitions, sensemaking, culture, and employee identification.

In the organizational studies literature, since Walsh and Ungson's (1991) seminal work on organizational memory, the literature on the concept has taken a divergent path. Walsh and Ungson (1991) focused on the structure and functions of organizational memory and defined it as "stored information from an organization's history that can be brought to bear on present decisions" (p. 61). They primarily linked organizational memory to organizational change and decision making. Since 1991, organizational memory has been defined in many ways, from a repository of organizational knowledge or knowledge stocks and flows (Argote & Miron-Spektor, 2011) to shared interpretations of past events commemorated by members of an organization (Casey, 1997). Organizational memory as defined as commemoration and history has been connected to different forms of identity—national (Schwartz & Kim, 2002), group (Cuc, Ozuru, Manier, & Hirst, 2006), and organizational (Anteby & Molnar, 2012; Casey, 1997; Hatch & Schultz, 2017; Ravasi & Schultz, 2006; Schultz & Hernes, 2013)—but this relationship and its impact on organizational memory processes has not been explored. Organizational memory has primarily been linked to organizational learning (Argote & Miron-Spektor, 2011; Casey, 1997; Huber, 1991; Schwandt, 1997), knowledge management, and organizational forgetting (Casey & Olivera, 2011) and, to a lesser extent, organizational identity.

In this book, collective memory is the primary lens to address organizational memory. The focus on the concepts and relationship between them is at the collective level. In addition, the book offers evidence from organizational practices that are influenced by this relationship, such as corporate museums and visitor centers. Implications for managers are discussed with insights from organizational research and practices in creating corporate museums, galleries, visitor centers, and other displays of this relationship. In addition, implications of this relationship on organizational actions are considered following significant events such as a merger or acquisition.

Organization of the Book

The book is divided into three main parts, which (1) define the concepts individually, (2) discuss their relationships, and (3) provide implications. Part I provides an in-depth overview of the core concepts related to collective memory and identity. Chapter 1 focuses on organizational and collective memory, while Chapter 2 covers organizational identity and related concepts. The first part of each chapter provides the organizational theory definition of the collective concept, followed by a presentation of the work on the collective-level concepts across sociology, anthropology, and history. Chapter 3, in Part II, analyzes the nature of the multidisciplinary relationship, and Chapter 4 highlights the factors that influence the relationship. In Part III, Chapter 5 presents a theoretical framework and theoretical implications, while Chapter 6 discusses implications for practice.

Originally, it was planned to have a chapter on each discipline—anthropology, history, organizational studies, and sociology—presenting the theory and research related to the conceptual relationship from that discipline. The first draft of the book showed that the chapters had similar content. It was also challenging to determine the primary disciplinary focus or background of the contribution based on the author's background or the journal in which an article was published. For example, a scholar could have an academic background in social psychology but have an appointment in a sociology department and publish only in sociological journals, while another author could have an academic background in communications but publish in political science journals. Some articles were coauthored by individuals from different disciplines. The book was then restructured to present an overview of the organizational studies literature on the two concepts and the relationship between them followed by an integrated summary and synthesis of the social sciences literature. Disciplinary contributions are highlighted in the chapters or the summary as appropriate.

References

Albert, S., & Whetten, D. A. (1985). Organizational identity. In L. L. Cummings & B. M. Staw (Eds.), *Research in organizational behavior* (pp. 263–295). Greenwich, CT: JAI Press.

Anteby, M., & Molnar, V. (2012). Collective memory meets organizational identity: Remembering to forget in a firm's rhetorical history. *Academy of Management Journal, 55*(3), 515–540. https://doi.org/10.5465/amj.2010.0245.

Argote, L., & Miron-Spektor, E. (2011). Organizational learning: From experience to knowledge. *Organization Science, 22*(5), 1123–1137. https://doi.org/10.1287/orsc.1100.0621.

Berliner, D. (2005). The abuses of memory: Reflections on the memory boom in anthropology. *Anthropological Quarterly, 78*(1), 197–211. https://doi.org/10.1353/anq.2005.0001.

Brewer, M. B. (2003). Optimal distinctiveness, social identity and self. In M. R. Leary & J. P. Tangney (Eds.), *Handbook of self and identity* (pp. 480–491). New York, NY: Guilford.

Breakwell, G. M. (2010). Resisting representations and identity processes. *Papers on Social Representations, 19*, 6.1–6.11. Retrieved from www.psych.lse.ac.uk/Psr/PSR2010/19_06Breakwell.pdf

Brickson, S. (2013). Athletes, best friends, and social activists: An integrative model accounting for the role of identity in organizational identification. *Organization Science, 24*(1), 226–245. https://doi.org/10.1287/orsc.1110.0730.

Casey, A. (1997). Collective memory in organizations. In P. Shrivastava, A. Huff, & J. Dutton (Series Eds.), J. Walsh & A. Huff (Vol. Eds.), *Organizational learning and strategic management* (Advances in Strategic Management, Vol. 14, pp. 111–151). Greenwich, CT: JAI Press.

Casey, A., & Olivera, F. (2011). Reflections on organizational memory and forgetting. *Journal of Management Inquiry, 20*(3), 305–310. https://doi.org/10.1177/1056492611408264.

Corley, K. G., Harquail, C. V., Pratt, M. G., Glynn, M. A., Fiol, C. M., & Hatch, M. J. (2006). Guiding organizational identity through aged adolescence. *Journal of Management Inquiry, 15*(2), 85–99. https://doi.org/10.1177/1056492605285930.

Cuc, A., Ozuru, Y., Manier, D., & Hirst, W. (2006). On the formation of collective memories: The role of a dominant narrator. *Memory & Cognition, 34*(4), 752–762. https://doi.org/10.3758/BF03193423.

Daft, R. L., & Weick, K. E. (1984). Toward a model of organizations as interpretation systems. *Academy of Management Review, 9*(2), 284–295. doi: 10.2307/258441.

Erickson, E. H. (1968). *Identity, youth and crises*. New York, NY: Norton.

Erickson, E. H. (1980). *Identity and the life cycle*. New York, NY: Norton.

Espinoza, A. E., Piper, I., & Fernandez, R. A. (2014). The study of memory sites through a dialogical accompaniment interactive group method: A research note. *Qualitative Research, 14*(6), 712–728. https://doi.org/10.1177/1468794113483301.

Feindt, G. R., Krawatzek, F., Mehler, D. A., Pestel, F., & Trimcev, R. (2014). Entangled memory: Toward a third wave in memory studies. *History and Theory, 53*(1), 24–44. https://doi.org/10.1111/hith.10693.

Gillis, J. R. (1994). Introduction. Memory and identity: The history of a relationship. In J. R. Gillis (Ed.), *Commemorations: The politics of national identity* (pp. 3–24). Princeton, NJ: Princeton University Press.

Gioia, D. A., & Chittipeddi, K. (1991). Sensemaking and sensegiving in strategic change initiation. *Strategic Management Journal, 12*(6), 433–448. https://doi.org/10.1002/smj.4250120604.

Haas, V., & Levasseur, E. (2013). Rumour as a symptom of collective forgetfulness. *Culture and Psychology, 19*(1), 60–75. https://doi.org/10.1177/1354067X12464986.

Halbwachs, M. (1980). *The collective memory* (F. J. Ditter, Jr. & V. Y. Ditter, Trans.). New York, NY: Harper and Row. (Originally published in 1950)

Hall, S. (1996). The question of cultural identity. In S. Hall, D. Held, D. Hubert, & K. Thompson (Eds.), *Modernity: An introduction to modern societies* (pp. 595–634). Cambridge, UK: Blackwell Publishers.

Hatch, M. J., & Schultz, M. (2017). Toward a theory of using history authentically: Historicizing in the Carlsberg Group. *Administrative Science Quarterly*, 62, 657–697. https://doi.org/10.1177/0001839217692535.

Haukanes, H., & Trnka, S. (2013). Memory, imagination, and belonging across generations: Perspectives from postsocialist Europe and beyond. *Focaal— Journal of Global and Historical Anthropology*, 66, 3–13.

Hewer, C. J., & Roberts, R. (2012). History, culture and cognition: Towards a dynamic model of social memory. *Culture and Psychology*, *18*(2), 167–183. https://doi.org/10.1177/1354067X11434836.

Huber, G. (1991). Organizational learning: The contributing processes and the literature. *Organization Science*, *2*(1), 88–115. https://doi.org/10.1287/orsc.2.1.88.

Kelman, H. C. (1997). Nationalism, patriotism, and national identity: Social psychological dimensions. In D. Bar-Tal & E. Staub (Eds.), *Patriotism in the lives of individuals and nations* (pp. 165–189). Chicago, IL: Nelson-Hall.

Kelman, H. C. (2001). The role of national identity in conflict resolution. In R. D. Ashmore, L. Jussim, & D. Wilder (Eds.), *Social identity, intergroup conflict, and conflict reduction* (pp. 187–212). Oxford: Oxford University Press.

King, B. G., Felin, T., & Whetten, D. A. (2010). Finding the organization in organizational theory: A meta-theory of the organization as a social actor. *Organization Science*, *21*, 290–305.

King, B. G., & Whetten, D. A. (2008). Rethinking the relationship between reputation and legitimacy: A social actor conceptualization. *Corporate Reputation Review*, *11*(3), 192–207. https://doi.org/10.1057/crr.2008.16.

Kreiner, G. E., Hollensbe, E., Sheep, M. L., Smith, B. R., & Kataria, N. (2015). Elasticity and the dialectic tensions of organizational identity: How can we hold together while we are pulling apart? *Academy of Management Journal*, *58*(4), 981–1011. https://doi.org/10.5465/amj.2012.0462.

Loveday, V. (2014). Flat-capping it: Memory, nostalgia and value in retroactive male working class identification. *European Journal of Cultural Studies*, *17*(6), 721–735. https://doi.org/10.1177/1367549414544117.

Morgeson, F. P., & Hofmann, D. A. (1999). The structure and function of collective concepts: Implications for multilevel research and theory development. *Academy of Management Review*, *24*(2), 249–265. https://doi.org/10.5465/amr.1999.1893935.

Nissley, N., & Casey, A. (2002). The politics of the exhibition: Viewing corporate museums through the paradigmatic lens of organizational memory. *British Journal of Management*, *13*(S2), S35–S44. https://doi.org/10.1111/1467-8551.13.s2.4.

Ocasio, W., Mauskapf, M., & Steele, C. W. (2016). History, society, and institutions: The role of collective memory in the emergence and evolution of societal logics. *Academy of Management Review*, *41*(4), 676–699. https://doi.org/10.5465/amr.2014.0183.

Olick, J. K., Vinitzky-Seroussi, V., & Levy, D. (2011). Introduction. In J. K. Olick, V. Vinitzky-Seroussi, & D. Levy (Eds.), *The collective memory reader* (pp. 3–62). New York, NY: Oxford University Press.

Radstone, S. (2000). Introduction. In S. Radstone (Ed.), *Memory and methodology* (pp. 1–22). Oxford and New York, NY: Berg.

Ravasi, D., & Schultz, M. (2006). Responding to organizational identity threats: Exploring the role of organizational culture. *Academy of Management Journal*, *49*(3), 433–458. https://doi.org/10.5465/amj.2006.21794663.

Rowlinson, M., Booth, C., Clark, P., Delahaye, A., & Procter, S. (2010). Social remembering and organizational memory. *Organization Studies, 31*(1), 69–87. https://doi.org/10.1177/0170840609347056.

Schultz, M., & Hernes, T. (2013). A temporal perspective on organizational identity. *Organization Science, 24*(1), 1–21. https://doi.org/10.1287/orsc.1110.0731.

Schwandt, D. R. (1997). Integrating strategy and organizational learning: A theory of action perspective. *Advances in Strategic Management, 14*, 337–360.

Schwartz, B. (2000). *Abraham Lincoln and the forge of national memory*. Chicago, IL: University of Chicago Press.

Schwartz, B. (2005). The new Gettysburg Address: Fusing history and memory. *Poetics, 33*(1), 63–79. https://doi.org/10.1016/j.poetic.2005.01.003.

Schwartz, B., & Kim, M. (2002). Honor, dignity and collective memory. In K. Cerulo (Ed.), *Culture in mind* (pp. 209–226). London, UK: Routledge.

Scott, W. R., & Meyer, J. W. (1994). *Institutional environments and organizations*. Thousand Oaks, CA: Sage.

Sørensen, B. M. (2014). Changing the memory of suffering: An organizational aesthetics of the dark side. *Organization Studies, 35*(2), 279–302. https://doi.org/10.1177/0170840613511930.

Walsh, J. P., & Ungson, G. R. (1991). Organizational memory. *Academy of Management Review, 16*(1), 57–91. https://doi.org/10.5465/amr.1991.4278992.

Whetten, D. A., & Mackey, A. (2002). A social actor conception of organizational identity and its implications for the study of organizational reputation. *Business & Society, 41*(4), 393–414. https://doi.org/10.1177/0007650302238775.

Whetten, D. A., Felin, T., & King, B. G. (2009). The practice of theory borrowing in organizational studies: Current issues and future directions. *Journal of Management, 35*(3), 537–563. https://doi.org/10.1177/0149206308330556.

Part I
The Concepts

1 Organizational and Collective Memory

Prior to Walsh and Ungson's (1991) seminal work on organizational memory, the term *organizational memory* was occasionally referenced in the organizational studies literature but was not explored in depth. For example, Weick (1979) referenced organizational memory in relationship to organizational learning. Organizational memory was also noted in terms of corporate history, with Smith and Steadman (1981) highlighting the role of corporate history in an organization's adaptation to change and the value of understanding the past, including corporate heritage and traditions, in relationship to present actions. Lawrence (1984) took a different perspective, emphasizing the value of a historical perspective in examining organizational studies phenomena.

Since Walsh and Ungson's (1991) work, researchers (Casey & Olivera, 2007) have asserted the importance of multidisciplinary theorizing and empirical work in the exploration of organizational memory, yet most of the work on organizational memory since Walsh and Ungson (1991) has taken either a managerial functionalist approach (Anteby & Molnar, 2012; Rowlinson, Booth, Clark, Delahaye, & Procter, 2010) or has drawn extensively from psychological theories of individual memory (Sorensen, 2014). Sociological theory on collective memory and related components of memory such as commemoration and history (Halbwachs, 1950/1980; Schwartz, 2000, 2005) have begun to emerge as a theoretical foundation for exploring organizational memory as a collective process (Casey, 1997; Feldman & Feldman, 2006; Ocasio, Mauskapf, & Steele, 2016) and, in connection to organizational history, providing a theoretical lens upon which to build theory and research on organizational memory as a collective process. In particular, this work has served to help understand the processes of commemoration or remembering together, as well as how organizations use their history to sustain, change, or manage their organizational identity (Hatch & Schultz, 2017; Schultz & Hernes, 2013). These theories have also surfaced factors that influence memory and its relationship to identity. In addition, they take into consideration the social and historical nature of organizational memory (Rowlinson et al., 2010). For example, the sociological lens suggests the important role of power in recollection of past events and commemoration (Nissley & Casey, 2002; Sorensen, 2014).

This chapter first provides the theoretical foundations and definitions of organizational memory from an organizational studies perspective, presenting two literature reviews on organizational memory in organizational studies and use of the concept in discussions of knowledge management and organizational learning. The next section shows how the organizational studies literature began to draw on the theoretical lens of collective memory. The chapter then turns to the scholarship on collective memory across the social sciences, including anthropology, history, and sociology. The chapter concludes with a discussion of the factors that influence organizational and collective memory.

Organizational Memory

Walsh and Ungson (1991) were the first to review the literature on organizational memory. They defined organizational memory as "stored information from an organization's history that can be brought to bear on present decisions" (p. 61) and noted that although the term was foundational in theoretical domains, including organizational learning and information systems, the concept was "fragmented and underdeveloped" (p. 57). In the more than 25 years since this article was published, organizational memory has continued to serve as a foundation for theorizing and research in areas such as organizational learning (Anderson & Sun, 2010; Argote, 2013; Argote & Miron-Spektor, 2011; Casey, 1997; Santos-Vijande, López-Sánchez, & Trespalacios, 2012; Schwandt & Marquardt, 2000; Schwartz, 1997), organizational forgetting (Casey & Olivera, 2011; Lopez & Sune, 2013; Mena, Rintamaki, Fleming, & Spicer, 2016), knowledge management (Barros, Ramos, & Perez, 2015), and, to a lesser extent, organizational identity (Anteby & Molnar, 2012; Casey, 2010; Casey & Byington, 2013; Schultz & Hernes, 2013), as well as the more recent work on historicizing organizations (Hatch & Schultz, 2017).

Since 1991, there have been three literature reviews on organizational memory: those of Casey and Olivera (2007) and Anderson and Sun (2010) in organizational studies and a third by Barros et al. (2015) in the information systems literature. This chapter presents an overview of Walsh and Ungson's work (1991), followed by a discussion of the major findings from the two literature reviews in organizational studies and a synopsis of the review of Barros et al. (2015). This serves as a foundation for an analysis of the more recent work on organizational memory in organizational studies, particularly the turn toward history and historicizing (Hatch & Schultz, 2017) work in organizations since 2010.

The Seminal Text of Walsh and Ungson

In their 1991 article entitled "Organizational Memory," Walsh and Ungson (1991) noted that as early as 1979, Weick referenced the importance of organization memory in processes such as organizational learning as well as organizing as a whole and indicated that memory could constrain and enable organizational actions in the present and future. They acknowledged that at that time organizational memory was thought to have components of "mental and structural artifacts" (Walsh & Ungson, 1991, p. 58), from cause maps and standard operating procedures to memories and the history of past events. They also referenced Yates's (1990) historical work that provides an analysis of the evolution of one aspect of organizational memory: the written record and how it evolved from 1850 to 1920.

Walsh and Ungson (1991) surfaced the issues involved in drawing from psychological definitions of memory and the work on memory that had been conducted in biology and neurology to inform memory at the organizational level. Much of the work on organizational memory at that time treated it as a metaphor, and Walsh and Ungson (1991) acknowledged the construct validity, measurement, and consequentiality issues in employing concepts from one level of analysis to another. (See Morgeson and Hofmann [1999] and Kozlowski and Klein [2000] for further exploration of issues in multilevel theorizing.)

Underlying their analysis of organizational memory, Walsh and Ungson (1991) made three assumptions: that organizations are (1) information processing systems obtaining data from their environments, (2) interpretation systems, and (3) "a network of intersubjectively shared meanings that are sustained" (p. 60) through language and social interaction. They defined organizational memory as "stored information from an organization's history that can be brought to bear on present decisions" (Walsh & Ungson, 1991, p. 61) and conceptualized it in terms of retention facilities or bins, which included individuals, culture, transformations, organizational structures, ecology, and external archives. They proposed processes associated with the functioning of organizational memory (acquisition, retention, and retrieval) and the types of knowledge (what, why, who, etc.) in each retention bin.

In acquisition processes, Walsh and Ungson (1991) acknowledged the difficulties organizations have in acquiring and storing information about decisions, actions, and consequences. Information can be ambiguous and incomplete, and organizational schemas or filters work to interpret this information. Similar issues were identified in the retention process. They proposed that memory is retained in different types of storage facilities, including individuals, cultures (that which is learned and transmitted), transformations, structures, ecology, and external archives, with different patterns of retention associated with different mechanisms. Retrieval processes focused on how information can be recovered through automatic and controlled processes. They proposed that schemata are involved in both automatic and controlled retrieval.

Walsh and Ungson's (1991) propositions related to the use and misuse of memory suggested that organizational memory and history should be taken into account when decisions are made and in creating organizational change, as change is framed from the perspective of the past. Yet their propositions also acknowledged the time-consuming process of considering information from the past and how this process could take away from future actions. These processes are impacted by political action as well. One of the more important influences on these processes is the influence of the individual both in terms of tenure in the organization and continuity of this service.

Walsh and Ungson (1991) framed a research agenda to address the structure, process, and consequences of organizational memory, arguing that future research on organizational memory could inform our understanding of organizational change, design, and structure. Their perspective on organizational memory has been applied to a variety of organizational phenomena, including learning (Anderson & Sun, 2010; Argote, 1999), innovation (Hargadon & Sutton, 1997; Moorman & Miner, 1997), decision making (Loma, Larsen, & Ginsberg, 1997), and improvisation (Crossan, Cunha, Vera, & Cunha, 2005).

Literature Reviews on Organizational Memory in Organizational Studies

There have been two major reviews of the literature on organizational memory (Anderson & Sun, 2010; Casey & Olivera, 2003) in organizational studies. These reviews took different approaches to reviewing the literature since Walsh and Ungson's (1991) seminal article on organizational memory. Casey and Olivera used the search term *organizational memory*, while Anderson and Son completed a citation analysis. Both reviews positioned the significance of their work based on the interest in and related citations of organizational memory since Walsh and Ungson, as well as its conceptual relevance for organizational learning (Anderson & Sun, 2010).

In Anderson and Sun's (2010) citation and content analysis, they found that more than 300 articles had cited the original work by Walsh and Ungson (1991) by the end of 2006. Their analysis focused on those articles that had the largest number of citations of Walsh and Ungson, and they explored which assertions in the Walsh and Ungson article had been most cited and which ones had been the most critiqued. Anderson and Son addressed four research questions:

1. Who cites Walsh and Ungson (1991) most frequently (in terms of authors and fields), and how has the number of citations changed over time?
2. What content from Walsh and Ungson (1991) have subsequent authors retrieved?
3. How many citing authors are critical of claims made by Walsh and Ungson (1991), and what is the nature of these criticisms?
4. Which articles contain the greatest number of Walsh and Ungson (1991) citation contexts, and how have these works extended our understanding of organizational memory?

(pp. 133–134)

The 301 cited articles were published in 105 distinct journals, with the most representative disciplines being management (43 journals) followed by information technology (36 journals). A wide range of disciplines were included, from medicine to information technology to marketing. Citations of the article continued to increase through 2006, the end of the timeframe for their research. The most widely cited claim from the 1991 work was the metaphor of organizational memory storage bins. The next most cited claim (with almost half the number of citations) was the use and misuse of memory (Anderson & Sun, 2010). The discussion of these claims was fairly superficial, with little extension of the concepts. Relatively few of the citations in the 301 articles were critical of Walsh and Ungson's claims, with the few criticisms focusing on the storage bins approach, the lack of process or interconnectedness of the bins, and the minimal discussion of different forms of organizations (Anderson & Sun, 2010).

Despite the large number of citations of Walsh and Ungson (1991)—the article could be considered a "citation classic" (Anderson & Sun, 2010, p. 143)—most of the treatment of the knowledge claims was limited, and therefore Anderson and Sun (2010) concluded that "Walsh and Ungson's (1991) work has had much less impact than its high citation count implies" (p. 142). At the same time, though, they concluded that Walsh and Ungson's work "represents a milestone in our understanding of organizational memory" (Anderson & Sun, 2010, p. 143).

Casey and Olivera's (2003) review of the organizational memory literature reached some similar conclusions. They reviewed the organizational memory literature from 1991 to 2002. Their primary conclusion was that although organizational memory was widely cited, it was mostly cited in a peripheral manner, and few studies had attempted to develop or empirically examine the concept. Progress had been made, though, in the theoretical development of the concept and in empirical research, with an emphasis on what has been learned about the functions and structure of organizational memory and, in practitioner work, related to knowledge management and the learning organization (e.g., Wexler, 2002). Similar to Anderson and Sun (2010), Casey and Olivera (2003) noted an increasing number of articles using the term through 2003, the end of their review period.

Casey and Olivera (2003) searched the term *organizational memory* in peer-reviewed articles in ProQuest; their search yielded 806 articles. After eliminating those in which organizational memory was used only in the references, they coded the remaining articles as either central, substantial, or peripheral. In 44 articles, organizational memory played a substantial role as a concept to develop propositions or to understand findings. Articles were coded as central if organizational memory was the topic or central construct in the article. Thirty-seven articles were coded as central. Twenty-four articles were empirical studies, of which most used qualitative methods. Articles in which organizational memory was an important theme mainly appeared in organizational theory or organizational behavior journals; a few were in information technology. They suggested that the large number of articles in which the construct has played a peripheral role indicates that the concept has sufficient intuitive appeal to become part of the academic and practitioner conversation in many diverse communities and disciplines. In addition, in most of the articles, including those that were coded substantial, there were many untested assumptions about the nature of organizational memory that were based on understanding of individual-level memory, with little concern for the challenges of theorizing across levels (Ackerman, 1996; Corbett, 2000; Morgeson & Hofmann, 1999).

Casey and Olivera (2003) analyzed the articles in relationship to the structure and function of organizational memory using Morgeson and Hofmann's (1999) framework for collective concepts. Their analysis found that researchers primarily explored organizational memory in relationship functions such as decision making, learning, stability, adaptation, innovation, and improvisation. From a structure perspective, Casey and Olivera (2003) found that the literature began to move away from the original storage bin approach proposed by Walsh and Ungson to consider more emergent structures, including dispersed memory and microprocesses. Casey and Olivera (2003) proposed three future research directions: (1) the dynamic structure of memory emerging from patterns of interactions of individuals in organizations; (2) the role of time in these processes; and (3) the agency of the individual and its interaction with organizational goals and how that affects the structure and function of memory.

Literature Review in Information Systems

Organizational memory has also been a key concept in the information systems literature. A literature review on organizational memory in this literature proposed information systems as a support for organizational memory, in that they "enhance and support the creation, storage, and dissemination of knowledge in the organization over time in order to ensure an effective management" of organizational memory (Barros et al., 2015, p. 47). In their review, Barros et al. searched for the term *organizational memory* in information systems databases, including IEEEXplore and AIS Electronic Library. The authors took a knowledge-based view of organizational memory, defining it as the "set of accumulated knowledge . . . being preserved through time" (p. 46). They proposed that organizational memory fosters the development of individuals and organizations if information systems are readily accessible and knowledge is easily stored in them. The literature review was focused on information systems and how they store memory, with little theoretical development of the concept of memory.

The Organizational Memory Literature Since 2010

Anderson and Sun (2010) noted an increasing number of citations of Walsh and Ungson through their work in 2006, and Casey and Olivera (2003) documented an increasing number of articles using the term *organizational memory* through 2003. For the research for this book, in January 2016, a search for organizational/organisational memory in Pro-Quest led to over 3,500 "hits" without filters and 2,073 hits as filtered for peer-reviewed articles in English. In narrowing the search to these terms in the abstracts of peer-reviewed articles, the total was approximately 105. Thus, the number of peer-reviewed articles in which organizational memory appeared was fairly consistent: 95 in 2010 and 105 in 2015. Overall, organizational memory as a concept continues to be of interest to researchers across disciplines, but particularly in organizational studies. In the years since 2007, organizational memory has continued to emerge as a topic in many journals across disciplines, ranging from organizational studies to higher education and business ethics. Yet, similar to the conclusions noted in the two literature reviews (Anderson & Sun, 2010; Casey & Olivera, 2003), organizational memory remains an underdeveloped, undertheorized, and underresearched concept.

Since 2010, literature on organizational memory has continued to cite the original definition articulated by Walsh and Ungson (1991)—"stored information from an organization's history that can be brought to bear on present decisions" (p. 61)—as a foundation for exploration of the concept. The two primary literature streams in which the concept has surfaced are organizational learning and knowledge management. One related literature stream that has begun to emerge is the representation of organizational memory as a form of organizational history (Hatch & Schultz, 2017; Rowlinson, Hassard, & Decker, 2014). In addition, but a more distant connection, is the recent trend toward advocating for the value of historical methods in organizational studies (Maclean, Harvey, & Clegg, 2016; Rowlinson, Casey, Hansen, & Mills, 2014).

Knowledge Management

Despite the popularity of organizational memory as a concept in the knowledge management literature, there has been little theoretical development of the concept in this literature stream. Most scholars reference Walsh and Ungson (1991) as the foundation for their work, and they tend to refer primarily on the retention bin properties of organizational memory, with memory most referenced as an existing stock of organizational knowledge (Lin, 2015) and a component of knowledge management systems. For example, organizational memory has been framed as a significant variable and studied as part of how knowledge management systems foster human resource management (Obeidat, Masa'deh, & Abdallah, 2014). In this type of research, organizational memory as a part of knowledge management is correlated with learning and internal process measures but not financial performance and customer satisfaction (Lin, 2015). Scales have been developed to measure organizational memory (Lin, 2015; Templeton, Lewis, & Snyder, 2002) based on the early work of Moorman and Miner (1997) and Cross and Baird (2000). In Lin's (2015) empirical study of knowledge management orientation, organizational memory was one dimension of the orientation that was positively correlated with organizational learning and growth.

Fiedler and Welpe (2010) also took a storage bin approach to organizational memory, conceptualizing an organization as a "collective that stores information" (p. 382), and defined organizational memory as "a structure of repositories in which different forms of knowledge are stored, and from which knowledge can be retrieved" (p. 382). Their work focused on the structural dimensions of organizations such as specialization and standardization and how they positively influence organizational memory. Although they took an information processing perspective of organizations and organizational memory, they acknowledged the process of remembering and how interactions and interpretations made by organizational members can be shaped through knowledge repositories such as electronic files. They noted that organizational memory has been thought of as a metaphor and acknowledged the contributions of Argyris and Schon (1978) and Sandelands and Stablein (1987), who considered organizations to be mental entities that think (Fiedler & Welpe, 2010, p. 384).

Lastly, Dunham and Burt (2011) and Thomas and Vohra (2015, p. 852) also defined organizational memory using Walsh and Ungson's (1991, p. 610) definition, i.e., "the stored information from an organization's history that can be brought to bear on present decisions," and considered it as a component of knowledge management systems. As is the case in much of this literature, Dunham and Burt (2011) operationalized their definition as a property and action of the individual. They asserted that organizational memory is the tacit and explicit knowledge stored in individuals and developed through their experiences and tenure in the organization. Alternatively, Thomas and Vohra (2015) proposed organizational memory as one of the knowledge management subprocesses in their process-based view of organizational learning: "information acquisition, information distribution, information interpretation and organizational memory" (p. 126). They defined organizations as "relational processes" (p. 126) and took a social network theory approach to organizational learning. Organizational learning was defined in terms of shared knowledge and was differentiated from individual memory and learning. They defined organizational memory using a transactive memory approach; it is both networks and nonhuman repositories of knowledge.

Despite the conceptual work and robust line of empirical studies on organizational memory in the knowledge management field, the concept of memory remains theoretically underdeveloped and is often conceptually confused with individual actions and memory processes.

Organizational Learning

Organizational memory continues to have a strong presence in interdisciplinary theories and models of organizational learning (Argote, 2013; Argote & Miron-Spektor, 2011; Feldman & Feldman, 2006). The interest in organizational learning has been sustained, in part, because the process is critical to organizational adaptation and survival (Argote & Miron-Spektor, 2011). Yet robust theorizing and empirical work on organizational learning have not contributed to in-depth theorizing on organizational memory. In this literature, organizational memory was most frequently depicted as stored information or knowledge or, to a lesser extent, as a process.

Organizational memory was explored as a critical component of organizational learning models in the early 1990s. For example, Huber (1991) articulated the relationship between organizational memory and learning in his organizational learning framework, which included four constructs and processes: knowledge acquisition, information distribution, information interpretation, and organizational memory. In this framework, organizational memory is defined as "the means by which knowledge is stored for future use" (p. 90) and is further framed as processes of storing and retrieving information, with computer-based memory being one outcome. Importantly, Huber (1991) asserted that "the basic processes that contribute to the occurrence, breadth, and depth of organizational learning depend on organizational memory" (p. 107) and called for further research of organizational memory to understand its relationship with learning and decision making (p. 88). During the same time period, March (1991) investigated exploration and exploitation as learning processes; he referenced how organizations accumulate stored knowledge "in their procedures, norms, rules and forms" (p. 73) and the role of knowledge in exploration and exploitation. Organizational memory was also identified as one of the major subsystems of other early organizational learning models, including that of Schwandt (1997, 2000).

Since the 1990s, organizational memory has remained a frequently identified component of organizational learning theories and models, framed as either a stock of organizational knowledge (Flores, Zheng, Rau, & Thomas, 2012; Kyriakopoulos & de Ruyter, 2004) or as a process, subprocess, or system of processes. For example, Thomas and Vohra (2015) proposed memory as a core subprocess in a process-based social network view of organizational learning while Mena and Chabowski (2015) also proposed it as a component of organizational learning particularly in relationship to other outcomes or processes such as stakeholder marketing.

In recent reviews of the organizational learning literature (Argote, 2013; Argote & Miron-Spektor, 2011), organizational learning was framed in terms of three subprocesses—creating, retaining, and transferring knowledge (Argote & Miron-Spektor, 2011)—and organizational memory was considered key to all three processes in terms of its capacity to constrain or enhance (Argote & Miron-Spektor, 2011) learning. These reviews noted that organizational memory is most often discussed, though, in terms of the knowledge retention subprocess of organizational learning, because this subprocess is thought to be a stock or repository of knowledge. Argote and Miron-Spektor (2011) proposed that knowledge repositories are primarily individuals, routines, or transactive memory systems, and researchers have studied knowledge decay as well as knowledge creation in relationship to these components. For example, Argote (2013) offered that the research on transactive memory "emphasizes that as social systems gain experience, members acquire knowledge about which member is good at performing which task or operating which tool" (p. 99), thereby increasing the store of knowledge. Argote and Miron-Spektor (2011) asserted that at the core of most of the definitions of organizational learning is a change, usually referring to a change in organizational knowledge or memory through experience. They referenced knowledge both in terms of a stock of valued information as well as the process of knowing. In defining organizational memory as a "supraindividual repository"—either a structure or process—of knowledge, there are challenges with each of these repositories or components of the organization in terms of creating, transferring, and further embedding knowledge in memory systems (Argote, 2013).

The interest in memory has also been addressed in knowledge transfer, which at times is considered a component of organizational learning. The focus on knowledge transfer has become increasingly highlighted as organizations try to retain knowledge in the face of staff turnover and increasing baby boomer retirements (Argote, 2013; Argote & Miron-Spektor, 2011) or face strategic organizational change initiatives such as mergers or acquisitions. Knowledge is often differentiated from organizational memory in the knowledge transfer literature, in that knowledge is considered to be only one component of organizational memory (Argote & Miron-Spektor, 2011). As an example, Levine and Prietula (2012) employed a qualitative research approach using agent-based modeling to explore the relationship between knowledge transfer and performance. They found that broader access to organizational memory creates a weaker relationship between global knowledge transfer and performance. Levine and Prietula drew from Walsh and Ungson's (1991) definition of organizational memory and the related bins, and their modeling took into account both social and asocial memory, with the former being based on interactions with other people and the latter being based on interaction with technology like a database. They found, in part, that an overall understanding of the relationship between knowledge transfer and performance needed to take into account individual, organizational, and environmental factors as the costs of extensive computer systems and training to aid knowledge management, as these factors may far exceed the performance and cost benefits (Levine & Prietula, 2012).

Argote and Ingram (2000) developed a framework to organize and articulate the theoretical and empirical work on knowledge transfer. This framework considers organizational memory as knowledge embedded in the organization in components such as members, tools, and tasks and the networks across these elements. The knowledge embedded in individuals and connected to routines, for example, has been studied in relationship to turnover and its impact on performance. For a more detailed elaboration, see Argote (2013), particularly in connection with losing individual knowledge.

While some authors, such as Argote and Miron-Spektor (2011), have argued that there has been significant progress in the theory and research on organizational learning, this has not translated into more robust theorizing and empirical research on the concept of organizational memory. Despite organizational memory being key to these processes, there has been little to no development of the concept itself or drawing from the rich theoretical literature on collective memory in other disciplines such as sociology and anthropology.

Collective Memory as a Theoretical Lens for Organizational Memory

In part to respond to the sustained interest in organizational memory as a concept in organizational studies and practice, to address the lack of substantive theorizing on organizational memory, and to expand beyond definitions and theories of knowledge, theorizing about organizational memory in the 2000s turned toward the sociological literature on collective memory, framing memory as history and commemoration in organizations and focusing on these processes in organizations and the relationship to identity.

This section begins with some of the early work on collective memory in organizational studies in the late 1990s and early 2000s followed by more recent work on commemoration as a part of collective memory, represented in two special issues of *Organization* (2014, 2016) on memory, narrative, and commemoration. The role of history as another key part of collective memory is then discussed, primarily through the special topics forum of the *Academy of Management Review* (2016) on history in organizational studies. The section concludes with related work on social memory and forgetting during this period.

Commemoration and Remembering as a Theoretical Lens for Organizational Memory

Early traces of this shift toward the sociological theorizing in organizational memory surfaced in Casey's (1997) empirical study of organizational memory. Casey built on Walsh and Ungson (1991), defining memory as shared interpretations of past events, and integrated the theoretical work on collective memory (Schwartz, 1991a, 1991b) from sociology to serve as a theoretical foundation for her research. In her case study of collective memory of an organization, Casey found shared recollections and interpretations of past events in the multisite organization that served as the research site. In addition, organizational identity was a critical factor in how and why events were recalled. Building on this work, Nissley and Casey (2002) theorized about the role of power and politics in what is remembered in organizations, taking a multidisciplinary approach (involving organizational studies, sociology, psychology, museum studies, and history) and drawing primarily from the work of Schwartz (1991a, 1991b) and Halbwachs (1950/1980). Since these early works, studies of organizational history framed as traditions or legacy as well as commemoration or coremembering as facets of organizational memory or collective memory have surfaced in organizational studies theory and have been linked with identity.

The role of power dynamics and politics also emerged in empirical work on commemoration and remembering in organizational studies, particularly in how collective memory is formed, shaped, and recalled in organizations in relationship to history and remembering. These studies often took a critical theory approach to memory, framing power as a managerial or dominant force. As an example, Sorensen (2014) noted that organizational studies began to "confront the role organizations play in creating and maintaining the memory of the darker sides of organization" (p. 283), which are often minimized or normalized (p. 279). In referring to how events of the past are recalled, Sorensen (2014) asserted that "history today is often represented as kitsch" (p. 279). He continued: "History tends to be organized by a majoritarian system—in this case what has been termed 'the Holocaust industry'—through collective instruction in how to interpret events," and he outlined "alternative ways for exposing and resisting this process, resulting in the creation of counter-narratives" (p. 279). He proposed the critical role organizations play in preserving and producing memory, particularly "kitsch" (p. 281), with processes influenced by the political and social forces that shape memory in organizations. This emphasis on power, politics, commemoration, and history continued to emerge throughout the early 2000s. Examples of this interest are the three special issues on memory, history, and identity in two key organizational studies journals.

Special Issues Focused on Organizational Memory as Collective Memory and Commemoration

Many of the ideas relative to organizational memory as a form of collective memory, commemoration, and history in organizational studies in the 2000s described thus far were captured in two special issues of *Organization* (2014, 2016) and a third in the *Academy of Management Review* in 2016. These three special issues contributed to and expanded our understanding of the relationship between memory and identity. The special issues in *Organization* enhanced understanding of social memory, commemoration, and connection with historical methods, while the special issues in *Academy of Management Review* highlighted a turn toward bringing history as a discipline and research methods from history such as historiography into organizational studies.

The two special issues of *Organization* on commemoration and remembering were directed toward considering how collective memory, narratives, and commemoration could be used as ways to explore memory primarily and identity secondarily. The editors acknowledged some of the issues in integrating history as a discipline—with its epistemology, ontology, and related methods—with organizational studies. In 2014, the special issue drew attention to narrative and memory, and in 2016 the special issue focused on commemoration. Rowlinson, Casey, et al. (2014), in the introduction to the first special issue, highlighted the intersection between organizational studies, memory studies, and historiography and the role that narratives play in organizational memory such as heritage. Similar to Walsh and Ungson (1991), they asserted that narratives as a form of memory may enable or constrain organizational actions (Rowlinson, Casey, et al., 2014) and that memory processes, whether conscious or unconscious, may intentionally or unintentionally shape recollections of the past. They acknowledged both the extensive work on social memory in sociology as well as the relatively minimal theory development of organizational memory in organizational studies. This special issue also highlighted the importance of exploring and incorporating research methods from history—from microhistory to ethnography and archival research. In acknowledging the "historic turn in organizational theory" (Rowlinson, Casey, et al., 2014, p. 443), they noted that the engagement of both business historians and organizational theorists offers the opportunity to expand the scope of research methods in studying stories and other forms of memory and history in and about organizations.

As an example, in this issue, Adorisio (2014) theorized an alternative to the storage bin approach to organizational memory as framed by Walsh and Ungson (1991), suggesting framing organizational memory as narrative or stories and as a process of remembering or coremembering influenced by both the subjective nature of individual memory as well as the importance of the context in which this process happens. Researchers have proposed that as a group recalls stories of the past through remembering together, these stories are continuously shaped as they are told and retold. This process of narratives is a way to "organize the selection and interpretation of the past" (Adorisio, 2014, p. 465). This work defined narrative and organizational stories following the work of Herrnstein Smith (1981, as cited in Adorisio, 2014) with an emphasis on social interaction. The role of the narrator in the story and how meaning is constructed (Linde, 2000, 2001) are critical to these approaches to stories and narrative. Theorists have proposed that stories of the organization's past live in the present and are shaped by the individual's past as well. Adorisio (2014) asserted that combining a "storying perspective" with antenarrative and microhistory methods enhances our understanding of the remembering process and the relationship of the past to the present (p. 475).

In the introduction to the 2016 special issue of *Organization* on commemoration in organizations, Cutcher, Dale, Hancock, and Tyler (2016) asserted that despite the importance of the relationship between organizational memory and organizational actions, commemoration and the process of memory have been overlooked as research topics. The articles in this issue revealed the importance of where and when stories are recalled and the critical role of power and politics in this process. Materiality, spatiality, and embodiment surfaced as major themes in this issue in relationship to what, when, and how we commemorate the past in organizations.

For example, in this issue, Allen and Brown's (2016) work explored how material objects play a significant role in the coremembering or commemoration process. Specifically, they theorized about how memorials "are attempts to preserve a contemporary account of a past event" (p. 11). In their study of the Hyde Park memorial in London, they investigated the often conflicting views regarding how the memorial should be constructed, how the event itself occurred, which communities were the benefactors of the memorial, and whether the memorial and the process of remembering sustained the values of that community. They conceptualized and described spatial mnemonic practices and how they preserved memories (Allen & Brown, 2016, p. 14), concluding that the past is always with us in the present.

Stories were also highlighted in their importance to material objects such as memorials, in that memorials are only meaningful in relationship to the stories that are told about them and their ability to connect with the present (Allen & Brown, 2016). Allen and Brown linked memorials and the process of remembering with the identity of collectives as well as the individuals who are remembering the events or people represented by a memorial. They described it as a fluid, emergent process: "The identity, meaning, purpose and use of a memorial—what it is, what it means, what and who it is for—do not seem to be fixed by the design process, but rather emerges and fluctuates over time" (Allen & Brown, 2016, p. 13). They compared and contrasted the perdurance approach (Ingold, 2013, as cited in Allen & Brown, 2016)—where identity is a process, with the identity of memorials and other material objects of memory being transformed through time—with the endurance approach, where the essence of the identity endures over time. As individuals interact with these memorials, the multiple identities of each individual become intertwined with the memory and identity processes (Allen & Brown, 2016, p. 17). Memory of the events continues to emerge and change through individual interactions and activities around and including the site, yet it is a process of both endurance and transformation of both the memories of the events and the identity of the collectives involved.

In this issue, power also surfaced as key to the process of commemoration or remembering together as well as forgetting (Mena et al., 2016; Rodgers, Petersen, & Sanderson, 2016), and it occurs in relationship to material objects as well as the dynamics of legitimation. As an example, in her study of commemoration of the Chattri memorial in Brighton in the United Kingdom, Ashley (2016) took a postcolonial theoretical approach to understand the meaning-making process and the shifting of meaning in the evolution of the story of Chattri "from colonial instrument to symbol and space for ethnic-Indian group activities" (p. 30). Her work demonstrates how memorializing can be seen as a complex combination of objects and practices that organize both meaning and value, engaging affect (p. 43), and highlights the critical role of physical space such as structures in the "official and everyday organizing and legitimation of what is accepted and valued as 'normal'" (p. 43) in this commemoration process.

Power dynamics as part of the dynamics of legitimation in organizations surfaced in the memorializing as well as forgetting. As an example, in Bell and Taylor's (2016) study of the vernacular mourning of the death of Steve Jobs, the authors asserted that this type of commemoration is frequently controlled by the corporation in an attempt to ensure its survival. They connected Foucault's work on heterotopia with impromptu mourning spaces as another form of commemoration that involves properties of space and time and the importance of power relations in these practices.

The dynamics of legitimation of memory as well as forgetting processes also were researched (Mena et al., 2016; Rodgers et al., 2016) in more public spaces in how people or memory sites are forgotten or minimalized in histories and commemorative practices. Public commemoration can be dominated by national schemas such as capitalism, which can minimize and at times erase the accomplishments of some parts of a society. Similar to social memory approaches that take a constructionist approach to memory (Schwartz, 2016) and organizational studies of memory and commemoration (Rowlinson, 2002; Rowlinson & Hassard, 1993), both Rodgers et al. and Mena et al. asserted that while organizational commemoration and forgetting processes can be passive and unintentional, most are intentional, active, and influential in forgetting and memory work that impact organizational processes and have the potential to shape or change the identity of the collective.

The third special issue related to organizational memory, commemoration, and history took a different approach. The focus of the special issue of the *Academy of Management Review* (2016) was a call to integrate history into organizational studies research. Specifically, the purpose of the special topic forum was to explore how organizational studies theorizing and research can be enhanced by incorporating history and historical methods (Godfrey, Hassard, O'Connor, Rowlinson, & Ruef, 2016), acknowledging the long line of theory that has worked toward this end, including Usdiken and Kieser (2004), Kipping and Usdiken (2014), and Booth and Rowlinson (2006). Articles in the issue highlighted the similarities and differences of the disciplines, and the major themes are discussed next.

In their introduction to the issue, Godfrey, Hassard, O'Connor, Rowlinson, and Ruef (2016) portrayed the field of organizational history as a "synthesis of organizational theory and historiography" and offered three arguments to position future research on "historical work within organizational studies" (p. 590). First, they asserted that organizational history and historical research are critical parts of organizational studies, with this "historic turn" in organizational studies drawing on the "theory and philosophy of history" (p. 591). History should be more than a context for studies, as it can also be a strategic resource (p. 590). Second, they proposed that "organization theory needs to provide a theoretical account of the past" instead of relying on history to "test or illustrate theory" (p. 591). Lastly, they advocated for incorporating history into organizational theory studies to investigate critical societal issues such as racism and social responsibility. In their introduction, they traced the development of the historic turn in organizational studies (p. 591) and the debates that emerged in this development regarding the relative value of history in organizational studies.

Godfrey et al. (2016) differentiated organizational history studies from business history and management history as subfields of organizational studies. They defined "organizational history loosely as research and writing combining history and organizational theorizing" (p. 592). Business history as a subfield is dedicated to research using archival records (p. 592), and management history is "the history of management thought" (p. 593). They noted the challenges in interdisciplinary or multidisciplinary fields and recommended a transdisciplinary approach, as originally developed by Leblebici; citing Maclean et al. (2016), they proposed theorizing that considers "history and organizational studies . . . of equal status" (Maclean et al., 2016, p. 610) and that would be accepted in both disciplines.

To further a transdisciplinary research agenda, Maclean, Harvey, and Clegg (2016) defined historical organizational studies as "organizational research that draws extensively on historical data, methods, and knowledge embedding organizing and organizations in their sociohistorical context to generate historically informed theoretical narratives attentive to both disciplines" (p. 609). They offered that historians emphasize deductive and inductive reasoning and their analytic methods are minimized or not apparent, while organizational studies of narrative and other facets of memory and history focus on theorizing, analysis, and explication of methods and findings relative to theory and research. As a partial solution to these differences, the authors proposed a model building on the commonalities between the disciplines for future research in historical organizational studies (p. 612). The model portrays four categories of historical organizational studies: history as evaluating, history as explicating, history as conceptualizing, and history as narrating (p. 612) and has five underlying principles: dual integrity, pluralistic understanding, representational truth, context sensitivity, and theoretical fluency (p. 617). Maclean et al. (2016) advocated that "the theoretical possibilities that uses of the past may stimulate within the field of organizational studies are potentially substantial" (p. 627).

In this special issue, the relationship between collective memory and identity surfaced in the work of Ocasio et al. (2016). They theorized about how collective memory processes shape our understanding of events as well as societal institutions, in particular societal logics, and then how collective memory is in turn shaped by societal logics. In exploring the historicity of societal logics such as family, religion, and the state (Thornton et al., 2012, as cited in Ocasio et al., 2016), they defined societal logics as "historically constituted cultural structures generated through collective memory-making" (p. 677). Drawing from Schwartz's work (2005), they defined collective memory as "a system of values, identities, and practices that shape the commemoration and (re)interpretation of historical events" (p. 677) and history as the "accumulation of past events and . . . the documents, narratives, and memories attached to them" (p. 677). They proposed that organizational-level logics can serve as the foundation for organizational identity. They also suggested that collective memory has a role in "mediating the influence of societal logics" (p. 694) that shape how historical events are recalled and will serve as a guide for the evolution of organizational identity.

Outside of these three special issues, there was additional discussion of this turn toward history and commemoration in organizational theorizing about memory. Greenwood and Bernardi (2014) suggested that the move is not without complications, due in part to three primary differences between these disciplines: the historian's perspective on methodology, relationship to practice, and the "ideal of objectivity" (p. 915). Organizational studies' turn away from history has been attributed to the social sciences' turn in general toward natural science norms of objectivity, evidence, and truth in the 1960s, particularly in the United States (Usdiken & Kieser, 2004, p. 321). Rowlinson, Hassard, et al. (2014) also noted an aspect of this issue, highlighting the focus on and use of different research methods to study a phenomenon.

In expanding on these critical methodological differences, Greenwood and Bernardi (2014) suggested that researchers can exploit them rather than try to integrate and minimize them. They suggested that the scholarship of historians can provide important data to the theorizing and research in organizational studies by contextualizing organizational phenomena in past events (Greenwood & Bernardi, 2014, p. 923). Maclean et al. (2016) suggested that despite the differences between organizational studies and history, there is much to be gained through their integration. Overall, these theorists acknowledged that "history matters" for understanding collectives such as organizations (Rowlinson, Hassard, et al., 2014).

Rowlinson, Hassard, et al. (2014) suggested that differences are seen in three "epistemological dualisms derived from historical theory": history tends to focus on "narrative construction, whereas organizational theorists subordinate narrative to analysis" (p. 250); history focuses on facts or verifiable sources, while most organizational theories focus on "constructed data" (p. 250); and history theorizes time by focusing on periodicity, while organizational theory treats time "as constant for chronology" (p. 250).

Organizational Memory as Social Remembering

In addition to the organizational memory work in the early 2000s that drew from collective memory theory and linked with organizational identity, theorizing about memory through the similar lens of social memory began to surface in the mid-2000s. For example, Feldman and Feldman (2006) and Booth and Rowlinson (2006) noted that efforts to theorize about organizational memory have been diminished by the narrow approach of a storage bin that doesn't capture the complexity of the concept and the more nuanced processes of organizational remembering

(Feldman & Feldman, 2006). Acknowledging that organizational memory is a uniquely appealing concept, they commented that "despite continued efforts to dismantle the concept's mystery, it has not lost its essentially baffling quality" (Feldman & Feldman, 2006, p. 864). They theorized about memory as a verb, or the process of remembering, and the factors that influence this process, supported by the work on social remembering. In this effort, they defined organizational remembering "as a collective, culture and time-specific process and practice, hinged on the concept of tradition as the cradling framework of meaning" (p. 862) and indicated that historicity is a defining quality of remembering (p. 868). The act of remembering is inherently social interaction influenced by power, space, and time, including the present, past, and future, which constitute a "chaining of remembering" (p. 868). Collective remembering is how tacit and explicit knowledge is passed along to old and new members of the organization. This process may be guided by traditions, a form of memory, yet these traditions can be flexible and a foundation for change.

Rowlinson et al. (2010), in their critique and analysis of the relationship between the literature on social remembering and organizational memory, noted the importance of the level of analysis and, in particular, the methods used for studying collective-level concepts such as organizational memory and collective memory in organizations. They highlighted sites of corporate memory—i.e., museums and visitor centers—and the research conducted about these sites. They took exception with Nissley and Casey's (2002) analysis of the collective memory in corporate museums as well as Casey's (1997) study of collective memory, asserting that these studies represented examples of *collected* memory versus *collective* memory. They highlighted that in the latter study in particular, Casey collected stories from more than 50 interviews, but the stories were from individuals. They identified accounts that they noted more directly surfaced collective memory, including Barndt's (2007) and Rowlinson's (2002) historical accounts of The Henry Ford Museum and Cadbury World, respectively. For an extensive comparison of organizational memory and social remembering, see Rowlinson et al. (2010).

In summary, the theory and research on organizational memory in the early 2000s that drew from the robust literature on collective memory to theorize about commemoration and history in organizations provided substantially more depth to the concept and, most importantly, provided a theoretical framework for future work in organizational memory and its relationship to other concepts, such as organizational identity. This work also began to surface the empirical relationship between organizational memory and identity and the factors that influence this relationship, including power, space, and material objects. The relationship between components of collective memory, i.e., history and commemoration and identity, also began to surface in this research in organizations.

In addition, this trend enhanced and expanded the research methods used to study organizational memory and its relationship to identity, including historiography.

Collective Memory: Social Science Perspectives From Anthropology, History, and Sociology

In addition to organizational studies, other social sciences such as sociology, anthropology, and history theorize and empirically research memory at the group, societal, or national levels. This research is most frequently conceptualized and defined from the perspective of collective memory. In the past 30 years, this work on collective memory has primarily been conducted by Western scholars (Schwartz, 2010, p. 619) and more frequently in sociology and anthropology.

Collective memory is an integral part of the broader field of memory studies, which crosses the social sciences. Collective memory is also, at times, referred to as social or cultural memory in these disciplines. Broadly, collective memory as a form of social memory is a study of not just what people recall but also how they interpret the memory as a form of knowledge (Schwartz, 2014). As early as 1998, the field of social memory studies was characterized by Olick and Robbins (p. 106) as "a nonparadigmatic, transdisciplinary, centerless enterprise." They were referring primarily to the work on collective memory in sociology and anthropology.

Olick, Vinitzky-Seroussi, and Levy (2011) highlighted that some of the issues in the study of collective memory stem from the terms used in these studies. For example, the term *collective memory* frequently raises the conflicts in interpretation of Halbwachs's work, in particular the level of analysis—i.e., is it "socially framed individual memory" or is it the "common memory of a group" (Olick et al., 2011, p. 41). Olick and colleagues (2011) proposed that the term *social memory studies* best captures this research in that it is "presuppositionally open to a variety of phenomena while pointing out that all remembering is in some sense social" (p. 41). Although there are varying interpretations of the term used for research in memory studies, the interest in collective or social memory remains strong across the social sciences.

Organizational researchers have contended that much of the work on collective memory from sociology and anthropology does not study organizations as sites of memory and identity but instead focuses on other collectives such as families, ethnic groups within countries or societies, nations, or societies as a whole (Godfrey, Hassard, O'Connor, Rowlinson, & Ruef, 2016; Rowlinson et al., 2010; Sorensen, 2014) without giving consideration to the uniqueness of an organization as a collective with memory and history.

There are many well-recognized scholars of collective memory in the past 50 years, particularly in sociology, and research across the fields of history, anthropology, and sociology has been significant. It is beyond the scope of this section to adequately cover this extensive work. This chapter reviews several major theoretical approaches to collective memory scholarship and related theorists in sociology and provides a limited overview of some of this work, with a focus primarily on Schwartz (1991a, 1991b, 1997, 2000, 2010, 2014, 2016). Schwartz is considered by many to be the father of collective memory studies in contemporary American sociology through his seminal writing on Halbwachs's work in a series of papers beginning in the early 1980s (Olick et al., 2011).

Origins of Collective Memory Theories: Halbwachs

Theories of collective memory are drawn primarily from Halbwachs's (1950/1980) work (Loveday, 2014; Olick et al., 2011). Halbwachs was a student of Durkheim (Beim, 2007). Durkheim's work on collective representations (Olick, 1999) and social facts set the stage for Halbwachs's thinking. Durkheim asserted that "collective memory is part of society's 'intellectual and moral framework'" (Durkheim, 1925, 1973, as cited in Schwartz, 2000, p. 8). Halbwachs was also a student of Henri Bergson, "who emphasized the subjective aspects of time, thought and reality" (Schwartz, 2014, p. 18). Schwartz (2014) asserted that Halbwachs's work on memory drew more from Bergson's philosophy of time than Durkheim, although Halbwachs took the subjective experience of time and memory a step further and centered the differences in perception of memory and time in the influence of social organizations (Olick et al., 2011). Halbwachs's focus on time and memory was in contrast to other philosophers of his time, who concentrated more on space as a way to determine the passage of time (Douglas, 1980, p. 1).

Halbwachs later left Bergson and became a student of Leibnitz. Halbwachs, similar to Leibnitz, thought that "our perceptions lose their clarity but they remain active and thanks to them we have the notion of our own identity. Nothing is forgotten; once attention is renewed these little perceptions become clear once more, and so we remember" (Douglas, 1980, p. 5). Drawing from Liebnitz's influence, Halbwachs also attributed the development of personal identity to social influences, including interaction with others as well as interactions with physical space and artifacts. "Individual consciousness is not the only way in which personal identity is constituted: contacts with other people and with other things can supplement it" (Douglas, 1980, p. 5). Halbwachs proposed the relationship between identity and memory in asserting that identity is core to collective memory. Historians (Megill, 1998) have asserted that Halbwachs presupposed that a preestablished identity, individual or collective, determines collective and historical memory.

Halbwachs began his work with Durkheim in Paris and moved toward sociology and Durkheim's conceptualization of time as a social construct.

He was a student and collaborator with Durkheim until Durkheim died in 1917. Durkheim's central concern was to "uncover the sources of social solidarity through a theory of collective consciousness" (Douglas, 1980, p. 7), and he believed that human understanding depended on the "social condition" (p. 8) in addition to time and space. Durkheim also provided a sociological framework of "cognitive order (time perception) with social order (division of labor)" upon which Halbwachs could build his collective memory theory.

Halbwachs's work on collective memory developed later during his work with Durkheim. He published *Les Cadres sociaux de la mémoire* in 1925, in which he differentiated dreams from memories. He asserted that memories are shared, sustained by others, public, and linked to physical space and artifacts (Douglas, 1980, p. 12). He emphasized the critical importance of social order and conditions on what is recalled, indicating that each social segment will have a "different historical past, will have different memories attached to their respective landmarks" (Douglas, 1980, p. 12). His later book, *La Topographie légendaire des évangiles en terre sainte*, focused on the relationship between space and memory and how memories can be shaped by the concerns of those remembering at a later date and in a different space. Halbwachs was one of several sociologists in France at that time to conduct empirical research; his early studies focused on urban areas and the working class (www.buchenwald.de/en/1219/ accessed 11/26/17). Halbwachs is credited with moving the concept of collective memory from an inherited or racial memory and a biological framework to a cultural lens (Assmann & Czaplicka, 1995).

Halbwachs's work on memory during this period was referenced by Bartlett, who was conducting laboratory studies of memory. In Bartlett's (1932) text, *Remembering*, he referenced Halbwachs and critiqued this research as "accepting from Durkheim a unitary conception of society and for reifying collective memory into a quasi-mystic soul with its own existence" (Douglas, 1980, p. 16). Douglas alleged that this was misleading and that Bartlett wrongly asserted that Halbwachs theorized about "memory of the group," where instead Halbwachs's contribution was to acknowledge and explicate the influence of social groups who sustain their partial memories of an event through interaction over time. "Our memories remain collective, however, and are recalled to us through others even though only we were participants in the events or saw the things concerned. In reality we are never alone" (Halbwachs, 1950/1980, p. 23).

Halbwachs strove for a synthesis of his thinking on collective memory in his final book, *La Mémoire collective*, published posthumously in 1950. He also interweaved his theorizing on time with a credit to Bergson in this text. He drew from the idea of the "conflation of the future and the past in the present" (Douglas, 1980, p. 18) and how we socially reconstruct history because large amounts of information "are forgotten, not from spite or intention but merely because the groups which used to remember them have disappeared" (Douglas, 1980, p. 18); further, "the divisions of time in the collective memory correspond to the divisions in society" (Douglas, 1980, p. 18). Halbwachs (1950/1980) explained the social reconstruction:

> A remembrance is gained not merely by reconstituting the image of a past event a piece at a time. That reconstruction must start from shared data or conceptions. These are present in our mind as well as theirs, because they are continually being passed back and forth. This process occurs only because all have been and still are members of the same group. This is the only way to understand how a remembrance is at once recognized and reconstructed. . . .
> We will clearly see that the "starting points," or the elements of these personal remembrances that seem to be uniquely our own, can easily be found preserved in definite social milieus.
>
> (pp. 31, 47)

In this work, Halbwachs clearly differentiated between memory and history. He considered collective memory as social, while he considered written history as objective (Burke, 2011). In comparing individual memory and collective memory, he noted that the latter "evolves according to its own laws, and any individual remembrances that may penetrate are transformed within a totality having no personal consciousness" (Halbwachs, 1950/1980, p. 51). He further distinguished them as autobiographical memory and historical memory (p. 52), with the latter representing "the past only in a condensed and schematic way" (p. 52). In the following text he elaborated on the differences between history and collective memory:

> Collective memory differs from history in at least two respects. It is a current of continuous thought whose continuity is not at all artificial, for it retains from the past only what still lives or is capable of living in the consciousness of the groups keeping the memory alive. . . . By definition it does not exceed the boundaries of this group. . . . Situated external to and above groups, history readily introduces into the stream of facts simple demarcations fixed once and for all. . . . In effect there are several collective memories. This is the second characteristic distinguishing the collective memory from history. History is unitary, and it can be said that there is only one history.
>
> (Halbwachs, 1950/1980, pp. 80, 81, 83)

Halbwachs's work was interrupted by deportation because of his resistance to the Nazis, and he died in the Little Camp at Buchenwald on March 15, 1945. In 1950, his daughter published his book on collective memory (www.buchenwald.de/en/1219/ accessed 11/26/17).

As Olick et al. (2011) noted, the early sociological theorizing of Durkheim and Halbwachs did not surface in a vacuum. They recognized links to classical philosophers such as Aristotle and Plato, who created metaphors of memory like "the mind as a wax tablet or of memorization as a sorting into bins" (p. 8). Much later, Locke proposed that memory is key to identity, as did Erikson (1994) and Mead (1934) (as cited in Olick et al., 2011). Early foundations of theory and research in psychology with Wundt and Ebbinghaus's (as cited in Olick et al., 2011) memory studies with individuals and, later, with Freud's work, also contributed to our understanding of the social foundations of memory. These dimensions are acknowledged in this early memory work even if the focus was for the most part on the individual and how memory functioned.

Collective Memory Literature Building on Halbwachs

Halbwachs's work was ignored for many decades but became prominent with the resurgence of interest in memory across the social sciences in the late 1980s and 1990s (Rowlinson et al., 2010). Theorizing that has followed Halbwachs's philosophical approach steers away from a concentration on the individual through the lens of psychology (Rowlinson et al., 2010). The research instead centers on the "genuinely collective nature of remembering" and "the degree to which it takes place in and through language, narrative and dialogue" (Olick, 1999, p. 343). Collective memory is more than an aggregation of individuals' memories (Olick, 1999; Rowlinson et al., 2010); it includes the meaning and interpretation of the memory to groups or collectives.

The renewed interest in social or collective memory in the social sciences, particularly in anthropology, has been attributed in part to "decolonization," with an emphasis on surfacing the multiple voices and memories of collectives that emerge (Berliner, 2005; Haukanes & Trnka, 2013), as well as a postmodern turn toward interpreting the relationship between memory and identity (Berliner, 2005; Hall, 1996). This focus on the collective was in contrast to the prevailing dominant trend toward individual and psychological perspectives (Hewer & Roberts, 2012) in the social sciences. It highlights the idea "that individual minds are the product of culture and history" (Hewer & Roberts, 2012, p. 169). In addition, this "memory boom" (Connerton, 2006, p. 317), particularly in sociology and anthropology, has moved toward the social process of commemoration or coremembering and the relationship to sustaining cultural or social memory rather than factual accounts in documents or other repositories. Lebow (2008), in reflecting on the "memory boom" in history, noted that this work also raises the importance of memory politics and memory as a political resource. Winter (2000, as cited by Lebow, 2008) called memory "the new paradigm of history, overpowering and restructuring other frames of reference like class and gender" (p. 26).

One challenge that has emerged from this "memory boom" in the social sciences is that the pervasive use of the term *memory* has led to its overuse, bringing with it "semantic exhaustion" (White, 2006, p. 325) or "semantic overload" (Klein, 2000), as noted in anthropology. With overuse, the term "seems to be losing precise meaning in proportion to its growing rhetorical power" (Gillis, 1994, p. 3, as cited in Olick et al., 2011). Memory as a concept has the potential of becoming less useful to researchers as it becomes more difficult to distinguish from culture or identity (Fabian, 1999, p. 51). More recently, Schwartz (2016) acknowledged that the study of memory is in an "ambiguous state," with studies of collective memory focusing more on its fallibility and much less on how it is useful to humankind. "Knowledge of collective memory's *normal* working is underdeveloped" (Schwartz, 2016, p. 10) in theory and research.

Theoretical Approaches to Collective Memory

Schwartz (2000) delineated several different theoretical approaches to collective memory based on his research on the collective memory of key U.S. historical figures, Western and Eastern cultures, and critical events; different approaches address the *how* of collective memory and not necessarily the content, or the *what* (Schwartz, 2010). The revisionist or presentist (Schwartz, 2010) approach is representative of Mead (1934) and Halbwachs (1950/1980) and asserts that the images of historical figures are reconfigured within present issues and are in transition and precarious (Schwartz, 2010, p. 621). Frequently, power is identified as a major factor in how memory is reconfigured (Schwartz, 2000, 2010).

The second approach, as addressed by Schwartz, frames collective memory as representing the politics of collective memory. This view is grounded in multiculturalism and "treats memory as a contested object of differently empowered communities" and a way by which "the privileged maintain their hegemony" (Schwartz, 1997, p. 23). Related to this view is that power is diffused and that memory emerges across groups of people and "makes the past hostage to the mentalities and structures of the present" (Schwartz, 1997, p. 23).

Schwartz (2016) proposed that these two approaches favor a constructionist approach, with collective memory depending "more on the contingencies of social experience than on qualities of the entities remembered" (p. 17). In discussing these approaches, Schwartz also cited the limitations of these approaches in supporting their premise that that past is malleable and easily distorted. He asserted that the distortion is limited by "reality's constraint on the malleability of perception" (Schwartz, 2016, p. 18). "Once a memory is established within a collectivity, it is difficult to modify let alone ignore" (Schwartz, 2016, p. 15).

The presentist approach has dominated the research on collective memory since World War I, when people began to question "absolutes of time, space and knowledge" (Schwartz, 2010, p. 621), and the approach continued into the 1960s, when traditions and stories from the past were discredited (Schwartz, 2010). This wave of research continued into the 1990s with research on power, relativism, global changes in multiculturalism, and differentiated values. The more traditionalist view sees memory as an independent variable and focuses on the "reality of the past" (Schwartz, 2010, p. 621).

Schwartz suggested a compromise between these approaches to collective memory, surfacing the role of collective identity in our remembrances and interpretations of the past. "Modern societies represent the past for their members through history and commemoration" (Schwartz, 2005, p. 64). History and commemoration represent the core elements of collective memory and are the two primary ways we access the past (Schwartz, 2000). Schwartz (2010) noted that research on collective memory is reacknowledging the "obduracy of history" in that "what is known about the past limits what can be done with it interpretively" (p. 622). He asserted that "memory is path dependent: earlier representations of the past affect the availability and resources required for present representations" (p. 622). Collective memory serves as a model *for* society and a model *of* society (Schwartz, 2014, p. 15), as it is built on values that define meaning, which shapes interpretations of the past. Schwartz (2014) noted that "social memory's contribution to humanity's survival is not its malleability; memory enhances our ability to survive because it permits us to retain and retrieve so much of the past" and "human society becomes impossible without it" (Schwartz, 2014, p. 313).

Differentiating Between Collective Memory and Other Related Terms

Numerous terms have been used to reference a shared past or collective memory across the social sciences. Following a brief discussion of related terms, this section focuses primarily on how history and commemoration have been discussed in definitions of collective memory.

Similar to sociology, in anthropology, a number of similar terms have been used to refer to a shared past or collective memory (Hewer & Roberts, 2012), such as *social memory, heritage*, and *history*. Earlier theorizing about memory in anthropology thought of it as a storehouse where recollections were static and could be withdrawn or deposited (Cipolla, 2008). More recently, definitions of collective memory in sociology and anthropology have been more process focused (Cipolla, 2008) and have described it in terms that are more similar to commemoration or remembering together. For example, Jedlowski (2001, p. 33) defined collective memory as "a set of *social representations concerning the past* which each group produces, institutionalizes, guards and transmits through the interaction of its members." In proposing collective memory as a social process, several factors have been identified that impact this process, including time, space, and identity (Espinoza, Piper, & Fernandez, 2014); power or political dynamics as well as group dynamics; and whether the group is a religious group, social class, or a team. It is through these social interactions or this remembering process that individuals and groups determine what and how memories are recalled (Russell, 2006).

Heritage and *legacy* are also frequently used to refer to aspects of collective memory and are often used in conjunction with each other. Haladewicz-Grzelak and Lubos-Koziel (2014) proposed that heritage is a more ambiguous term used to discuss the past and is embedded with emotion. This term has been used primarily by Western theorists. As cited in Haladewicz-Grzelak and Lubos-Koziel (2014), Lowenthal (1996) also differentiated history from heritage, with heritage more linked with emotion. The two terms employ different means to persuade: history relies on facts and truth, while heritage elaborates upon some aspects and forgets or invents others (Lowenthal, 1996). Heritage as a process has been connected with legitimizing collective identities (Lowenthal, 1996).

Differentiating Between History and Collective Memory

Halbwachs (1950/1980) referenced both history and commemoration as integral components of collective memory. These components and their relationship have been further theorized. For example, Schwartz (2000) defined collective memory as "the representation of the past embodied in *both* historical evidence and commemorative symbolism" (p. 9). He asserted that these components have different functions, in that history provides the "causes and consequences of events" while commemoration selects the events based on a "community's distinctive values" and identity (Schwartz, 2010, p. 620). These two components are intertwined, as commemoration is a social process grounded in historical evidence or knowledge and cannot be separated from it (Adamczyk, 2002; Schwartz, 2000, 2010). For example, Adamczyk noted that traditions and collective memory such as those associated with Thanksgiving are based on historical events (Adamczyk, 2002, p. 347), yet are recalled through a process that continues to shape how Thanksgiving and this initial specific event is remembered.

Kansteiner (2002), a historian, also agreed that memory and history are distinctly different. He noted that collective memory is a "collective phenomenon but it only manifests itself in the actions and statements of individuals," which tend to "privilege" the interests of the present and can be manipulated or mediated through conscious efforts and absorbed unconsciously (p. 180). He noted that most historians who study collective memory work from Halbwachs's theories yet often take exception with Halbwachs's distinctly "anti-individualism" approach and the assumption that all memory is social memory when the focus of history is frequently on the individual and his or her objectives and actions in particular critical events (Kansteiner, 2002, p. 181). He claimed that many historians have unsuccessfully tried to find alternatives to the "sociologically 'occupied' conception of collective memory" (p. 181) with terms such as *social memory* or even *myth*.

In Kansteiner's critique of collective memory scholarship in sociology and other disciplines, he defined collective memory as

> the result of the interaction among three types of historical factors: the intellectual and cultural traditions that frame all our representations of the past, the memory makers who selectively adopt and manipulate these traditions, and the memory consumers who use, ignore, or transform such artifacts according to their own interests.
>
> (2002, p. 180)

He also faulted the media culture of the 21st century with images and representations of the past that have little relationship to traditions or history. "Perhaps history should be more appropriately defined as a particular type of cultural memory" because "this selection, interpretation and distortion is socially conditioned" (Kansteiner, 2002, p. 184). The focus on identity suggests that "our modern crises of memory may not be as exceptional as we tend to assume" (p. 184). One of the significant contributions of sociological work on collective memory has been to differentiate between history and memory and propose a structure of collective memory and the factors that influence it. In addition, this sociological work has surfaced the relationship between collective memory and the identity of collectives such as nations, communities, and nationalities.

The difference between terms has been discussed across the social sciences. Historian Peter Novick outlined the distinction between history and collective memory in the following terms: "To understand something historically is to be aware of its complexity and to have sufficient detachment to see it from multiple perspectives and to accept the ambiguities, including moral ambiguities, of protagonists' motives and behavior. Collective memory simplifies; sees events from a single, committed perspective; is impatient with ambiguities of any kind; and reduces events to mythic archetypes" (Novick, 1999, pp. 3–4 as cited in Wertsch, 2008).

The difference between history and memory has also been explored in recent work in anthropology (Adamczyk, 2002; De Lugan, 2013) and social psychology (Hewer & Roberts, 2012). De Lugan (2013) proposed that there is a "dynamic tension between history and memory" (p. 978). She defined history in terms of the "official representations about the past, so important to asserting nation state legitimacy" (p. 7), while memory consists of recollections that are distinct from the official history of a country or a people. This differentiation between history and collective memory was also considered by Hewer and Roberts (2012). Building on Wertsch and Roediger's (2008) work, they asserted that history may be "willing to change a narrative in order to be loyal to facts" (p. 171); its overall purpose is to "provide an accurate representation of the past where the emphasis is on the transformation of knowledge" (Hewer & Roberts, 2012, p. 171). Collective remembering or commemoration, in contrast, "is willing to change information (even facts) in order to be loyal to a narrative" (Hewer & Roberts, 2012, p. 171).

As noted in the definitions above, collective memory is differentiated into several components, with history and commemoration, or coremembering, the most frequently articulated components. Distinguishing history and collective memory is difficult at times, and it quickly becomes clear that the distinction is both necessary and yet challenging to sustain. This issue has been part of the discussion for decades. In the 1920s, Maurice Halbwachs outlined the difference between "formal history" and collective memory (Halbwachs, 1950/1980, p. 78), and related claims emerged even earlier in debates about nations and national memory.

Schwartz on Commemoration and History

Schwartz's work (2000, 2005) on collective memory highlights many of the differences in how collective memory and history are defined that emerge from the discussion across the social sciences. He too proposed a dynamic tension between history and commemoration, with both defined as two facets of collective memory. Similar to other scholars, he described history as more objective or factual, while commemoration involves remembering together; he didn't privilege one as having more power than another or representing a dominant group. History is "objectively conceived" (Schwartz, 2000, p. 10) and upheld and limited by evidence or facts. History is external to a collective (Schwartz, 2016) and is the process of "establishing and propagating of facts about the past" (Schwartz, 2008, p. 76). This record is portrayed in museums, monographs, or other researched or analytic documents that are independent of a group's present interests and concerns. These accounts of events, often before one's lifetime, may often be produced as part of a commemorative activity or occasion (Schwartz, 2005). Once the essence of history is stabilized in evidence over time, Schwartz proposed that it remains essentially the same, while peripheral elements may change to meet present needs and understanding (Schwartz, 2000, 2016). Commemoration or remembering together, as a facet of collective memory, is grounded in the idea that "historical knowledge can be represented in the mind by means of physical objects and ritual forms, the most common of which include scriptural (hagiographic) accounts, icons (including painting and statuary), music, monuments, shrines, naming conversations and ritual observances" (Schwartz & Schuman, 2000, p. 2).

The word *commemoration* stems from the "Latin term *com*, together, and *memorare*, to remember" (Schwartz, 2000, p. 9). Commemoration, or remembering together, selects events from history that are most reflective of the identity of the collective and affirms "its members' mutual affinity" (Schwartz, 2000, p. 10). At the same time, commemoration is grounded in historical evidence. Commemoration leads to new patterns of perception or thinking in a culture while maintaining old ones. Commemoration is the process of coremembering, or remembering together (Schwartz, 2000, 2005).

Schwartz distinguished two types of commemoration: the first is remembering historical events that affirm a society's ideals and positive accomplishments (Schwartz, 2015, p. 1), and the second is remembering traumatic or negative events that are "weighing on the present as sources of shame and dishonor" (Schwartz, 2015, p. 1). In discussing current theories of commemoration, Schwartz proposed that some assume commemoration is based on politics and power about what is remembered and "the tastes, values, and interests of society's elite" (Schwartz, 2015, p. 11), while others are framed from the diffusion of power across "a matrix of cross-cutting coalitions and enterprises rather than a ruling" elite (Schwartz, 2015, p. 11).

Schwartz suggested that both history and commemoration "shape what ordinary individuals believe about the past; they are the vehicles of collective memory" (2005, p. 64). Commemorative patterns of interpretations are formed through redundancy as accounts of the past and symbols accumulate, are "stored in social institutions," and are "transmitted across generations and sustained outside the mind of the individual" (Schwartz & Schuman, 2000, p. 1). Schwartz and Schuman proposed that history and commemoration are interdependent in that "commemorative symbols mark the morally relevant zones of history—events reflecting our values and ideals most vividly—while historical accounts ground commemoration factually" (2000, p. 2). Schwartz (2015) also acknowledged a second wave of commemoration theories, which focus on commemoration as meaning making and are less influenced by manipulation of a powerful group; these theories present commemoration more as a moral framework for people to use as a guide for interpretation and action (Schwartz, 2015). In these theories, commemoration is a model *of* and a model *for* society (Schwartz, 2015).

Schwartz theorized that an essential tension exists between commemoration and history and acknowledged that the two terms are easy to confuse with one another (2005, p. 64). He asserted that this tension must be maintained in a reciprocal relationship that creates collective memories, and the two should not be fused together. He noted that "commemorative occasions are sites of memory, not history; yet historians are now legitimating such sites as ritual participants" and that "what we take to be exciting new ways of knowing history are in fact episodes of history being absorbed by memory" (Schwartz, 2005, p. 75).

In his research on the representation of the Gettysburg Address, Schwartz (2005) explained how current historians recall parts of the speech to emphasize present-day civil rights concerns rather than understanding the words and associated meaning in the context of the time. In focusing on Lincoln's actual words and aspects of history, Schwartz asserted that Lincoln's emphasis was on the survival of the nation, yet by the end of the 20th century, racial justice, not national survival, was America's preoccupation. The meaning of Lincoln's dedication then shifted to phrases in the speech that supported the civil rights movement and in doing so destroyed the "vibrant opposition between history and commemoration" that is a "necessary condition for protection of historical truth" (Schwartz, 2005, p. 77).

This view of collective memory and identity rebuts the revisionist history perspective and asserts that we address "how" and "why" an event is recalled in addition to the content of the story itself. Schwartz noted that reducing stories about historical figures to the influence on current politics cannot explain the "deep cultural continuities" (Schwartz, 2000, p. 310), such as identity, that live in the stories. Diverse aspects of the stories of a critical historical event may emphasize different points depending on present events or subgroups, but the remembrances are framed "within a common sense of identity" (2000, p. 310). Schwartz's work asserted that theories of collective memory that rest on revisionist history ideas or conflict and hegemony cannot explain why Lincoln's values are received and accepted by different cultures or groups across time. Schwartz (1997) proposed that these stories of Lincoln remain because they are part of a "deeper and more permanent part of a collective consciousness" (p. 43) that extends and connects generations in collectives such as organizations. Schwartz (2005) asked:

> What are the limits to the past's capacity to frame and make present situations meaningful? Can we assume, as Karl Mannheim (1936) does, that there are few false perceptions of history since every generation sees aspects of the past that are less visible to other generations, or are some generations despite Mannheim's optimism so constituted as to inculcate a fundamentally false past?
>
> (p. 64)

These questions are at the heart of the collective memory discussions that focus on how the past is used to understand and frame the present and future and the challenges in theorizing about collective memory, history, and commemoration.

Factors That Influence Collective Memory

In reviewing the literature on collective memory across the social sciences, several factors emerged that influence how collective memory forms, is constructed, and is sustained. This section identifies these factors and discusses their influence. These factors include the impact of social interaction, individuals, language, time, physical space, and cognitive templates.

Social Interaction and the Role of the Individual in Collective Memory

Collective memory is increasingly defined as a social process that involves remembering and history and is influenced by social interaction. For example, in history, Lebow (2008) defined collective memory as a socially constructed process that is linked with identity. This social process is also portrayed as malleable, as it can be influenced by "counterfactual history" that emerges in different types of press (Lebow, 2008, p. 30). These works "often address the outcome of wars, like the American Civil War and World War II, that are central to contemporary problems of identity and memory" (Lebow, 2008, p. 30). Lebow (2008) projected that there will be increased resistance to institutional memory, and this in turn may be problematic for identity at the "national and supranational levels where it relies so heavily on institutional memories" (p. 31). It may also be problematic for other types of identity, such as family, generational, or religious identity, "that cut across national boundaries" and yet "will become correspondingly more important, as will the collective memories on which they rest" (Lebow, 2008, p. 31).

This can also be an issue in other types of collectives, such as organizations, when multiple accounts of a critical event become fused into one collective memory that is understood and acknowledged across much of the organization and provides evidence for "who we are" as an organization. Resistance to the memory of this event may emerge if new evidence or facts emerge about an event and then there is a shift in what the events means to the organization (Casey & Byington, 2013).

The importance of social interaction to collective memory is also linked to what Feindt, Krawatzek, Mehler, Pestel, and Trimcev (2014) proposed as a critical juncture in social memory studies. They suggested that a "third wave" of memory studies has begun, following the first wave initiated by Halbwachs (1950/1980) and the second wave with works by Nora (1989) and Assmann and Czaplicka (1995). In this third wave, the purpose is to enrich the connections between the theory and research in social memory studies through four areas: "chronology against time, conflict, generations, and self-reflexivity" (p. 24). They also suggested that this next wave of research is bringing enhanced focus on the individual and his or her perceptions, as well as the interrelationships between the individual and the collective in the process. The third wave of research assumes that collective memory is a process of social construction and should be studied as such rather than focusing on the content of memory as a homogenous entity—the view that drove much of the early empirical work. The meaning attached to memories of critical events may shift depending on how and when the memories are recalled; there may be multiple, competing interpretations at one time in a collective, but not all may be equally visible. The individual and his or her identity and the salient aspects of that individual identity in a given context are important in this process, as individuals have multiple identities or social groups that impact their recollections at any time, as well as the language that is used (Feindt et al., 2014). This is often referred to as the "plurality of memory at any given moment" (Feindt et al., 2014, p. 32) and is a little explored area of Halbwachs's (1950/1980) work.

Language also contributes to this process in that memory and the process of collective remembering are constituted by language. Memories are symbols with meanings that emerge through collective remembering and the language used in the process. These meanings may shift depending on how and when the memories are recalled, and there may be multiple competing interpretations at one time in a collective.

Feindt et al. (2014) also encouraged collective memory scholars to work across disciplines to understand the larger processes of change and the debates that cut across fields. Feindt et al. (2014) referenced the interaction between the individual and the group as entangled memory, as a memory becomes institutionalized with the past, present, and future, as well as space. Much of this research focuses on differences in interpretations over conflicts from different social groupings, such as generations. Although scholarship on memory and identity often researches and exposes plurality, the outstanding resources and coercive power of political groups are often overshadowed in these memory conflicts.

Crane (1997) and others (Zerubavel, 1996) also asserted that the collective memory process is influenced by the interactions of individuals participating in the process. For example, Zerubavel (1996, p. 294) stated that collective memory involves the integration of many different personal pasts into a single common past that all members of a particular community come to remember collectively through interactions with each other. In addition, Linde (2000) acknowledged that memory is not only neurological but also a social process of construction and reconstruction, noting:

> Even so, we must still problematize the question of what it means for a person to remember something that she did not experience, or indeed, to be encouraged or exhorted to remember it as a national or religious duty (Yerushalmi, 1989). Memory in this sense is a key to identity, and to the acquisition of identity.
>
> (p. 608)

In summary, both the role of the individual in collective memory and that role as part of a social process is being theorized across the social science disciplines. Overall, collective memory, in particular, commemoration, can be further investigated through the theory and research on how individuals and the multiple identities held by individuals may influence this process of remembering. As collectives, whether they are organizations or nations, there is increasing pluralism. This pluralism is represented by multiple voices which at times surface rapidly through increasingly diverse technologies such as social media platforms. These voices influence this process of commemoration through different knowledge and interpretations of critical events.

Schemas as Cognitive Tools in Collective Memory

Researchers have also taken a more cognitive approach to the process of social construction of memory and proposed the role of schemata in this process (Beim, 2007; Casey, 1997; Di Maggio, 1997; Zerubavel, 1995, 2003) as well as a link to identity (Casey, 1997; DiMaggio, 1997) as a form of schema. Bartlett's (1932) work on schema is an early reference to the role of these cognitive organizing structures in memory at the individual level, and the idea is that they help individuals organize their recollections of the past (Schwartz, 2015). Schwartz warned that many researchers take a simplistic view of these structures in that there are many ways that individuals are motivated to remember events and aspects of these events, citing Fiske and Taylor's (1991, p. 13) idea of individuals as "motivated tacticians." Overall, he acknowledged that in much of the experimental work on individual memory "memory regularly distorts reality to some degree . . . but within a limited range," which further supports the idea that reality constrains "the vulnerability of perception" (Schwartz, 2015, p. 25).

The idea of a master narrative that influences collective and individual memory surfaces in history and sociology. Sociologist Zerubavel (1995) proposed the importance of a master commemorative narrative that is created through historical sources and individual narratives of commemoration. This master narrative structures collective memory and is focused on a "group's distinct social identity and highlights its historical development" (Zerubavel, 2011, p. 237). Similarly, historian Paabo (2014) also referenced a master narrative that represents a nation and to which individuals connect their own individual narratives. Paabo maintained that this socially constructed narrative is always emerging. He also brought power into the memory process in asserting that the "master narrative is a tool that makes hegemonic collective memory functional" (Paabo, 2014, p. 191). Paabo drew from Bourdieu's work on historical narratives or myths that are central to exercise of power by the state.

Wertsch (2002, 2008) proposed the importance of cultural tools as a type of schema or narrative and their use in shaping the process of deep collective memory. He referenced these tools as shaping "the speaking and thinking of individuals to such a degree that they can be viewed as serving as 'coauthors' when reflecting on the past" (Wertsch, 2008,

p. 139). In explaining how these tools work, he theorized that there are two levels of collective memory and two levels of these tools. These tools are not simple representations of a group but are active parts of the process of the social construction and reconstruction of these groups.

Wertsch's (2008) work was based on Bruner's (1990) ideas of a "cultural tool kit," where these tools are created through education, families, public ceremonies, etc. Wertsch (2008) described these tools as generalized structures that provide a "basic schematic narrative template" or plot from which multiple more specific and varied narratives can emerge for events (p. 140). These narrative templates influence how and when community members may describe an event, and it can be difficult to decide whether the members are reporting what they believe to be true or are "harnessing the narrative tools in a cultural tool kit"—i.e., schematic narrative templates—to develop a meaning of the past. These schematic templates mold the "deep collective memory" because they have "deeply held emotional resonance and are a fundamental part of the identity claims of a group" (p. 142). They are fundamental in how we recall and retell the past, particularly when they are related to critical or significant past events representing the identity of the collective (Wertsch, 2008).

Time and Collective Memory

Time—past, present, and future—is critical to theorizing about memory as a social process. Time is represented in the recollection of past events that are significant or critical to a collective (Espinoza et al., 2014; Halbwachs, 1950/1980), and studies have focused on how memories of events are transmitted across generations. In some studies (Jelin, 2003), experiencing an event firsthand has led to differences in memories, but other studies have shown little difference in the recollection of significant events (Casey, 1997). These are often cross-level approaches employing both macro- and micro-sociological theories (Espinoza et al., 2014; Fine & Beim, 2007; Halbwachs, 1950/1980).

Other theorists have acknowledged that the collective memory process shapes the identity and the actions of the group (Cuc, Ozuru, Manier, & Hirst, 2006) over time, and therefore, it's important to understand the process of how these memories arise and are shared. Collective memory is linked with how people make meaning of the present, past, and future (Beim, 2007), and as Rowlinson et al. (2010, p. 82) acknowledged, it's critical to study how groups create the founding stories because it in turn influences how their identity is constructed through time.

Physical Space in Collective Memory

In the discussion of collective memory as a socially constructed process, theories also highlight the influence of physical space in shaping social interactions and repeated practices (Espinoza et al., 2014) that create a knowledge base or framework that sustains memories through generations. This memory may be realized in memorials or physical artifacts or in commemorations or celebrations of past events in these physical spaces and is linked to the identity needs of a collective over time. These spaces are critical because events are often commemorated in memorials, sites, and museums that house physical evidence from the collective's history about significant events. People use these spaces to remember together and make meaning of the past. These examples of physical space, as well as texts and performative institutions such as rites or celebrations, are sustained in societies across generations, and "they are symbols with meaning that may be reconstructed as the identity needs of society may change" (Struve, 2013, p. 7).

Summary

Overall, studies of collective memory across the social sciences of anthropology, sociology, and history that take a social constructionist perspective suggest it is a political, dynamic, changing social process and is related to the identities of the collectives which it serves. Patterns in social science theorizing about collective memory are similar to patterns seen in theorizing on collective concepts in organizational theory. Both macro and micro perspectives, and sometimes a combination, are discussed. Collective memory has been theorized as a process, i.e., collective remembering (Olick & Robbins, 1998; Wertsch, 2002), and as an outcome, i.e., a set memory of a past event (Young, 1993). Collective memory is differentiated from collected memory or an aggregation of individual memories that may have social influences (Olick & Robbins, 1998). In each approach, the discussion, and, at times, debate, are most often around the degree to which it is a social fact or supraindividual construct or entity and the degree to which it is malleable or evolves over time. There are middle approaches suggesting that collective memory is a supraindividual construct that is formed through social interactions of individuals and institutions, as well as fragmented approaches that assert that collective memories are located in the individual, "placing the responsibility to remember in the hands of the individual rather than the state or other cultural or political institutions" (Beim, 2007, p. 15). Contemporary historians such as Confino (1997) have argued that overemphasizing the role of power and politics in creating and determining what is remembered reduces our understanding of the function and meaning of collective memory and, ultimately, ignores the social role in collective memory. "By sanctifying the political while underplaying the social, and by sacrificing the cultural to the political, we transform memory into a 'natural' corollary of political development and interests" (Confino, as cited in Olick et al., 2011, p. 198). This is supported by Schwartz's work, which maintains there is a limit to the malleability of memory; it is constrained by the events from the past and the history of these events.

References

Ackerman, M. S. (1996). Definitional and contextual issues in organizational and group memories. *Information Technology & People, 9*(1), 10–24. https://doi.org/10.1108/09593849610111553.

Adamczyk, A. (2002). On Thanksgiving and collective memory: Constructing the American tradition. *Journal of Historical Sociology, 15*(3), 343–365. https://doi.org/10.1111/1467-6443.00182.

Adorisio, A. L. M. (2014). Organizational remembering as narrative: 'Storying' the past in banking. *Organization, 21*(4), 463–476. https://doi.org/10.1177/1350508414527248.

Allen, M., & Brown, S. D. (2016). Memorial meshwork: The making of the commemorative space of the Hyde Park 7/7 Memorial. *Organization, 23*(1), 10–28. https://doi.org/10.1177/1350508415605103.

Anderson, M., & Sun, P. Y. T. (2010). What have scholars retrieved from Walsh and Ungson (1991). A citation context study. *Management Learning, 41*(2), 131–145. https://doi.org/10.1177/1350507609341091.

Anteby, M., & Molnar, V. (2012). Collective memory meets organizational identity: Remembering to forget in a firm's rhetorical history. *Academy of Management Journal, 55*(3), 515–540. https://doi.org/10.5465/amj.2010.0245.

Argote, L. (1999). *Organizational learning: Creating, retaining and transferring knowledge.* Norwell, MA: Kluwer.

Argote, L. (2013). *Organizational learning: Creating, retaining and transferring knowledge* (2nd ed.). New York, NY: Springer. https://doi.org/10.1007/978-1-4614-5251-5.

Argote, L., & Ingram, P. (2000). Knowledge transfer: A basis for competitive advantage in firms. *Organizational Behavior and Human Decision Processes, 82*(1), 150–169. https://doi.org/10.1006/obhd.2000.2893.

Argote, L., & Miron-Spektor, E. (2011). Organizational learning: From experience to knowledge. *Organization Science, 22*(5), 1123–1137. https://doi.org/10.1287/orsc.1100.0621.

Argyris, C., & Schon, P. (1978). *Organizational learning.* Reading, MA: Addison-Wesley.

Ashley, S. L. T. (2016). Re-colonizing spaces of memorializing: The case of the Chattri Indian Memorial, UK. *Organization, 23*(1), 29–46. https://doi.org/10.1177/1350508415605101.

Assmann, J., & Czaplicka, J. (1995). Collective memory and cultural identity. *New German Critique, 65*, 125–133. https://doi.org/10.2307/488538.

Barndt, K. (2007). Fordist nostalgia: History and experience at The Henry Ford. *Rethinking History, 11*(3), 379–410. https://doi.org/10.1080/13642520701353330.

Barros, V. F., Ramos, I., & Perez, G. (2015). Information systems and organizational memory: A literature review. *Journal of Information Systems and Technology Management, 12*(1), 45–63. https://doi.org/10.4301/S1807-17752015000100003.

Bartlett, F. (1932). *Remembering. A study in experimental and social psychology.* Cambridge, UK: Cambridge University Press.

Beim, A. (2007). The cognitive aspects of collective memory. *Symbolic Interaction, 30*(1), 7–26. https://doi.org/10.1525/si.2007.30.1.7.

Bell, E., & Taylor, S. (2016). Vernacular mourning and corporate memorialization in framing the death of Steve Jobs. *Organization, 23*(1), 114–132. https://doi.org/10.1177/1350508415605109.

Berliner, D. (2005). The abuses of memory: Reflections on the memory boom in anthropology. *Anthropological Quarterly, 78*(1), 197–211. https://doi.org/10.1353/anq.2005.0001.

Booth, C., & Rowlinson, M. (2006). Management and organizational history: Prospects. *Management & Organizational History, 1*(1), 5–30.

Bruner, J. (1990). *Acts of meaning.* Cambridge, UK: Harvard University Press.

Casey, A. (1997). Collective memory in organizations. In P. Shrivastava, A. Huff, & J. Dutton (Series Eds.), J. Walsh & A. Huff (Vol. Eds.), *Organizational learning and strategic management* (Advances in Strategic Management, Vol. 14, pp. 111–151). Greenwich, CT: JAI Press.

Casey, A. (2010). *The role of collective memory in organizational identity.* Presented at the annual conference of the Academy of Management, Montreal, Quebec, Canada.

Casey, A., & Byington, L. (2013). *Nike: A case study of identity claims in a complex global world.* Presented at the annual conference of the Academy of Management, Lake Buena Vista, FL. https://doi.org/10.5465/ambpp.2013.12456abstract.

Casey, A., & Olivera, F. (2003). *Organizational memory remembered: A look back and future directions.* Paper presented at the annual meeting of the Academy of Management, Seattle, WA.

Casey, A., & Olivera, F. (2007). *Organizational memory remembered: A look back and future directions.* Unpublished paper.

Casey, A., & Olivera, F. (2011). Reflections on organizational memory and forgetting. *Journal of Management Inquiry, 20*(3), 305–310. https://doi.org/10.1177/1056492611408264.

Cipolla, C. (2008). Signs of identity, signs of memory. *Archaeological Dialogues, 15*(2), 196–215. https://doi.org/10.1017/S1380203808002675.

Confino, A. (1997). Collective memory and cultural history: Problems of method. *The American Historical Review, 102*(5), 1386–1403. https://doi.org/10.2307/2171069.

Connerton, P. (2006). Cultural memory. In C. Tilley, W. Keane, S. Küchler, M. Rowlands, & P. Spyer (Eds.), *Handbook of material culture* (pp. 315–324). Thousand Oaks, CA: Sage. doi: 10.4135/9781848607972.n21.

Corbett, J. M. (2000). On being an elephant in the age of oblivion: Computer-based information systems and organisational memory. *Information Technology & People, 13*(4), 282–297. https://doi.org/10.1108/09593840010359482.

Crane, S. (1997). Writing the individual back into collective memory. *The American Historical Review, 102*(5), 1372–1385. https://doi.org/10.2307/2171068.

Cross, R., & Baird, L. (2000). Technology is not enough: Improving performance by building organizational memory. *Sloan Management Review, 41*(3), 69–78.

Crossan, M., Cunha, M. P. E., Vera, D., & Cunha, J. (2005). Time and organizational improvisation. *Academy of Management Review, 30*(1), 129–145. https://doi.org/10.5465/amr.2005.15281441.

Cuc, A., Ozuru, Y., Manier, D., & Hirst, W. (2006). On the formation of collective memories: The role of a dominant narrator. *Memory & Cognition, 34*(4), 752–762. https://doi.org/10.3758/BF03193423.

Cutcher, L., Dale, K., Hancock, P., & Tyler, M. (2016). Places and spaces of remembering and commemoration. *Organization, 23*(1), 3–9. https://doi.org/10.1177/1350508415605111.

De Lugan, R. M. (2013). Commemorating from the margins of the nation: El Salvador 1932, indigeneity and transnational belonging. *Anthropological Quarterly, 86*(4), 965–994. https://doi.org/10.1353/anq.2013.0046.

DiMaggio, P. (1997). Culture and cognition. *Annual Review of Sociology, 23*(1), 263–287. https://doi.org/10.1146/annurev.soc.23.1.263.

Douglas, M. (1980). Introduction. In M. Halbwachs (Ed.), *The collective memory* (F. J. Ditter, Jr. & V. Y. Ditter, Trans.). New York, NY: Harper and Row.

Dunham, A. H., & Burt, C. D. B. (2011). Organizational memory and empowerment. *Journal of Knowledge Management, 15*(5), 851–868. https://doi.org/10.1108/13673271111174366.

Espinoza, A. E., Piper, I., & Fernandez, R. A. (2014). The study of memory sites through a dialogical accompaniment interactive group method: A research note. *Qualitative Research, 14*(6), 712–728. https://doi.org/10.1177/1468794113483301.

Fabian, J. (1999). Remembering the other: Knowledge and recognition in the exploration of Central Africa. *Critical Inquiry, 26*, 49–69.

Feindt, G. R., Krawatzek, F., Mehler, D. A., Pestel, F., & Trimcev, R. (2014). Entangled memory: Toward a third wave in memory studies. *History and Theory, 53*(1), 24–44. https://doi.org/10.1111/hith.10693.

Feldman, R. M., & Feldman, S. P. (2006). What links the chain: An essay on organizational remembering as practice. *Organization, 13*(6), 861–887. https://doi.org/10.1177/1350508406068500.

Fiedler, M., & Welpe, I. (2010). How do organizations remember? The influence of organizational structure on organizational memory. *Organization Studies, 31*(4), 381–407. https://doi.org/10.1177/0170840609347052.

Fine, G. A., & Beim, A. (2007). Introduction: Interactionist approaches to collective memory. *Symbolic Interaction, 30*(1), 1–5. https://doi.org/10.1525/si.2007.30.1.1.

Flores, L. G., Zheng, W., Rau, D., & Thomas, C. H. (2012). Organizational learning: Subprocess, identification, construct validation, and an empirical test of cultural antecedents. *Journal of Management, 38*(2), 640–667. https://doi.org/10.1177/0149206310384631.

Godfrey, P. C., Hassard, J., O'Connor, E., Rowlinson, M., & Ruef, M. (2016). What is organizational history? Toward a creative synthesis of history and organizational studies. *Academy of Management Review, 41*(4), 590–608. https://doi.org/10.5465/amr.2016.0040.

Greenwood, A., & Bernardi, A. (2014). Understanding the rift, the (still) uneasy bedfellows of history and organization studies. *Organization, 21*(6), 907–932. https://doi.org/10.1177/1350508413514286.

Haładewicz-Grzelak, M., & Lubos-Koziel, J. (2014). Story-ing memory in the Lichen-Pilgrimage Centre (Poland). *European Journal of Cultural Studies, 17*(6), 647–664. https://doi.org/10.1177/1367549414544119.

Halbwachs, M. (1980). *The collective memory* (F. J. Ditter, Jr. & V. Y. Ditter, Trans.). New York, NY: Harper and Row. (Originally published in 1950)

Hall, S. (1996). The question of cultural identity. In S. Hall, D. Held, D. Hubert, & K. Thompson (Eds.), *Modernity: An introduction to modern societies* (pp. 595–634). Cambridge, UK: Blackwell Publishers.

Hargadon, A. R., & Sutton, R. (1997). Technology brokering and innovation in a product development firm. *Administrative Science Quarterly, 42*(4), 716–750. https://doi.org/10.2307/2393655.

Hatch, M. J., & Schultz, M. (2017). Toward a theory of using history authentically: Historicizing in the Carlsberg Group. *Administrative Science Quarterly, 62*, 657–697. https://doi.org/10.1177/0001839217692535.

Haukanes, H., & Trnka, S. (2013). Memory, imagination, and belonging across generations: Perspectives from postsocialist Europe and beyond. *Focaal—Journal of Global and Historical Anthropology, 66*, 3–13.

Hewer, C. J., & Roberts, R. (2012). History, culture and cognition: Towards a dynamic model of social memory. *Culture and Psychology, 18*(2), 167–183. https://doi.org/10.1177/1354067X11434836.

Huber, G. (1991). Organizational learning: The contributing processes and the literature. *Organization Science, 2*(1), 88–115. https://doi.org/10.1287/orsc.2.1.88.

Jelin, E. (2003). *State repression and the labors of memory.* Minneapolis, MN: University of Minnesota Press.

Jedlowski, P. (2001). Memory and sociology: Themes and issues. *Time and Society, 10*(1), 29–44.

Kansteiner, W. (2002). Finding meaning in memory: A methodological critique of collective memory studies. *History and Theory, 41*(2), 179–197. https://doi.org/10.1111/0018-2656.00198.

Kipping, M., & Üsdiken, B. (2014). History in organization and management theory: More than meets the eye. *The Academy of Management Annals, 8*(1), 535–588. https://doi.org/10.5465/19416520.2014.911579.

Klein, K. L. (2000). On the emergence of memory in historical discourse. *Representations, 69*, 127–150.

Kozlowski, S. W. J., & Klein, K. J. (2000). A levels approach to theory and research in organizations. In K. J. Klein & S. W. J. Kozlowski (Eds.), *Multilevel theory, research and methods in organizations* (pp. 3–90). San Francisco, CA: Jossey-Bass.

Kyriakopoulos, K., & de Ruyter, K. (2004). Knowledge stocks and information flows in new product development. *Journal of Management Studies, 41*, 1469–1498. https://doi.org/10.1111/j.1467-6486.2004.00482.x.

Lau, K.-W. (2015). Organizational learning goes virtual?: A study of employees' leaning achievement in stereoscopic 3D virtual reality. *The Learning Organization, 22*(5), 289–303. https://doi.org/10.1108/TLO-11-2014-0063.

Lawrence, B. S. (1984). Historical perspective: Using the past to study the present. *Academy of Management Review, 9*(2), 307–312. https://doi.org/10.5465/amr.1984.4277663.

Lebow, R. N. (2008). The future of memory. *Annals of the American Academy of Political and Social Science, 617*(1), 25–40. https://doi.org/10.1177/0002716207310817.

Levine, S. S., & Prietula, M. J. (2012). How knowledge transfer impacts performance: A multilevel model of benefits and liabilities. *Organization Science, 23*(6), 1748–1766. https://doi.org/10.1287/orsc.1110.0697.

Lin, H.-F. (2015). Linking knowledge management orientation to balanced scorecard outcomes. *Journal of Knowledge Management*, 19(6), 1224–1249. https://doi.org/10.1108/JKM-04-2015-0132.

Linde, C. (2000). The acquisition of a speaker by a story: How history becomes memory and identity. *Ethos*, 28(4), 608–632. http://doi.org/10.1525/eth.2000. 28.4.608.

Linde, C. (2001). Narrative and social tacit knowledge. *Journal of Knowledge Management*, 5(2), 160–171. https://doi.org/10.1108/13673270110393202.

Loma, A., Larsen, E. R., & Ginsberg, A. (1997). Adaptive learning in organizations: A system dynamics-based exploration. *Journal of Management*, 23(4), 561–582. https://doi.org/10.1177/014920639702300404.

Lopez, L., & Sune, A. (2013). Turnover-induced forgetting and its impact on productivity. *British Journal of Management*, 24(1), 38–53. https://doi.org/10. 1111/j.1467-8551.2011.00785.x.

Loveday, V. (2014). Flat-capping it: Memory, nostalgia and value in retroactive male working class identification. *European Journal of Cultural Studies*, 17(6), 721–735. https://doi.org/10.1177/1367549414544117.

Lowenthal, D. (1996). *Possessed by the past: The heritage crusade and the spoils of history*. Cambridge, UK: Cambridge University Press.

Maclean, M., Harvey, C., & Clegg, S. R. (2016). Conceptualizing historical organizational studies. *Academy of Management Review*, 41(4), 609–632. https:// doi.org/10.5465/amr.2014.0133.

March, J. (1991). Exploration and exploitation in organizational learning. *Organization Science*, 2(1), 71–87. https://doi.org/10.1287/orsc.2.1.71.

Mead, G. H. (1934). *Mind, self and society*. Chicago, IL: University of Chicago Press.

Megill, A. (1998). History, memory and identity. *History of the Human Sciences*, 11(3), 37–62. https://doi.org/10.1177/095269519801100303.

Mena, J. A., & Chabowski, B. R. (2015). The role of organizational learning in stakeholder marketing. *Journal of the Academy of Marketing Science*, 43, 429–452.

Mena, S., Rintamaki, J., Fleming, P., & Spicer, A. (2016). On the forgetting of corporate irresponsibility. *Academy of Management Review*, 41(4), 720–738.

Moorman, C., & Miner, A. (1997). The impact of organizational memory on new product performance and creativity. *Journal of Marketing Research*, 34(1), 91–106. https://doi.org/10.2307/3152067.

Morgeson, F. P., & Hofmann, D. A. (1999). The structure and function of collective concepts: Implications for multilevel research and theory development. *Academy of Management Review*, 24(2), 249–265. https://doi.org/10.5465/ amr.1999.1893935.

Nissley, N., & Casey, A. (2002). The politics of the exhibition: Viewing corporate museums through the paradigmatic lens of organizational memory. *British Journal of Management*, 13(S2), S35–S44. https://doi.org/10.1111/1467-8551. 13.s2.4.

Nora, P. (1989). Between memory and history: Les lieux de memoire. *Representations (Berkeley, Calif.)*, 26(Spring), 7–24. https://doi.org/10.2307/2928520.

Obeidat, B. Y., Ra'ed, M., & Abdallah, A. B. (2014). The relationships among human resource management practices, organizational commitment and knowledge management processes: A structural equation modeling approach.

International Journal of Business and Management, 9(3). doi: 10.5539/ijbm. v9n3p9.

Ocasio, W., Mauskapf, M., & Steele, C. W. (2016). History, society, and institutions: The role of collective memory in the emergence and evolution of societal logics. *Academy of Management Review, 41*(4), 676–699. https://doi.org/10.5465/amr.2014.0183.

Olick, J. K. (1999). Collective memory: The two cultures. *Sociological Theory, 17*, 333–348.

Olick, J. K., Vinitzky-Seroussi, V., & Levy, D. (2011). Introduction. In J. K. Olick, V. Vinitzky-Seroussi, & D. Levy (Eds.), *The collective memory reader* (pp. 3–62). New York, NY: Oxford University Press.

Olick, J. K., & Robbins, J. (1998). Social memory studies: From "collective memory" to the historical sociology of mnemonic practices. *Annual Review of Sociology, 24*(1), 105–140. https://doi.org/10.1146/annurev.soc.24.1.105.

Paabo, H. (2014). Constructing historical space: Estonia's transition from the Russian civilization to the Baltic Sea region. *Journal of Baltic Studies, 45*(2), 187–205. https://doi.org/10.1080/01629778.2013.846929.

Rodgers, D. M., Petersen, J., & Sanderson, J. (2016). Commemorating alternative organizations and marginalized spaces: The case of forgotten Finntowns. *Organizations, 23*(1), 90–113. doi: 10.1177/1350508415605110.

Rowlinson, M. (2002). Public history review essay: Cadbury World. *Labour Review, 67*(1), 101–119.

Rowlinson, M., Booth, C., Clark, P., Delahaye, A., & Procter, S. (2010). Social remembering and organizational memory. *Organization Studies, 31*(1), 69–87. https://doi.org/10.1177/0170840609347056.

Rowlinson, M., Casey, A., Hansen, P. H., & Mills, A. J. (2014). Narratives and memory in organizations. *Organization, 21*, 441–446.

Rowlinson, M., & Hassard, J. (1993). The invention of corporate culture: A history of the histories of Cadbury. *Human Relations, 46*, 299–326.

Rowlinson, M., Hassard, J., & Decker, S. (2014). Research strategies for organizational history: A dialogue between historical theory and organization theory. *Academy of Management Review, 39*(3), 250–274. https://doi.org/10.5465/amr.2012.0203.

Russell, N. (2006). Collective memory before and after Halbwachs. *French Review (Deddington), 79*(4), 792–804.

Sandelands, L. E., & Stablein, R. E. (1987). The concept of organization mind. In N. DiTomaso & S. Bachrach (Eds.), *Research in the sociology of organizations* (Vol. 5, pp. 135–161). Greenwich, CT: JAI Press.

Santos-Vijande, M. L., López-Sánchez, J. Á., & Trespalacios, J. A. (2012). How organizational learning affects a firm's flexibility, competitive strategy, and performance. *Journal of Business Research, 65*(8), 1079–1089. https://doi.org/10.1016/j.jbusres.2011.09.002.

Schultz, M., & Hernes, T. (2013). A temporal perspective on organizational identity. *Organization Science, 24*(1), 1–21. https://doi.org/10.1287/orsc.1110.0731.

Schwandt, D. R. (1997). Organizational learning and strategy: An action theory perspective. In A. Huff & J. Walsh (Eds.), *Advances in strategic management* (Vol. 14). New York, NY: JAI Press.

Schwandt, D. R., & Marquardt, M. J. (2000). *Organizational learning: World class theories to global best practices.* New York, NY: St. Lucie Press.

Schwartz, B. (1997). Collective memory and history. *The Sociological Quarterly, 38*(3), 469–496. https://doi.org/10.1111/j.1533-8525.1997.tb00488.x.

Schwartz, B. (1991a). Iconography and collective memory: Lincoln's image in the American mind. *The Sociological Quarterly, 32*(3), 301–319. https://doi.org/10.1111/j.1533-8525.1991.tb00161.x.

Schwartz, B. (1991b). Social change and collective memory: The democratization of George Washington. *American Sociological Review, 56*(2), 221–236. https://doi.org/10.2307/2095781.

Schwartz, B. (2000). *Abraham Lincoln and the forge of national memory.* Chicago, IL: University of Chicago Press.

Schwartz, B. (2005). The new Gettysburg Address: Fusing history and memory. *Poetics, 33*(1), 63–79. https://doi.org/10.1016/j.poetic.2005.01.003.

Schwartz, B. (2008). Collective memory and abortive commemoration: Presidents' Day and the American holiday calendar. *Social Research, 75*, 75–110.

Schwartz, B. (2010). Culture and collective memory. In J. R. Hall, L. Grindstaff, & M.-C. Lo (Eds.), *Handbook of cultural sociology* (pp. 619–629). Abingdon, UK: Routledge.

Schwartz, B. (2014). Where there's smoke, there's fire: Memory and history. In T. Thatcher (Ed.), *Memory and identity in Ancient Judaism and Early Christianity: A conversation with Barry Schwartz* (pp. 7–37). Atlanta, GA: SBL Press.

Schwartz, B. (2015). Commemoration. In J. D. Wright (Ed.), *International encyclopedia of the social and behavioral sciences* (2nd ed., pp. 235–242). Cambridge, UK: Elsevier Ltd. https://doi.org/10.1016/B978-0-08-097086-8.10404-0.

Schwartz, B. (2016). Rethinking the concept of collective memory. In A. Tota & T. Hagen (Eds.), *Routledge international handbook of memory studies* (pp. 9–21). London, UK: Routledge.

Schwartz, B., & Schuman, H. (2000). The meanings of collective memory. *Newsletter of the Sociology of Culture Section, American Sociological Association, 14*, 1–3.

Smith, G. D., & Steadman, L. E. (1981). Present value of corporate history. *Harvard Business Review, 59*(6), 164–173.

Sørensen, B. M. (2014). Changing the memory of suffering: An organizational aesthetics of the dark side. *Organization Studies, 35*(2), 279–302. https://doi.org/10.1177/0170840613511930.

Struve, L. A. (2013). Chinese memory makes a martyr. The case of Huani Chunyao (1605–1645). *History & Memory, 25*(2), 5–31. https://doi.org/10.2979/histmemo.25.2.5.

Templeton, G. F., Lewis, B. R., & Snyder, C. A. (2002). Development of a measure for the organizational learning construct. *Journal of Management Information Systems, 19*(2), 175–218. https://doi.org/10.1080/07421222.2002.11045727.

Thomas, N., & Vohra, N. (2015). Development of network measures for knowledge processes: A relational framework. *Knowledge and Process Management, 22*(2), 126–139. https://doi.org/10.1002/kpm.1465.

Usdiken, B., & Kieser, A. (2004). Introduction: History in organization studies. *Business History, 46*(3), 321–330. https://doi.org/10.1080/0007679042000219166.

Walsh, J. P., & Ungson, G. R. (1991). Organizational memory. *Academy of Management Review, 16*(1), 57–91. https://doi.org/10.5465/amr.1991.4278992.

Weick, K. E. (1979). *The social psychology of organizing* (2nd ed.). New York, NY: McGraw-Hill.

Wertsch, J. V. (2002). *Voices of collective remembering.* Cambridge, UK: Cambridge University Press. https://doi.org/10.1017/CBO9780511613715.

Wertsch, J. V. (2008). Collective memory and narrative templates. *Social Research, 75*(1), 133–155.

Wertsch, J. V., & Roediger, H. L., III. (2008). Collective memory: Conceptual foundations and theoretical approaches. *Memory (Hove, England), 16*(3), 318–326. https://doi.org/10.1080/09658210701801434.

Wexler, M. N. (2002). Organizational memory and intellectual capital. *Journal of Intellectual Capital, 3*(4), 393–414. https://doi.org/10.1108/14691930 210448314.

White, G. (2008). Epilogue: Memory moments. *Ethos, 34*(2), 325–341.

Yates, J. (1990). For the record: The embodiment of organizational memory, 1850–1920. *Business and Economic History, 19*, 172–182.

Young, J. E. (1993). *The texture of memory.* New Haven, CT: Yale University Press.

Zerubavel, Y. (1995). *Recovered roots: Collective memory and making of Israeli national tradition.* Chicago, IL: University of Chicago Press.

Zerubavel, E. (1996). Social memories: Steps to a sociology of the past. *Qualitative Sociology, 19*(3), 283–299. https://doi.org/10.1007/BF02393273.

Zerubavel, E. (2003). *Time maps: Collective memory and the social shape of the past.* London, UK: University of Chicago Press. https://doi.org/10.7208/chicago/9780226924908.001.0001.

Zerubavel, E. (2011). Recovered roots: Collective memory and the making of Israeli national tradition. In J. K. Olick, V. Vinitzky-Seroussi, & D. Levy (Eds.), *The collective memory reader* (pp. 237–241). New York, NY: Oxford University Press.

2 Organizational and Collective Identity

This chapter first provides the theoretical foundations and definitions of organizational identity from an organizational studies perspective, including the social actor perspective as defined by the seminal work of Albert and Whetten (1985) and the social constructionist perspective (Gioia, Schultz, & Corley, 2000; Hatch, 2010; Ravasi & Schultz, 2006). The chapter then reviews the scholarship on collective identity—with a focus on national identity—across the social sciences, including anthropology, sociology, and history.

Organizational Identity

Social Actor Perspective

The organizational identity literature can be traced to the seminal definition of organizational identity by Albert and Whetten (1985):

> We propose, by way of a preliminary definition, that an adequate statement of organizational identity satisfies the following criteria:
>
> 1. The answer points to features that are somehow seen as the essence of the organization: *the criterion of claimed central character.*
> 2. The answer points to features that distinguish the organization from others with which it may be compared: *the criterion of claimed distinctiveness.*
> 3. The answer points to features that exhibit some degree of sameness or continuity over time: *the criterion of claimed temporal continuity.*
>
> For the purposes of defining organizational identity as a scientific concept, we treat the criteria of central character, distinctiveness and temporal continuity as each necessary and as a set sufficient.
>
> (p. 265)

Organizational identity answers the question, "Who are we as an organization?" (Whetten & Mackey, 2002). As noted in the definition, all three attributes—core, distinctive, and temporal continuity—are needed to be considered organizational identity. These attributes are often referred to in the literature as CED (central, enduring, and distinctive). Organizational identity scholarship builds from work in psychology on individual identity, which is

> encoded as a distinctive pattern of similarities and differences, encompassing both social comparisons (self-other) and temporal comparisons (self-self). Similarity and difference can thus be thought of as dimensions of the identity concept. The posited need for "optimal distinctiveness" set forth in this literature highlights an inherent tension between these dimensions.
>
> (Whetten, 2013, p. 2)

Albert and Whetten's (1985) definition of organizational identity is grounded in institutional theory and assumes that organizations are social actors in a field and legal entities with responsibilities (Scott, 2001) that take actions to meet goals. An organization is defined and its characteristics are formed through its founding and its history as it evolves over time. Whetten (2013) noted that this "sociological view is based on the supposition that among the myriad types of social entities within modern society, only 'corporate' organizations (exemplified by, but not limited to, business corporations) are granted roughly the same rights and responsibilities as individuals" (p. 3).

Identity rarely surfaces in everyday matters in organizations; it becomes conscious and matters during crises or when decisions need to be made that will profoundly affect the organization (Albert & Whetten, 1985). Albert and Whetten listed different times in the life cycle of an organization when identity becomes more salient, including the founding of the organization, the loss of a founder, rapid growth, a change in "collective status" such as a merger or acquisition, and "retrenchment" (Albert & Whetten, 1985, p. 275).

From the social actor perspective, organizational identity claims are also temporally continuous and serve as a stable foundation for the organization over time (Albert & Whetten, 1985). Organizational identity is "formed by ordered inter-organizational comparisons over time (Albert, 1977)" (Albert & Whetten, 1985, p. 273). Identity claims frame "an organization's self-determined (and 'self' defining) unique social space and [are] reflected in its unique pattern of binding commitments" (Whetten, 2006, p. 220) that endure over time. Organizations "perpetuate their central and distinguishing features, preserving for tomorrow what has made them what and/or who they are today" (Whetten, 2006, p. 224). These coherent claims are "historical frames of reference"

(Whetten, 2006, p. 223) that guide organizational strategic actions in the past, present, and future (Whetten & Mackey, 2002).

Albert and Whetten (1985) also addressed organizations with mono or dual identities in their initial work. They proposed that most organizations might be composed of multiple types and defined a hybrid as an organization "with two or more types that would not normally be expected to go together" (p. 269), such as a church and a bank. These dual-identity organizations may take a holographic or ideographic form. In addition, Albert and Whetten suggested that organizations can evolve from mono to dual identities, and the "key to understanding the evolution of an organization is to track the shifts in its identity over time" (p. 276)—particularly the shift from A or B to AB.

In 2006, Whetten expanded on the definition of organizational identity by articulating three components of organizational identity: definitional, phenomenological, and ideational. The *definitional* component of organizational identity is represented by the central, enduring, and distinct (CED) features of an organization. He proposed that history—in particular, the founding commitments of an organization—serves as the foundation for the identity claims that endure. These founding commitments are commemorated in recollections of critical events in the organization's history (Casey, 1997) and also surface in statements about the organization from organizational members. Whetten referred to the recollections of critical events as the *phenomenological* component of organizational identity, while the organizational members' view of organizational identity is the *ideational* component. Although the examples or stories used to exemplify these commitments may change, the claims or commitments themselves and the labels used to describe them often remain the same (Casey, 2010; Casey & Byington, 2013).

Social Constructionist Perspective

Scholars who define organizational identity from a social constructionist perspective address the question "Who are we as an organization?" from the perspective of the shared interpretations of organizational members (Gioia & Chittipeddi, 1991; Hogg & Terry, 2001; Kreiner, Hollensbe, Sheep, Smith, & Kataria, 2015; Ravasi & Schultz, 2006). The social constructionist perspective defines organizational identity as "shared emergent beliefs" or "identity understandings" (Ravasi & Schultz, 2006, p. 436) about what is core and distinctive about the organization. Most social constructionist views recognize the influence of official organizational identity claims but emphasize the critical role of members' interpretations of these claims. This perspective, as articulated by Hatch and Schultz (1997, 2000, 2002) and others (Corley & Gioia, 2004; Dutton & Dukerich, 1991; Fiol, 1991; Gioia & Thomas, 1996; Hatch, 2010; Nag, Corley, & Gioia, 2007), defines organizational identity as a dynamic process involving an ongoing dialogue among organizational stakeholders, organizational culture, and the external environment (Gioia et al., 2000; Hatch, 2010; Hatch & Schultz, 2002; Kreiner et al., 2015). The majority of the theorizing and research on organizational identity since its introduction in 1985 has been from a social constructionist perspective.

From the social constructionist perspective, organizational identity claims evolve to adapt to significant changes occurring in the internal or external environment (Fiol, 1991; Gioia & Chittipeddi, 1991; Ravasi & Schultz, 2006). Formal claims or the labels may endure, but they are often in name only, as the meaning and interpretation have changed (Gioia, Patvardhan, Hamilton, & Corley, 2013). Multiple identities can also coexist in an organization (Besharov, 2014; Pratt & Foreman, 2000). This perspective emphasizes the individual members' roles in shaping interpretations about the identity of an organization. From this perspective, organizational identity can be viewed as both an internal and external concept (Brickson, 2013), as organizations need to engage with both internal and external actors and stakeholders. It can also be viewed from the idea of the expected or future identity (Foreman & Whetten, 2002; Gioia et al., 2000; Hsu & Hannan, 2005; King & Whetten, 2008) and the current identity (Brickson, 2013).

Within the social constructionist perspective, organizational identity has also been theorized from a process perspective. This process has been described as one of "identity elasticity" (Kreiner et al., 2015, p. 981), in which tensions both stretch and constrain the social construction process of organizational identity, as compared to a set of claims or attributes of an organization. Similarly, Hatch (2010) defined organizational identity as a "distributed phenomenon, best depicted as occurring within dynamic webs of material and meaning (i.e., cultures) produced, carried, communicated, and remembered in various forms by all those involved" (p. 346). This view is in line with the recent trend in organizational studies toward more process-based approaches (Langley, Smallman, Tsoukas, & Van de Ven, 2013; Schultz & Hernes, 2013). This work often takes a microdynamics approach and studies the organizational mechanisms at play in creating or re-creating organizational identity. The assumption supporting this view is that organizations are changing rapidly, and it is therefore reasonable to assume that organizational identity must evolve, or organizations would not survive.

Work on organizational identity as a socially constructed process has been conducted in the context of mergers and acquisitions. Łupina-Wegener, Schneider, and van Dick (2015) asserted that the research on organizational identity in this context has been minimal in the past decade, with the exception of the work of Chreim (2007) and Clark, Gioia, Ketchen, and Thomas (2010). Studies of this context often focus on identity conflict and organizational identity processes over time, i.e., premerger and postmerger. In Łupina-Wegener et al.'s (2015) study of the temporal dimensions of identity construction during a merger, they focused on intergroup and intragroup dynamics in identity construction in a longitudinal grounded theory study of the merger of two Mexican subsidiaries as part of two European multinational corporations. This study found that ingroup and outgroup dynamics were a significant influence in organizational identity dynamics.

The organizational identity construction process has also been studied in the context of other types of organizational change. For example, Kreiner et al. (2015) studied the process of identity construction during significant change in the Episcopal Church. They examined how organizational members experienced the changes and how these experiences impacted the perception of organizational identity over time. In this paper, organizational identity was both a process and a set of attributes. Kreiner et al. (2015) maintained that it is critical to look at all three components of the original definition, i.e., central, distinctive, and enduring. They asserted that most of the work has focused on the enduring component, with assumptions about centrality and little focus on the distinctiveness component of the definition. From a process approach, their work creates a case for addressing how or why enduringness occurs as well as what constitutes centrality.

In this research, Kreiner et al. (2015) found that "tensions emerged as members discussed identity, often using 'thing-like' labels, but imbuing those labels with different features and processual, tensional descriptions" (p. 990). This is similar to ideas proposed by Gioia et al. (2013), which explicate the difference between labels and meanings in connection to organizational identity. Kreiner et al. (2015) introduced the concept *organizational identity elasticity*, defining it as the "socially constructed tensions that simultaneously stretch identity while holding it together, akin to the boundaries of a balloon or rubber band expanding and contracting" (p. 982). They discussed this process as organizational identity work, i.e., "the cognitive, discursive, and behavioral processes in which individuals engage to create, present, sustain, share, and/or adapt organizational identity" (p. 985). The multiple constructions of identity claims coexist as they are "held in an ongoing interplay, a dynamic 'both/and' tension" (p. 992), without one claim dominating "at the expense of its opposite" (p. 992). This is in contrast to literature that asserts that one identity claim resonates more for some members than for others (Besharov, 2014; Brickson, 2013; Solomon & Casey, 2017).

Bridging the Two Perspectives of Organizational Identity

Recent theorizing on organizational identity suggests that these two views of organizational identity that appear to be contradictory may be complementary, and the integration of these views provides a more complete articulation of organizational identity (Elstak, 2008; Kreiner et al., 2015; van Rekom, Corley, & Ravasi, 2008). Kreiner et al. (2015) noted that their work supports the "fluidity of identity," yet it also explains the paradox of how it can endure over time. The "elastic dialectic," they found, allowed for expansion, constriction, and stasis (p. 997). In adding to the discussion regarding the enduringness of organizational identity, they found that "organizational identity work was to construct identity as both enduring and fluid" (p. 999), with enduring and evolving present at the same time. "We therefore contribute to the emerging debate on whether identity is a process or characteristic by agreeing with Gioia and Patvardhan's (2012) call for a 'both-and framing' and providing empirical evidence showing that it is both, and should be treated as such" (Kreiner et al., 2015, p. 1004). Similarly, Hatch and Schultz (2017) asserted that the understanding and use of an organization's history to support or facilitate the evolution of organizational identity needs to stay close to the original meaning of the claims to be authentic.

In relationship to history and time, Kreiner et al.'s work (2015) supported Suddaby and Greenwood's (2005) assertions that members of organizations draw on past organizational events to advance their own constructions of identity that link with who they are as individuals. From an organizational identity elasticity perspective, an individual's interpretation of past events helps one to frame expanding or constraining organizational identity. This work along with others taking a social constructionist perspective assumes that interpretations of the past are malleable and attests to what Gioia et al. (2000) called the "adaptive instability of identity" (Kreiner et al., 2015, p. 1000).

Organizational Identity Research in Related Fields

The interest in organizational identity crosses other areas of organizational studies, including business ethics and organizational communications, and related disciplines such as higher education and social work, when the focus is on organizations versus individuals. Organizational identity is frequently used as an explanatory concept. Most of this work has cited Albert and Whetten's (1985) seminal definition of organizational identity, i.e., identity claims that are central, distinct, and enduring. For example, in business ethics there has been empirical work on organizational identity and image as related to corporate social responsibility (CSR), and the interest in these concepts is increasing (Martínez, Pérez, & Rodríguez del Bosque, 2014).

In this work, the social constructionist perspective prevails. Other definitions of organizational or corporate identity framed from this perspective are employed or cited, such as Brown and Humphreys's (2006) depiction of organizational identity as an "extremely fluid discursive construction" (p. 233). Also in this research there is frequently an assumption that organizational identity can be developed and managed. Organizational identity and image and the interaction between the two are also highlighted and, in particular, the need for organizations to align identity and image to be effective (Morsing & Roepstorff, 2015). Multiple organizational identities have also been proposed and explored, for example, in the context of multinational companies (Rajan & Casey, 2015), addressing how a local and a global identity can exist to guide CSR strategy and practices (Huermer, 2010). Much of the research work across these different fields and disciplines offers a theoretical contribution to other concepts such as CSR but little to the concept of organizational identity.

In the higher education literature (Bastedo, Samuels, & Kleinman, 2014; Steiner, Sundstrom, & Sammalisto, 2013), organizational identity has been studied as a variable and as a process, yet the definitions of organizational identity used in this research are often unclear. For example, in Bastedo et al.'s (2014) study of college presidents, organizational identity was explored as a variable that mediates between charismatic leadership and performance. Yet the definition of organizational identity in this study was closer to a definition of organizational identification, as the authors cited Ashforth and Mael (1989) and stated that identity was "the perception among organizational stakeholders that their membership in a given organization defines themselves and their beliefs" (Bastedo et al., 2014, p. 399).

Also in the higher education literature, Steiner et al. (2013) took a social constructionist perspective of organizational identity and developed a multidimensional model of university identity to explore the internal and external factors that influence the university identity and related reputation. Similar to Hatch and Schultz (1997, 2002), they expanded on the relationships between image, identity, culture, and reputation and the importance of understanding the reciprocal relationships to respond to changing external environments and the diverse stakeholder groups associated with universities. Similar to the study of Bastedo et al. (2014), this study offered no theoretical contributions to the scholarship on organizational identity but was more focused on the context and explaining a phenomenon in a particular setting.

In information systems, organizational identity has been linked to how organizations develop information and communication systems (Tyworth, 2014), defining organizational identity as "who we are as an organization" and how this understanding differentiates the organization from others. Tyworth (2014) drew on various perspectives on organizational identity, citing Dutton and Dukerich (1991), Reger et al. (1994), Elsbach and Kramer (1996), Gioia and Thomas (1996), Dukerich, Golden, and Shortell (2002), and Corley and Gioia (2004), yet at the same time also referencing Whetten's (2006) three components of organizational identity, i.e., definitional, phenomenological, and ideational. Tyworth (2014) asserted that organizational identity drives organizational actions and therefore would be relevant to information technology actions as well, with organizational identity "acting as a deep structure providing the foundation for higher-level organizational arrangements and technologies" (p. 70). Again, organizational identity was used to explain information technology actions and strategies with little theoretical or empirical development of the concept of identity.

The corporate communications literature has also explored organizational identity from the perspective of concepts and phenomena that are important to that discipline. For example, Evans (2015) suggested that organizational identity is responsible for how organizations communicate about themselves, particularly in relationship to strategic communication. Grounded in Albert and Whetten's definition of organizational identity, Evans (2015) proposed that organizational identity functions in differentiating the organization from other organizations and that it is enacted through communication in organizations. It is also a factor in framing strategy and decision making in relationship to positioning the organization in its environment.

In summary, when organizational identity has been explored in related fields, it has frequently been mistakenly defined and operationalized in terms of other closely related concepts such as organizational identification (Ashforth & Mael, 1989). It has also been conflated with organizational image and reputation and used as a variable to explain other organizational phenomena or the relationship between two concepts. This work has offered minimal contribution to the theoretical development of the concept of organizational identity.

Differentiating Organizational Identity From Other Concepts

Since the early work on organizational identity in organizational studies, it has been differentiated from similar concepts such as organizational culture (Albert & Whetten, 1985; Hatch & Schultz, 2002; Ravasi & Schultz, 2006; Whetten, 2006), reputation, image (Hatch, 2010), and brand. In differentiating it from organizational culture, scholars (Cian & Cervai, 2014; Hatch & Schultz, 2002; Hatch, Schultz, & Skov, 2015; Ravasi & Schultz, 2006; Whetten, 2006) have proposed that it serves as the foundation for organizational culture, while others have pointed to the idea that organizational identity emerges from organizational culture, and yet others (Cian & Cervai, 2014) have asserted that organizational culture and organizational identity are independent concepts. Despite the interest in framing the similarities between organizational identity and other concepts, it remains a separate and significant concept for organizational theorizing.

Literature reviews of organizational identity (Cian & Cervai, 2014) and related terms such as image (corporate, projected, and construed) and organizational culture have been conducted from the perspective of other disciplines, such as corporate communications, with the goal of facilitating discussions across disciplines studying organizational identity (Cian & Cervai, 2014). Cian and Cervai (2014) proposed an umbrella framework, with reputation as the overarching term because it frames perceptions of the organization from both internal and external perspectives. Similar to Hatch (2010), they differentiated between image and identity, noting that image is most often linked with external perceptions of the organization, while identity focuses more on the internal perceptions of the members of the organization.

Conclusion

Early theorizing on organizational identity drew from theories of psychology and human development and, to a lesser extent, sociological theories such as institutional theory. For example, Albert and Whetten referenced Erickson (1968, 1980) and Mead (1934) as well as others. Yet the original articulation of the concept is grounded in institutional theory (Albert & Whetten, 1985) with the organization as a social actor in society. A key facet of the debate regarding the enduring nature of identity is what constitutes an organization or how an "organization" is defined (Whetten, 2013). The paradigmatic underpinnings of the definition of organization are critical in the concept of organizational identity. At times it is difficult to discern what constitutes the definition of an organization in studies such as that of Kreiner et al. (2015) that take a social constructionist perspective.

A related key distinction in the scholarship on organizational identity is how the components of the definition of organizational identity—i.e., core, distinctive, and enduring—are defined along with the criteria for these definitions (Corley et al., 2006), particularly the enduring component or the extent to which organizational identity changes over time and the forces that shape it. This debate is evolving and is reshaping the literature (Elstak, 2008; Kreiner et al., 2015; van Rekom et al., 2008). Corley et al. (2006) suggested that there may be "two different parts to the organization's identity" (p. 95), while Ravasi and Schultz (2006) suggested that the "two perspectives—institutional claims and collective understandings—represent different aspects of the construction of organizational identities" (p. 436). The view of organizational identity as a process proposes that organizational identity can "simultaneously be enduring *and* fluid—a more robust, flexible view of identity as a set of dialectic tensions allowing holding together *while* pushing apart" (Kreiner et al., 2015, p. 1004).

The maturation of the work on organizational identity is providing a promising reconceptualization of organizational identity for future theory and research and its link to collective memory through its focus on time. As noted above, most perspectives and definitions of organizational identity reference history, founders, tradition, and legacy at different times, yet the role of collective memory is underdeveloped (Casey, 2010). More recent work is beginning to expand and draw on the rich theories and empirical work on collective memory from a variety of theoretical foundations and is using it to explore organizational identity from multiple levels (micro dynamics, meso and macro levels).

As noted earlier, most of the theory and research on organizational identity has taken a social constructionist approach and most recently proposes organizational identity as a process. More theorizing and elaboration on alternative perspectives or on organizations as social actors and organizational identity from a social actor or institutional perspective is needed to further advance the work on organizational identity. While institutional theory is increasingly looking at micro dynamics, what constitutes an organization and its unique social space remains the foundational question in much of the organizational identity research (King, Felin, & Whetten, 2010).

Other Perspectives on Collective Identity: Social Science Perspectives From Anthropology, History, and Sociology

Identity is explored at the collective level of analysis in anthropology, history, and sociology. Across these social sciences, it is frequently defined in terms of the identity of a nation or a society, or groups in societies. The purpose of this section is to offer some perspectives on how collective identity is researched in these disciplines to serve as a foundation for exploring the relationship with collective memory, but it is beyond the scope of this book to address in depth the expansive literature on collective identity across these disciplines.

National Identity

Definitions of national identity cross disciplines from communications to history (Kelman, 1997) to social psychology and conflict resolution. At the core of the discussion regarding national identity is the debate about how a nation itself is defined and, in sociology and history, when, how, and why the concept or idea of a nation emerged (Smith, 2002). Some, such as Hobsbawm and Gellner, have asserted that the concept emerged as part of the discussion of nationalism and is fairly modern (Smith, 2002). Hobsbawm and Ranger's (1983) "invention of tradition" thesis explored how European states prior to World War I created a "sense of historical endurance" for their practices as a way to signal legitimacy (Olick, Vinitzky-Seroussi, & Levy, 2011, p. 13), while Anderson (1991) described these states as "imagined communities" with invented traditions. Burke, a British historian, suggested that the late 19th century

marked the "invention of tradition," and national monuments and rituals associated with national histories were created as a way to legitimate
the nation-state (Burke, 2011, p. 191). As nations sought legitimacy
and resources to support their work, their "memory thus served as the
handmaiden of nationalist zeal, history its high counsel" (Olick et al.,
2011, p. 14).

Smith (2002) asserted that the concepts of nation-state and national
identities have a longer history and did not emerge with the theories of
nationalism that are more modern and more oriented toward Western
culture. These properties exclude ethnic nations with a focus on geneal-
ogy and commonly understood stories or history. These characteristics
also raise questions regarding when a nation begins to exist and whether
it needs all the properties or only a set of them or a core group.

Several defining characteristics of nations emerged from these early
discussions, including a nation as "a territory with clear boundaries, a
community that shares a code of law, legitimate, international or part
of a global system, and people who are aware they are part of the community" (Smith, 2002, p. 7). It is "a named community possessing an
historic territory, shared myths and memories, a common public culture,
and common laws and customs" (Smith, 2002, p. 15). Building on the
idea of shared myths and memories, others have taken a more ethnosymbolic approach in defining a nation with a focus on the social and symbolic components that constitute cultural identity (Smith, 2002). Smith
concluded that there is a need to address "the institutional expression"
of these ethnosymbolic elements such as recorded myths, history, and
legal aspects (p. 30). Ethnosymbolists might define nation by highlighting more subjective aspects of the definition, and this more fluid and
boundaryless condition can be tied to symbols. Kelman (1997, p. 168)
asserted that a nation is an "ethnic-cultural unit that has a meaning apart
from the shape of political boundaries" and has a territory, or a shared
memory of a territory, and other cultural elements such as language and
history that unify them. Guibernau (2004) also framed a nation in the
context of a culture in defining nation as "a human group conscious of
forming a community, sharing a common culture, attached to a clearly
demarcated territory, having a common past and a common project for
the future, and claiming the right to rule itself" (p. 132).

In summary, some of the common elements in these definitions of
nation include the importance of shared ethnosymbolic aspects of memory such as myths, stories, and a written history that create a shared sense
of culture and that draw from language to unify and communicate them.
The physical space such as territory may be real or imagined from their
past or their future, but the component of physical space is critical to the
idea of nation.

National identity surfaces from these definitions of a nation. National
identity establishes and exhibits itself through a combination of structures

such as laws, physical boundaries of countries, and physical space, such as monuments, as well as "culturally through public memories, dominant ideologies, literary, artistic and religious traditions, and educational systems" (Bruner, 2011, p. 403). Kelman expanded on the definition of national identity with the following:

> Insofar as a group of people have come to see themselves as constituting a unique, identifiable entity, with a claim to continuity over time, to unity across geographical distance, and to the right of various forms of self-expression, we can say that they have acquired a sense of national identity. National identity is a group's definition of itself as a group—its conceptions of its enduring characteristics and basic values; its strengths and weaknesses; its hopes and fears; its reputation and conditions of existence; its institutions and traditions; and its past history, current purposes and future prospects.
>
> (Kelman, 1997, p. 171)

Others, like Bruner (2011) and Kelman (2001), added the importance of language and narratives to national identity, in particular rhetoric as intentionally or unintentionally focused on persuasion. Rhetoric has implicit and often explicit tones of power and hegemony as it has been used to shape national identities. National identity is also supported by "a national narrative—an account of the group's origins, its history, and its relationship to the land" (Kelman, 2001, p. 191). These forces work together to create national identity, which is sustained particularly in discourse in memorialization. Bruner (2011) asserted that "all human subjectivity including collective identity . . . is thoroughly rhetorical inasmuch as human meaning and identity presupposes entry into symbolic worlds whose overwhelming influence usually goes unnoticed" (p. 404). Rhetoric can be a variable in national identity and memory and is useful to consider in analysis of public memory or commemoration, as memorials are often sites of "public discursive contestation" (p. 408). Rhetoric scholars began researching the relationship between history, memory, and identity in the 1960s, particularly in relationship to national identity.

Collective Identity Among Other Groups

Other ways to consider and define collective identity and its relationship to memory are through social groups or other types of collectives. Burke (2011), a British historian, suggested that it is more "fruitful to think in pluralistic terms about the uses of memories to different social groups" (p. 191) and what they determine is important to remember about who they are as a collective. These memories also influence what is officially recorded as history. Contemporary historians such as Megill (1998) have asserted that the evolving nature of collective identity is intertwined with the evolving construction of memory of a collective. These can be "imagined communities" (Anderson, 1991) in contrast to those determined by national boundaries.

Zerubavel, a sociologist, also theorized about collective identities and their relationship to memories of a social group. He theorized that much of what we remember as individuals is filtered through interpretation that happens in the context of a social group (Zerubavel, 1996). Remembering is "regulated by unmistakably social *rules of remembrance*" (Zerubavel, 1996, as cited in Olick et al., 2011, p. 222). He noted that identifying with the collective past of a group and acquiring that group's memories is part of the process of assuming a social identity. To assimilate into a social group requires active engagement with the past of the community (Zerubavel, 2003, p. 3). He referred to these social groups who have a common identity through recollections of significant past events as mnemonic communities (Zerubavel, 2003, p. 4). These groups create and commemorate a collective past. For example, one of the key significant events for a social group is its founding, and this significant event becomes part of the recollections. The constructed narratives about the origins or founding often include references to specific places such as the town or community in which a group was founded, and this place becomes linked to its identity through commemoration, celebrating its history. The place of origin becomes part of the group's collective identity.

Cultural Identity

There is also cross-disciplinary interest in cultural identity through the work of sociologists and cultural anthropologists. For example, Hall (1996), a sociologist and cultural theorist, explored the concept of collective identity, and in particular cultural identity through theorizing in part regarding identity at the individual level. Hall, in citing Mercer (1990), suggested that identity is tacit, only surfacing during crises, when something that is considered to be stable is suddenly in doubt or in crisis. Hall proposed three different conceptualizations of identity. The first is based on the individual person, the "Enlightenment Subject." The individual is a "human person as being a fully centered, unified individual, endowed with capacities of reason, consciousness and action" and with an inner core or essence that begins to emerge when the individual is born. This identity is relatively stable or unchanging, referred to as "his identity" (p. 597). The second view of identity is that of the "Sociological Subject," with the idea that this essence is formed through interaction with the environment or culture. With a foundation in symbolic interactionism, this view holds a core self but one that evolves in interaction with society. Lastly, he suggested that the postmodern view assumes that identity changes as needed in relationship to the culture in which we are embedded, as there is no coherent or uniform self.

Thus, identity is "historically, not biologically, defined" (Hall, 1996, p. 598). "If we feel we have a unified identity from birth to death, it is only because we construct a comforting story, or narrative of the self" about ourselves (p. 598). The assumption is that societies are in chronic rapid change, and there are multiple power centers that are constantly changing or being dislocated. Citing Laclau (1990), Hall asserted that there is constant disruptive change due to the external environment. These divisions and change can produce a variety of identities for individuals. These different divisions that make up societies are not unified but hold together to some degree because certain elements or identities can be expressed together under certain circumstances.

Hall (1996) suggested that this process is how national identities are formed. He asserted that "national identities are not things we are born with, but are formed and transformed within and in relationship to *representation*" (p. 612). Representations are sets of meanings, and nations produce these meanings. Nations are more than simply political "entities" but also create representations that produce meanings, "*a system of cultural representations*" (p. 612). Nations are symbolic communities that generate identities and loyalty through discourses that create meaning through stories and memories of the past.

Summary

In summary, definitions of collective identity, whether as part of a nation or a social group, have distinct similarities to definitions of organizational identity. For example, national identity is defined as a "collective phenomenon" and a "property of a group" (Kelman, 2001, p. 191) that has boundaries, common values, and stories of critical events that are important to the collective. These elements serve as a foundation for the culture of the group. Yet similar to the literature on organizational identity and the concept of organization, there is debate in the literature on national identity regarding how a nation is defined or constituted. Organizational identity also has a degree of continuity over time, i.e., it is temporally continuous (Albert & Whetten, 1985). Definitions of both organizational identity and collective identity offer some unity across the group yet acknowledge that multiple interpretations of the values may be present at different times. Despite how identity is defined in relationship to a nation, group, or organization, scholars assert that identity is mostly tacit and surfaces during crises of identity or when the collective is threatened. These definitions of collective identity, whether for a nation, social group, organization, or other type of collective, serve several functions, including creating a sense of unity, presenting a positive image of the collective, clarifying ownership or source of resources, and offering a foundation upon which to develop culture.

References

Albert, S., & Whetten, D. A. (1985). Organizational identity. In L. L. Cummings & B. M. Staw (Eds.), *Research in organizational behavior* (pp. 263–295). Greenwich, CT: JAI Press.

Anderson, B. (1991). *Imagined communities: Reflections on the origin and spread of nationalism*. London, UK: Verso.

Ashforth, B. E., & Mael, F. (1989). Social identity theory and the organization. *The Academy of Management Review*, *14*(1), 20–39. doi: 10.2307/258189.

Bastedo, M. N., Samuels, E., & Kleinman, M. (2014). Do charismatic presidents influence college applications and alumni donations? Organizational identity and performance in US higher education. *Higher Education*, *68*(3), 397–415.

Besharov, M. (2014). The relational ecology of identification: How organizational identification emerges when individuals hold divergent values. *Academy of Management Journal*, *57*(5), 1485–1512.

Brickson, S. (2013). Athletes, best friends, and social activists: An integrative model accounting for the role of identity in organizational identification. *Organization Science*, *24*(1), 226–245. https://doi.org/10.1287/orsc.1110.0730.

Brown, A. D., & Humphreys, M. (2006). Organizational identity and place: A discursive exploration of hegemony and resistance. *Journal of Management Studies*, *43*, 231–257. doi: 10.1111/j.1467–6486.2006.00589.x.

Bruner, M. L. (2011). Rhetorical studies and national identity construction. *National Identities*, *13*(4), 403–414. https://doi.org/10.1080/14608944.2011.629428.

Burke, P. (2011). History as social memory. In J. K. Olick, V. Vinitzky-Seroussi, & D. Levy (Eds.), *The collective memory reader* (pp. 188–192). New York, NY: Oxford University Press.

Casey, A. (1997). Collective memory in organizations. In P. Shrivastava, A. Huff, & J. Dutton (Series Eds.), J. Walsh & A. Huff (Vol. Eds.), *Organizational learning and strategic management* (Advances in Strategic Management, Vol. 14, pp. 111–151). Greenwich, CT: JAI Press.

Casey, A. (2010). *The role of collective memory in organizational identity*. Presented at the annual conference of the Academy of Management, Montreal, Quebec, Canada.

Casey, A., & Byington, L. (2013). *Nike: A case study of identity claims in a complex global world*. Presented at the annual conference of the Academy of Management, Lake Buena Vista, FL. https://doi.org/10.5465/ambpp.2013.12456abstract.

Chreim, S. (2007). Social and temporal influences on interpretations of organizational identity and acquisition integration: A narrative study. *Journal of Applied Behavioral Science*, *43*, 449–480. doi: 10.1177/0021886307307345.

Cian, L., & Cervai, S. (2014). Under the reputation umbrella: An integrative and multidisciplinary review for corporate image, projected image, construed image, organizational identity, and organizational culture. *Corporate Communications*, *19*(2), 182–199. https://doi.org/10.1108/CCIJ-10-2011-0055.

Clark, S. M., Gioia, D. A., Ketchen, D. J., & Thomas, J. B. (2010). Transitional identity as a facilitator of organizational identity change during a merger. *Administrative Science Quarterly*, *55*(3), 397–438.

Corley, K. G., & Gioia, D. A. (2004). Identity ambiguity and change in the wake of a corporate spin-off. *Administrative Science Quarterly, 49*, 173–208. Retrieved from www.jstor.org/stable/4131471

Corley, K. G., Harquail, C. V., Pratt, M. G., Glynn, M. A., Fiol, C. M., & Hatch, M. J. (2006). Guiding organizational identity through aged adolescence. *Journal of Management Inquiry, 15*(2), 85–99. https://doi.org/10.1177/1056492605285930.

Dukerich, J., Golden, B., & Shortell, S. (2002). Beauty is in the eye of the beholder: The impact of organizational identification, identity, and image on the cooperative behavior of physicians. *Administrative Science Quarterly, 47*, 507–533.

Dutton, J. E., & Dukerich, J. M. (1991). Keeping an eye on the mirror: Image and identity in organizational adaptation. *Academy of Management Journal, 34*, 517–554.

Elsbach, K. D., & Kramer, R. M. (1996). Members' responses to organizational identity threats: Encountering and countering the *Business Week* rankings. *Administrative Science Quarterly, 41*, 442–476. Retrieved from www.jstor.org/stable/2393938

Elstak, M. N. (2008). The paradox of the organizational identity field. *Corporate Reputation Review, 11*(3), 277–281. https://doi.org/10.1057/crr.2008.22.

Erickson, E. H. (1968). *Identity, youth and crises.* New York, NY: Norton.

Erickson, E. H. (1980). *Identity and the life cycle.* New York, NY: Norton.

Evans, S. K. (2015). Defining distinctiveness: The connections between organizational identity, competition, and strategy in public radio organizations. *International Business Communication, 52*(1), 42–67. https://doi.org/10.1177/2329488414560280.

Fiol, C. M. (1991). Managing culture as a competitive resource: An identity-based view of sustainable competitive advantage. *Journal of Management, 17*, 191–211. doi: 10.1177/014920639101700112.

Foreman, P., & Whetten, D. A. (2002). Members' identification with multiple-identity organizations. *Organization Science, 13*(6), 618–635. https://doi.org/10.1287/orsc.13.6.618.493.

Gioia, D. A., & Chittipeddi, K. (1991). Sensemaking and sensegiving in strategic change initiation. *Strategic Management Journal, 12*(6), 433–448. https://doi.org/10.1002/smj.4250120604.

Gioia, D. A., & Patvardhan, S. (2012). Identity as process and flow. In M. Schultz, S. Maguire, A. Langley, & H. Tsoukas (Eds.), *Constructing identity in and around organizations* (pp. 50–62). New York, NY: Oxford University Press.

Gioia, D., Patvardhan, S., Hamilton, A., & Corley, K. (2013). Organizational identity formation and change. *The Academy of Management Annals, 7*(1), 123–193. https://doi.org/10.5465/19416520.2013.762225.

Gioia, D. A., Schultz, M., & Corley, K. G. (2000). Organizational identity, image, and adaptive instability. *Academy of Management Review, 25*(1), 63–81. https://doi.org/10.5465/amr.2000.2791603.

Gioia, D. A., & Thomas, J. B. (1996). Identity, image, and issue interpretation: Sensemaking during strategic change in academia. *Administrative Science Quarterly, 41*(3), 370–403. https://doi.org/10.2307/2393936.

Guibernau, M. (2004). Anthony D. Smith on nations and national identity: A critical assessment. *Nations and Nationalism, 10*(1–2), 125–141. https://doi.org/10.1111/j.1354-5078.2004.00159.x.

Hall, S. (1996). The question of cultural identity. In S. Hall, D. Held, D. Hubert, & K. Thompson (Eds.), *Modernity: An introduction to modern societies* (pp. 595–634). Cambridge, UK: Blackwell Publishers.

Hatch, M. J. (2010). Material and meaning in the dynamics of organizational culture and identity with implications for leadership of organizational change. In N. Ashkanasy, C. Wilderom, & M. Peterson (Eds.), *The handbook of organizational culture and climate* (2nd ed., pp. 341–348). Thousand Oaks, CA: Sage.

Hatch, M. J., & Schultz, M. (1997). Relations between organizational culture, identity, and image. *European Journal of Marketing, 31*(5), 356–365. https://doi.org/10.1108/03090569710167583.

Hatch, M. J., & Schultz, M. (2000). Scaling the tower of Babel: Relational differences between identity, image and culture in organizations. In M. Schultz, M. Hatch, & M. Larsen (Eds.), *The expressive organization: Linking identity, reputation, and the corporate brand*. Oxford, UK: Oxford University Press.

Hatch, M. J., & Schultz, M. (2002). The dynamics of organizational identity. *Human Relations, 55*, 989–1018. https://doi.org/10.1177/0018726702055008181.

Hatch, M. J., & Schultz, M. (2017). Toward a theory of using history authentically: Historicizing in the Carlsberg Group. *Administrative Science Quarterly, 62*, 657–697. https://doi.org/10.1177/0001839217692535.

Hatch, M. J., Schultz, M., & Skov, A. M. (2015). Organizational identity and culture in the context of managed change: Transformation in the Carlsberg Group, 2009–2013. *Academy of Management Discoveries, 1*, 58–90. https://doi.org/10.5465/amd.2013.0020.

Hobsbawn, E., & Ranger, T. (1983). *The invention of tradition*. Cambridge, UK: Cambridge University Press.

Hogg, M. A., & Terry, D. J. (2001). *Social identity process in organizational identity*. Philadelphia, PA: Psychology Press.

Hsu, G., & Hannan, M. T. (2005). Identities, genres, and organizational forms. *Organization Science, 16*, 474–490. doi: 10.1287/orsc.1050.0151.

Huermer, L. (2010). Corporate social responsibility and multinational corporation identity: Norwegian strategies in the Chilean aquaculture industry. *Journal of Business Ethics, 91*, 265–277.

Kelman, H. C. (1997). Nationalism, patriotism, and national identity: Social psychological dimensions. In D. Bar-Tal & E. Staub (Eds.), *Patriotism in the lives of individuals and nations* (pp. 165–189). Chicago, IL: Nelson-Hall.

Kelman, H. C. (2001). The role of national identity in conflict resolution. In R. D. Ashmore, L. Jussim, & D. Wilder (Eds.), *Social identity, intergroup conflict, and conflict reduction* (pp. 187–212). Oxford: Oxford University Press.

King, B. G., Felin, T., & Whetten, D. A. (2010). Finding the organization in organizational theory: A meta-theory of the organization as a social actor. *Organization Science, 21*, 290–305.

King, B. G., & Whetten, D. A. (2008). Rethinking the relationship between reputation and legitimacy: A social actor conceptualization. *Corporate Reputation Review, 11*(3), 192–207. https://doi.org/10.1057/crr.2008.16.

Kreiner, G. E., Hollensbe, E., Sheep, M. L., Smith, B. R., & Kataria, N. (2015). Elasticity and the dialectic tensions of organizational identity: How can we hold together while we are pulling apart? *Academy of Management Journal, 58*(4), 981–1011. https://doi.org/10.5465/amj.2012.0462.

Laclau, E. (1990). *New reflections on the revolution of our time*. London, UK: Verso.

Langley, A., Smallman, C., Tsoukas, H., & Van de Ven, A. H. (2013). Process studies of change in organization and management: Unveiling temporality, activity and flow. *Academy of Management Journal*, 15(1), 1–13. https://doi.org/10.5465/amj.2013.4001.

Łupina-Wegener, A., Schneider, S. C., & van Dick, R. (2015). The role of outgroups in constructing a shared identity: A longitudinal study of a subsidiary merger in Mexico. *Management International Review*, 55(5), 677–705. https://doi.org/10.1007/s11575-015-0247-6.

Martínez, P., Pérez, A., & Rodríguez del Bosque, I. (2014). Exploring the role of CSR in the organizational identity of hospitality companies: A case from the Spanish tourism industry. *Journal of Business Ethics*, 124(1), 47–66. https://doi.org/10.1007/s10551-013-1857-1.

Mead, G. H. (1934). *Mind, self and society*. Chicago, IL: University of Chicago Press.

Megill, A. (1998). History, memory and identity. *History of the Human Sciences*, 11(3), 37–62. https://doi.org/10.1177/095269519801100303.

Mercer, K. (1990). Welcome to the jungle. In J. Rutherford (Ed.), *Identity*. London, UK: Lawrence and Wishart.

Morsing, M., & Roepstorff, A. (2015). CSR as corporate political activity: Observations on IKEA's CSR identity-image dynamics. *Journal of Business Ethics*, 128(2), 395–409. https://doi.org/10.1007/s10551-014-2091-1.

Nag, R., Corley, K. G., & Gioia, D. A. (2007). The intersection of organizational identity, knowledge, and practice: Attempting strategic change via knowledge grafting. *Academy of Management Journal*, 50(4), 821–847. https://doi.org/10.5465/amj.2007.26279173.

Olick, J. K., Vinitzky-Seroussi, V., & Levy, D. (2011). Introduction. In J. K. Olick, V. Vinitzky-Seroussi, & D. Levy (Eds.), *The collective memory reader* (pp. 3–62). New York, NY: Oxford University Press.

Pratt, M. G., & Foreman, P. O. (2000). Classifying managerial responses to multiple organizational identities. *Academy of Management Review*, 25, 18–42. doi: 10.2307/259261.

Rajan, H. C., & Casey, A. (2015). "Who are we as an organization?" Organizational identity in a multinational company's subsidiary. *Academy of Management Annual Meeting Proceedings*, 2015(1), 15502–15502.

Ravasi, D., & Schultz, M. (2006). Responding to organizational identity threats: Exploring the role of organizational culture. *Academy of Management Journal*, 49(3), 433–458. https://doi.org/10.5465/amj.2006.21794663.

Scott, W. R. (2001). *Institutions and organizations* (2nd ed.). Thousand Oaks, CA: Sage.

Schultz, M., & Hernes, T. (2013). A temporal perspective on organizational identity. *Organization Science*, 24(1), 1–21. https://doi.org/10.1287/orsc.1110.0731.

Smith, A. D. (2002). When is a nation? *Geopolitics*, 7(2), 5–32.

Solomon, J., & Casey, A. (2017). A hierarchical model of organizational identification. *Journal of Organizational Psychology*, 17(3), 93–111.

Steiner, L., Sundström, A. C., & Sammalisto, K. (2013). An analytical model for university identity and reputation strategy work. *Higher Education*, 65(4), 401–415. https://doi.org/10.1007/s10734-012-9552-1.

Suddaby, R., & Greenwood, R. (2005). Rhetorical strategies of legitimacy. *Administrative Science Quarterly*, *50*(1), 35–67. https://doi.org/10.2189/asqu. 2005.50.1.35.

Tyworth, M. (2014). Organizational identity and information systems: How organizational ICT reflect who an organization is. *European Journal of Information Systems*, *23*(1), 69–83. https://doi.org/10.1057/ejis.2013.32.

van Rekom, J., Corley, K., & Ravasi, D. (2008). Extending and advancing theories of organizational identity [guest editorial]. *Corporate Reputation Review*, *11*(3), 183–188. https://doi.org/10.1057/crr.2008.21.

Whetten, D. A. (2006). Albert and Whetten revisited: Strengthening the concept of organizational identity. *Journal of Management Inquiry*, *15*(3), 219–234. https://doi.org/10.1177/1056492606291200.

Whetten, D. A. (2013). Organization identity. In E. H. Kessler (Ed.), *Encyclopedia of management theory* (pp. 560–563). Thousand Oaks, CA: Sage. https://doi.org/10.4135/9781452276090.n177.

Whetten, D. A., & Mackey, A. (2002). A social actor conception of organizational identity and its implications for the study of organizational reputation. *Business & Society*, *41*(4), 393–414. https://doi.org/10.1177/0007650302238775.

Zerubavel, E. (1996). Social memories: Steps to a sociology of the past. *Qualitative Sociology*, *19*(3), 283–299. https://doi.org/10.1007/BF02393273.

Zerubavel, E. (2003). *Time maps: Collective memory and the social shape of the past*. London, UK: University of Chicago Press. https://doi.org/10.7208/chicago/9780226924908.001.0001.

Part II

The Relationships Between Collective Memory and Identity

3 Relationships Between Collective Memory and Identity

This section highlights and integrates the multidisciplinary theory and research on organizational memory (Casey, 1997; Walsh & Ungson, 1991) and collective memory (Fine & Beim, 2007; Olick, 2007; Olick & Robbins, 1998; Schwartz, 1991a, 1991b, 1997, 2000, 2005; Wertsch, 2002, 2008) and their relationship to organizational identity (Albert & Whetten, 1985; Casey & Byington, 2013) and national and cultural identity (Hall, 1996; Kelman, 1997, 2001; Schwartz, 2000, 2005; Zerubavel, 2003). Collective memory is a significant research focus in the social sciences, as interest in it has grown across disciplines (Espinoza, Piper, & Fernandez, 2014; Loveday, 2014; Radstone, 2000). As this focus has emerged, the relationship between collective memory and identity itself has also surfaced as a topic for theory and research. Similarly, the interest in organizational and national or cultural identity has continued to grow and is a significant research focus. In this literature, the importance of memory to identity has been theorized and researched, as highlighted by Olick, Vinitzky-Seroussi, and Levy (2011) in their question, "How is the self of yesterday connected to the self of today and of tomorrow? Only by memory?" (p. 177). Although this quote is primarily referring to the individual level of analysis, it can also be theorized at the collective level and across levels and highlights the critical importance of memory in forming identity, particularly memory in the form of an organized narrative from birth or founding to death (Olick et al., 2011) of an individual or a collective. Individuals and groups are linked through the stories they tell (Olick et al., 2011) and collective identity is created, sustained, and at times evolves as it in turn influences what is recalled and why. Halbwachs's (1980) work serves as a foundation for the relationship between identity and memory and the importance of shared memories and commemoration to a collective's identity process.

This chapter first explores the relationship between identity and memory based on theory and research in organizational studies that link these concepts. The first section focuses on organizational identity literature and how the relationship between identity and memory is expressed, and the second section focuses on organizational memory literature and how the relationship between memory and identity has been researched. Both sections present the relationship as it surfaces in definitions and in empirical studies. The chapter then explores the relationship across the social sciences, addressing the iterative relationship between identity and memory. Two components of collective memory, history and commemoration, and their relationship to identity (Assmann & Czaplicka, 1995; Haas & Levasseur, 2013; Olick, 2007; Schwartz, 2000, 2005; Zerubavel, 2003) are highlighted.

As part of this discussion, this chapter elaborates on the "memory boom" beginning in the 1980s (McDonald, 2010) in sociology and other social sciences and in the 2000s in organizational studies. Part of the rationale offered for this increased interest in memory studies is the impact of global, political, and social changes and generational differences (Hewer & Roberts, 2012) on how collectives see themselves and their identity in relation to their past. Recent trends that emphasize a multivocal relationship between memory and identity are explored, as well as the relevant debates regarding this relationship (Gabel, 2013; Haas & Levasseur, 2013).

This connection between the concepts of memory and identity can be seen in some of the definitions discussed thus far. Collective memories are often defined as "representations of the past in the minds of members of a community that contribute to the community's sense of identity" (Manier & Hirst, 2008, p. 253, as cited in Rime, Bouchat, Klein, & Licata, 2015). The functions of collective memory are also discussed in relationship to identity, in that collective memory serves as the foundation for a collective's identity (Rime et al., 2015). In this sense, collective memories are not simply representations of the past shared across a social group but inherent to the identity of the group.

The presence of memory in understandings of identity is apparent in definitions of national identity. For example:

> National identity is a group's definition of itself as a group—its conceptions of its enduring characteristics and basic values; its strengths and weaknesses; its hopes and fears; its reputation and conditions of existence; its institutions and traditions; and its past history, current purposes and future prospects.
>
> (Kelman, 1997, p. 171)

National identity is also described as establishing and exhibiting itself through a combination of structures such as laws, physical boundaries of countries, and physical space, such as monuments, as well as "culturally through public memories, dominant ideologies, literary, artistic and religious traditions, and educational systems" (Bruner, 2011, p. 403).

The presence of memory also resides in definitions of organizational identity but is more implicit in that they reference the temporal nature of identity. For example, in their seminal work, Albert and Whetten (1985) noted: "For the purposes of defining organizational identity as a scientific concept, we treat the criteria of central character, distinctiveness and temporal continuity as each necessary and as a set sufficient" (p. 265).

Organizational Identity and Its Relationship to Memory

Until the mid-2000s, the organizational identity literature rarely mentioned sociological perspectives on collective memory or references to past work on organizational memory. If the history of an organization was noted, it was discussed in general terms, such as the founding of the organization or the historical binding commitments, or critical events in an organization's past. Historical binding commitments are what "has made them what and/or who they are today" (Whetten, 2006, p. 224). In the early theorizing of organizational identity from a social constructionist perspective, when history or memory was addressed, it was from revisionist history or postmodern theories of history that support the changing interpretations of past organizational events and identity claims (Gioia, Schultz, & Corley, 2000). More recently, in empirical research taking the social constructionist perspective on organizational identity, such as that of Ravasi and Schultz (2006), theorists have delved slightly more deeply into theories of collective memory, and in doing so the stabilizing influence of memory has surfaced. For example, Anteby and Molnar (2012) focused on collective memory, in particular an organization's recorded history, in researching how organizational identity might endure over time. Similarly, Hatch and Schultz (2017), in their research on organizational identity and history, explored the process of historicizing or authentically preserving parts of an organization's past and how it connected to and framed the identity of the organization. Other work (Schultz & Hernes, 2013) has taken a temporal view of organizational identity and the relationship between different types of memory forms and the impact on how identity is constructed. Despite the contributions of this more recent work, the relationships between memory and identity are yet to be explored in depth and remain theoretically and empirically underdeveloped.

The Relationship as It Surfaces in Definitions of Organizational Identity

Time is foundational in defining the essential components of organizational identity, i.e., core, enduring, and distinctive (CED) (Albert & Whetten, 1985). Organizational identity is framed within and over time, yet there is temporal continuity. Organizational identity surfaces during crises or forks in the road when a decision will profoundly affect the future direction of an organization. From the social actor perspective of organizational identity, these points in time and decisions are critical for the future of organizations and consequently become markers in history; they are often the foundation of stories that are told about key events in the past and are frequently preserved in recorded organizational histories. These CED features are preserved in the components of collective memory, i.e., commemoration and history, because the claims and related historical binding commitments are what "has made them what and/or who they are today" (Whetten, 2006, p. 224). These coherent claims are "historical frames of reference" (Whetten, 2006, p. 223) that guide organizational strategic actions in the past, present, and future (Whetten & Mackey, 2002). From a social actor perspective, memory as recorded history serves to sustain the knowledge of the organization and its identity through the years.

The social constructionist perspective of organizational identity also builds from the CED features of organizational identity but takes issue with how enduring is defined (Albert & Whetten, 1985). More recently, the dialectic of functioning to support both stability and change in identity has surfaced, discussed as part of the elasticity of organizational identity (Kreiner, Hollensbe, Sheep, Smith, & Kataria, 2015). In addition, the relationship between these concepts has been explored as a process, e.g., historicizing (Hatch & Schultz, 2017).

The relationship between identity and memory as expressed in this work highlights how memory functions to preserve identity and its core features, as well as how it can support the evolution of identity as memories of the past are revised to meet the needs of the present. The preservation aspect occurs particularly through recorded histories, while the revision process is more likely to occur through commemoration. The dialectic perspective and the view of both concepts as a process offer insight into both stability and change. How memory functions and the nature of the relationship is dependent on the theoretical and ontological perspectives taken relative to both concepts, i.e., identity and memory.

Empirical Studies of Organizational Identity Related to Memory

Research on organizational identity from the social constructionist perspective (Ravasi & Schultz, 2006) has explored the role of organizational culture in identity processes and suggested that history, as a part of organizational culture, functions as a stabilizing influence in the evolution of organizational identity. The interpretation of the characteristics or claims may change or evolve, but the interpretation may not fundamentally negate the past as reflected in the organization's history (Ravasi & Schultz, 2006) or commemorative practices. Ravasi and Schultz's (2006) empirical study of organizational identity and culture also found that an organization's history and traditions were closely linked to the organization's identity, particularly during times of change. Ravasi and Schultz took a constructionist perspective on history, citing Gioia et al. (2000), with the assumption that history can be reconstructed to meet the needs of the present. In this study, the sociological theoretical literature on collective memory, and in particular history, was not explicitly developed, nor was it used to explain the findings, therefore not adding to our theorizing about organizational memory and history as a form of memory.

More recently, Anteby and Molnar (2012) also explored the relationship between organizational identity and memory and drew more explicitly from the sociological work on collective memory. They used the theoretical work on collective memory (Halbwachs, 1992; Olick & Levy, 1997) as a foundation to understand how organizational identity endures over time. They highlighted that most theorizing about organizational identity has revealed how identity changes, yet little work has focused on how it endures. While their study proposed the connection with memory, or more specifically the organization's "rhetorical history," and how managers make meaning of the past (p. 515), it found that organizational forgetting processes were also critical to endurance of identity. Forgetting was defined as the "deliberate omission of potentially contradictory aspects of an organization's history (i.e., what we label 'structural omission') or the ongoing deliberate attempt to neutralize these contradictory aspects with valued identity cues (i.e., 'preemptive neutralization')" (p. 516). Drawing from Olick and Levy (1997) and Halbwachs (1992), collective memory is defined as "a reconstruction of the past that adapts images of ancient facts to present beliefs" (p. 517). Anteby and Molnar (2012) also incorporated other theoretical approaches to collective memory (Misztal, 2003; Schwartz, 2000; Wagner-Pacifici & Schwartz, 1991) to further explore the enduring aspects of organizational identity.

Anteby and Molnar (2012) noted that organizations are understudied collectives in the sociological literature on collective memory yet offer valuable opportunities for exploring the relationship between memory and organizational identity. Although their focus was primarily on how organizational memory sustains organizational identity, they concluded that through studying organizational identity we may further understand organizational memory and forgetting processes in organizations. Organizational identity "may be seen as constituting collective memories" (p. 532) or may be considered as "sites of memory, similar to flags, anthems, or geographical places (Nora, 1996)" (p. 532).

Schultz and Hernes (2013) also explored history as a form of organizational memory and in doing so acknowledged the role it can play in sustaining the depth of possible interpretations of identity for both stability and change. In their empirical study of the construction of organizational identity of the LEGO Group, they theorized that a longer and broader range of memory forms, such as textual, material, and oral memory

(Schultz & Hernes, 2013, p. 1), contributed to a depth of claims for future identity as organizational actors drew on the organization's past. Their study was framed from a social constructionist process perspective, in that organizations were defined as "an ongoing accomplishment" and were "seen as in a continuous state of creation, emergence and becoming while being shaped by a changing past and future ambitions" (Schultz & Hernes, 2013, p. 1). The authors assumed that time—past, present, and future—is subject to interpretation and is a key component of the identity construction process. This was one of the rare works in organizational identity that drew from Walsh and Ungson's original definition of organizational memory, particularly the storage bins approach.

Schultz and Hernes (2013) also contributed to our understanding of organizational memory through theorizing that the form or the context is important in the recall and use of memory. They suggested using the idea of memory forms instead of bins and indicated that the forms influence the meaning of the memory. They drew from Mead's (1934) discussion of different forms of memory but did not delve into these in depth using the sociological theory on memory. They also theorized that memory is evoked rather than invoked and that this is part of a sensemaking process (Weick, 1995).

The primary focus of Schultz and Hernes's work (2013) was to extend theorizing on organizational identity in relationship to temporal aspects, and their findings supported considering identity as both enduring and changing simultaneously. This "avoids the question of identity as either stable or enduring" (p. 16). A combination of memory forms "opened a path to deeper understanding of past identities, inspiring greater depth in the articulation of the intended future identity of the company" (p. 16). The contribution to organizational memory was limited, though. As the authors noted, although this paper began to develop a framework on how memory is used in relationship to identity, "the distinctions between the three forms remain coarse" (p. 18), with considerable overlap between the contents of the forms. In conclusion, their contribution to organizational or collective memory in organizations was minimal, but their paper did expand our understanding of how organizational identity is influenced by different types of memory held in organizations.

More recent process perspectives of organizational identity (Kreiner et al., 2015) have suggested that individuals in organizations may draw on past events both in their own lives as well as in organizational histories and shape them to address a current issue. The assumption is that the recollections and interpretations of the past are malleable. This malleability facilitates the "adaptive instability" of organizational identity (Gioia et al., 2000). Kreiner et al. (2015) also proposed that this "fluidity of identity" helps to explain why organizational identity appears to endure, in that it can be adapted to solve present problems yet still is linked to the past.

Taking a slightly different approach to the relationship of an organization's past or its history to organizational identity, Zundel, Holt, and Popp (2016) explored how organizations use history to construct identity. They, too, took a social constructionist approach to organizational identity, with the assumption that identity claims can be managed or influenced. They asserted that organizations use their history as well as that of their external environment to create and sustain identity claims as needed, particularly during times of uncertainty. Managerial power can shape and sustain recollections to maintain claims. Using speech act theory to support their work, they theorized that speech as a "performative action" can shape identity through the words used and their interpretation. To support their framework, they included examples from organizational websites that delineated how and when organizations used history to build the internal or external commitment of stakeholders and the degree to which organizations used their own history versus that of events in their external environment.

Overall, Zundel et al. (2016) assumed that history and identity are malleable and can be used with some degree of success depending on how history and the narratives are constructed to support organizational initiatives. They cited Suddaby, Foster, and Quinn's (2010) work, noting that "it is not just the meaning of events, but the facts themselves that become subject to 'active management,' resulting in highly utilitarian accounts" (Zundel et al., 2016, p. 17). Zundel et al. (2016) drew from the work of Nietzsche (1873–76/1995), the literature on use of history in organizational theory (Rowlinson, Hassard, & Decker, 2014; Suddaby et al., 2010; Suddaby & Greenwood, 2005), and seminal work on organizational memory (Walsh & Ungson, 1991) to theorize about history and memory, but the theorizing was primarily to clarify identity processes and did not draw directly from the theory and research on collective memory nor contribute to theorizing about organizational memory.

In contrast, while Hatch and Schultz (2017) acknowledged that managers may work to manipulate or use parts of an organization's history to achieve their goals, they surfaced the importance of sustaining the authenticity of history in management's actions and coined the term *organizational historicizing* (Hatch & Schultz, 2017, p. 1). Historicizing, they suggested, is composed of the microactivities of rediscovering, recontextualizing, reclaiming, renewing, and re-embedding an artifact (Hatch & Schultz, 2017, p. 1). In taking a process or temporal view of organizational identity and history, they expanded on the micro-level activities in which organizational actors use historical artifacts to develop organizational identity at different points in the life of an organization.

Hatch and Schultz (2017) noted that there has been limited work on how organizations use their histories. Most of the research in this area has focused on how managers use the history of the organization to manipulate strategic change or to sustain or reinforce an organization's identity. Other work has explored storytelling in organizations as a part of this process of legitimation (Wry, Lounsbury, & Glynn, 2011). Power has been a significant factor in these processes, especially as related to organizational identity, and they asserted that we need to take a closer look at power's role in the process. They noted that most of the organizational studies literature related to power and identity has taken a critical theory perspective, with the view that managers manipulate and reconfigure events from the past to meet managerial and organizational needs.

In their empirical investigation of the Carlsberg Company, Hatch and Schultz (2017) hypothesized that how organizations use history in relationship to organizational identity is nuanced and complex. They noted that "anyone who wishes to use history needs to authenticate the intended historical content in the eyes of those on whose acceptance of its uses they depend" (p. 33) and that other organizational actors beyond managers need to be studied in terms of how they use the history of the organization.

> We propose that manipulating history risks failure because it undermines the immediacy, intensity, and emotionality that history inspires in others and thereby denies its agency. Allowing history to have agency, in the sense of possessing the power to inspire those who use it, could bring additional insights into the field of organizational history research, such as those that informed this article.
>
> (p. 36)

Hatch and Schultz (2017) found that the latent history that exists in organizations has the "potential for its own rediscovery" (p. 30). As organizational members strive to "authenticate historical materials that they intend to use, actors expand their knowledge of history at the same time" (p. 33), and the artifacts and the history become more meaningful to them through the process. They proposed that future organizational memory research should use temporal tracking of how memories of events or artifacts are used at different points in the organization's life cycle.

Hatch and Schultz (2017) concluded that organizational historians can be "valuable partners for strategists, not because they can manipulate history to legitimate strategy already formulated but because they can guide managers to use history authentically to align their strategic choices with knowledge of and wisdom extracted from the past" (p. 692). This discussion is similar to Schwartz's delineation of commemoration and history as two components of collective memory. Commemoration needs to stay close to history as the factual account of events or it loses its meaning.

To summarize, four main ideas emerge from this important empirical work on organizational identity and its relationship to memory in organizations:

1. History and commemoration in organizations and the meaning that is derived from them need to stay close or congruent to be meaningful, and organizational identity functions to preserve what, why, and how history and memory are recalled.
2. Organizational memory can take multiple forms with different characteristics, and these forms have agency in themselves and can influence organizational identity.
3. Power dynamics can influence organizational memory, which in turn influences organizational identity processes.
4. More in-depth exploration of the relationship of organizational memory and identity in organizations can inform both areas of study.

In conclusion, the empirical work in organizational studies has offered minimal contributions to theories of organizational memory thus far. Instead, organizational memory is more frequently used to support our understanding of organizational identity.

Organizational Memory and Its Relationship to Identity

The Relationship as It Surfaces in Definitions of Organizational Memory

Memory in organizations continues to be researched in its many forms in organizational studies yet remains an underdeveloped, undertheorized, and underresearched concept. Memory in organizations has been studied from the perspective of organizational memory or, more recently, collective memory and history. The relationship between organizational or collective memory and organizational identity was proposed by Casey (1997) as part of her study on collective memory but has only recently been explored in the organizational studies literature, particularly when memory is conceptualized from the perspective of the two components of collective memory, i.e., history and commemoration, as highlighted in recent special issues on history and organizational studies. Organizational identity has not been linked with scholarship that has framed organizational memory as a type of knowledge or information system.

In organizational studies, definitions of organizational memory have minimal if any references to organizational identity. For the most part, organizational memory is defined as a repository of knowledge, and the repository can take many forms. Beginning with Walsh and Ungson (1991), organizational memory was defined as "stored information from an organization's history that can be brought to bear on present decisions" (p. 61). In this definition, history is not explicated in much detail using theories of history or literature from the disciplines of history. Huber (1991) also defined organizational memory as "the means by which knowledge is stored for future use" (p. 90). Later, building on

Casey's (1997) empirical study of collective memory in an organization, memory was defined as "a dynamic socially constructed phenomenon, or as a process" (Nissley & Casey, 2002, p. 37). More recently, different types of memory as explored in the work of Schultz and Hernes (2013) were explained as the following:

> Inspired by Mead's (1932, p. 352) distinction among "material documents, oral testimony, and historical remains" as the fundamental forms of memory from which people access the past, we suggest that organizational memory may be classified into textual, material, and oral forms (see usage by historians as described in the Library of Congress 2009, Olick, 2007).
>
> (p. 4)

Yet, knowledge-based and more functionalist views of organizational memory have predominated in the organizational studies literature since the concept was introduced by Walsh and Ungson (1991), with memory referenced primarily as a "set of accumulated knowledge . . . being preserved through time" (Barros, Ramos, & Perez, 2015, p. 46).

Empirical Studies of Organizational Memory Related to Identity

Empirical work on organizational memory has minimally drawn upon sociological theories on collective memory, either to create conceptual frameworks for their studies of organizational memory or to explore and extend their findings particularly in relationship to identity.

Early traces of this shift toward sociological theorizing in organizational memory surfaced in Casey's (1997) empirical study of organizational memory. Casey built on Walsh and Ungson (1991), defining memory as shared interpretations of past events, and integrated the theoretical work on collective memory (Schwartz, 1991a, 1991b) from sociology to serve as a foundation for her research. Nissley and Casey (2002) continued to theorize about this relationship, particularly in connection with the role of power in their conceptual work on corporate museums, taking a multidisciplinary approach (involving organizational studies, sociology, psychology, museum studies, and history), drawing from the work of Schwartz (1991a, 1991b) and Halbwachs (1980). Later, in Casey and Byington's case study (2013) of collective memory and identity at Nike, they found shared recollections and interpretations of past events in this vast multisite organization. Organizational identity was a critical factor in how and why events were recalled. Nike's organizational identity claims were embedded in memories of significant events in the organization's history that were recalled across generations of employees. This was an iterative relationship in that the identity claims were why events were considered critical and, therefore, why and how they were recalled, and then the commemoration, formal and informal, of these events evolved and in turn influenced the interpretation of the identity claims.

Since these early works, organizational history framed as traditions or legacy, as well as commemoration or coremembering as facets of organizational memory or collective memory, has surfaced in organizational studies theory and research, particularly in relationship to organizational concepts such as organizational identity and organizational culture (Gioia et al., 2000; Rindova, Dalpiaz, & Ravasi, 2011; Weber, Heinze, & DeSoucey, 2008). For the most part, in this initial work, organizational history and memory were primarily referenced to further explore or explain these concepts of identity (Anteby & Molnar, 2012; Schultz & Hernes, 2013) and culture. For example, Gioia et al. (2000) studied the relationship between organizational identity and image and proposed the unique adaptive instability of organizational identity. They highlighted the role of organizational history in this process, noting that history is inherent in the perspectives of organizational identity: the social actor perspective grounded in institutional theory portrays organizational identity as resistant to change, given that it is grounded in history, while the social constructionist perspective is supported by the revisionist history perspective or a postmodern approach to the past. Their theorizing focused on organizational identity and did not further our understanding of organizational history through in-depth analysis of the sociological literature on collective memory nor in how organizational identity might contribute to history or commemoration.

Memory or traditions are usually influenced by organizational identity in these studies (Casey, 1997; Zundel et al., 2016). It's both why events are remembered and why they are significant. More recent work on memory in organizations has operationalized memory as commemoration and history. This work was reviewed earlier in this book in the discussion of the special issues of *Organization* and the *Academy of Management Review*.

In conclusion, much of the empirical work on organizational memory since Walsh and Ungson (1991) has offered little to the theoretical development of memory as a concept and less to its relationship to identity or further theorizing about identity. This began to change with some of the work on social memory (Feldman & Feldman, 2006), leading to a more distinct focus on memory as commemoration and process in the mid-2000s, with the special issues discussed earlier in this text. This more recent work has offered insights into memory as a process, drawing from sociological theories and history, and into our understanding of the iterative nature of the relationship between memory and identity as a process. Identity functions both to shape what is recalled and why and can erase memory, while memory functions to further sustain or shape identity.

The Relationship Between Collective Memory and Identity: Social Science Perspectives From Anthropology, History, and Sociology

The relationship between collective memory and identity has been addressed across the disciplines of anthropology, history, and sociology. Similar to the work in organizational studies, sometimes the two constructs are defined in terms of each other while at other times the definitions are distinctly different and the focus is on the relationship between the two constructs. Also similar to the organizational studies literature, the relationship between the concepts is either described as interdependent or co-constructed. For example, Topp (2009), a historian, asserted that memory and identity are "two sides of the same coin not only among individuals but also among groups progressing through time" (p. 14); the two constructs have an interdependent relationship and need each other to survive. When identity and memory are discussed in this section, the focus is at the collective level—a group, organization, society, or nation.

How Memory Supports Identity

As discussed in early sections of this text, in looking across the disciplines of anthropology, history, and sociology, the definition of collective memory is framed in two primary ways. First, collective memory is defined as "the representation of the past embodied in *both* historical evidence and commemorative symbolism" (Schwartz, 2000, p. 9), and identity is acknowledged as a key factor in what is recalled. Second, collective memory is framed more as a multifaceted social and political process of meaning construction and is influenced by identity. In both cases, memory also serves several functions in this relationship.

First, memory functions to fuse and solidify identity; it forms the core of identity. For example, Figlio (2012), a psychoanalyst addressing identity and collective memory in the context of reconstructing a collective identity in post-World War II Germany, noted that collective memory is "the backbone that holds identity together" (p. 161), as "memories and histories consolidate the sense of identity" (p. 161). Overall, from a historical, sociological, and material culture perspective, memory is the core of identity and informs the construction of identity (De Jong, 2009; Krmpotich, 2010). De Jong (2009) also emphasized the intertwined nature of the relationship of collective memory and identity, maintaining that memory is at the heart of identity. DeJong asserted that "memory forms the fabric of human life, affecting everything from the ability to perform simple, everyday tasks to the recognition of the self" (p. 362); as "the means by which we remember who we are, memory provides the very core of identity" (p. 362).

Second, memory also facilitates the acquisition of identity. Linde, an anthropologist, proposed that memory is "key to identity, and to the acquisition of identity" (p. 608) because collective memory embeds and highlights the identity and identification of social groups (Murray, 2013, p. 103). Both the content and the process of memory are critically related to how identity is acquired and evolves in individuals, group, collectives, and societies (Murray, 2013).

Much of the theory and empirical work on the role of memory in identity processes in the fields of anthropology, sociology, and history has been done in relationship to the sweeping changes in Europe, particularly in the past 50 years. This work has described how new national identities are formed in part through the recollections of the past. How the past is recalled and which group's past is highlighted are part of the process and, at times, the struggle. For example, Avdikos (2013) and others have studied the relationship of national identity and history and the formation of national states in the Balkan Peninsula and have highlighted the importance of "tracing the historical route of these states" (Avdikos, 2013, p. 396). The past, both historical documents and recollections of events, is often reconfigured to create new national identities. This effort involves memory processes of remembering as well as forgetting, which can be problematic for collectives or parts of a collective (Lebow, 2008).

Third, memory supports identity by creating, unifying, and maintaining its uniqueness or distinctiveness from other groups through storing recollections of events that are most critical for a group to remember. Collective memory provides a group with a feeling of unity that differentiates it from other groups (Haas & Levasseur, 2013). Historians Assmann and Czaplicka (1995) further articulated this dynamic interdependence between the two concepts in their description of cultural memory as a collective's efforts to keep critical events from the past alive. "Cultural memory has its fixed point; its horizon does not change with the passing of time. These fixed points are fateful events of the past, whose memory is maintained" (p. 129) through texts, rituals, or memorials. Cultural memory is "a store of knowledge from which a group derives awareness of its unity and peculiarity" (Assmann & Czaplicka, 1995, p. 130) based on its past. The collective, therefore, constructs a stable identity through sharing its knowledge of the past, keeping its identity alive in the process. Stories of significant events may evolve over time, but they stay linked to the identity of the collective that creates them and the collective's unique history.

As part of this process of national identity, delineating borders and establishing differences are critical because they are used as a way to distinguish one new country and its identity from another. Avdikos (2013) noted that identity is about difference from other groups, similar to collective memories of a group that are often framed in terms of us versus them (Haebich, 2011). The function of memory "is not 'to preserve the past but to adapt it, so as to enrich and manipulate the present' (Lowenthal, 1985, p. 19)" (Avdikos, 2013, p. 398). History or recollections of the past are an anchor for the newly forming national identities. This national history can bond people together and is frequently intentional remembering or, at times, forgetting. At other times, it can also create divisions between subgroups in conflicts over national identity, as represented in contested recollections of the past when events represent different symbols and meaning (Levy, 1999). A nation's history and recollections of it are crucial for national identity to form and be sustained (Kratochwil, 2006, p. 16).

Avdikos (2013) raised the idea of micro and macro identities and the usefulness of both in the process of identity and memory. In this work, the more micro level is local or regional memories beyond the state or national memories. Avdikos proposed that more macro levels of identity such as cultural identity are more useful because they provide room for the more micro levels within it. Avdikos (2013) commented:

> Official memory as inscribed in national histories is the result of expediencies, particularly of the need to form national consciousness and to support the borderline. Consequently, only oral memory can shed light on contradictions, provided that the political conditions are favourable and the research framework facilitates the activation of memory.
>
> (p. 408)

Commemorating, or coremembering or remembering together, as a component of collective memory involves rituals that facilitate "order and continuity" and are connected with emotionally significant events that affirm and sustain "the identity of one's group and redefining membership with that group" (Frijda, 1997, p. 109). Significant events can be the founding or the origins of an organization or other type of collective or events that are turning points or critical situations threatening the essence or the identity of the community (Pennebaker & Banasik, 1997). In organizations, these events are the "fork-in-the road" decision points (Whetten, 2006) where the organization will be permanently changed if one path is taken over another.

In sociology, anthropology, and history, collective identity and memory usually refer to the identity and recollections of a community, nation, or society. Similarly, Lebow (2008), a political scientist and historian, noted that individuals and groups may protect their memories of identity when they are content but will "defend their memories with a particular vengeance" (p. 29) when threatened. Other theorists have proposed that memory serves as the foundation for the identity of a group (Rime et al., 2015) by facilitating the formation and structures of the identity of the collective (Gabel, 2013). "Memory is a central medium through which identities are constructed" (Olick & Robbins, 1998, p. 133). This structured or unified identity functions to guide actions for the present and strategic decisions for future actions (Rime et al., 2015).

Gillis (1994) also supported the idea that memory functions to sustain identity, or a "sense of sameness over time and space" (p. 3), and at the same time identity sustains the recollection. As generations experienced different events and their interpretation of past critical events in society changed, it was speculated that their identification with different groups would shift as well.

Forgetting some of the past while recalling other parts is a memory process that shapes identity. In relationship to national identity, Haebich (2011) cited Connerton's (1989) types of forgetting and said they shared the common denominator of "shaping and maintaining a group's identity (past, present, future) by adapting history, selecting what is stored from the present, and choosing what direction to take to preserve the (new) identity" (p. 6). Groups may forget part of their history in the process of remembering or commemorating other more salient events. These processes of remembering and forgetting are intertwined and influenced by political forces that create new master narratives in the process. The processes can also work to further create group identity through constructing new memories and silence about parts of their past (Connerton, 1989). These processes have been studied extensively, particularly in relationship to outgroups whose pasts are targets for political repression.

Schwartz (2010), in studying collective memory in Asia, stressed the importance of studying collective memory in Eastern cultures as a way to empirically test Western ideas like collective memory in a different context. More importantly, he noted that this research would offer "new theorizing placing less emphasis on the interests that distort history and more on the cultural traits that define the meaning of real historical events" (Schwartz, 2010, p. 627).

Greenwood and Bernardi (2014), citing historian Alan Bullock (1994), also described the interdependent, complex relationship between identity and history, a type of collective memory, in that "a culture or society that turns its back on the past falls into a cultural and historical amnesia which weakens its sense of identity" (p. 921). Identity is interlinked with memory.

Following more of a social constructionist perspective in sociology, these recollections carry the identity of the community, "allowing old values and truths to metamorphose into shapes that are appropriate in a new context" (Bigelow, 2011, p. 392) and facilitate meaning making (Bigelow, 2011). In Bigelow's research, memory systems were a part of a dynamic equilibrium of shifting memories that allowed space and voice to all. In this way, everyone was able to find his or her way to a stake in the process of memory making and identity construction (p. 401).

The relationship between national identity as a form of collective identity and history and commemoration was also explored in Andersen's (2014) work on understanding the Métis's history. He asserted, "National identities like those produced in official commemorative work . . . produce and solidify claims to cultural unity and homogeneity" that shape how we understand our world (p. 622), yet these histories can reflect the "violence of historical abstraction" (p. 623) that leaves gaps in the history of groups. In this research, the physical space, i.e., the Batoche national historic site, displays "unnecessarily abstracted and disembodied portraits of Métis community and identity" (p. 630). Anderson advocated for a multivocal history and commemoration that gives voice to the community, local, regional, and global, and to "commemorative, scholarly, and community histories" (p. 630).

In Kelman's view, national identities have the potential for change through reconstruction as an ongoing process of a collective but, in general, are constrained by a group's history (p. 194) and are resistant to change. Identities can be reconstructed through the different elements that compose it, as some become more important and others less so given the changing nature of the group's environment. Although elements can be added or deleted, at "its core, national identity is clearly non-negotiable" (Kelman, 2001, p. 196) and is "transmitted to group members in the course of their socialization" (Kelman, 1997, p. 172). Accommodation of others in the boundaries of national identity may change elements of the original identity as long as the core aspects of the identity are protected. The core elements are immutable (Kelman, 2001, p. 196). Similarly, when defining national identity, Hall (1996) also asserted the importance of history and memory, in that identity is "historically, not biologically, defined" (p. 598). Assmann and Czaplicka (1995) referred to cultural knowledge as a type of memory and as the "concretion of identity" (p. 128); "a group bases its consciousness of unity and specificity upon this knowledge and derives formative and normative impulses from it, which allows the group to reproduce its identity. In this sense, objectivized culture has the structure of memory" (p. 128).

In conclusion, this review of some of the social science literature on collective memory and its relationship to identity reveals multiple ways in which memory functions to support identity:

1. Memory functions to create and at times acquire identity, and then to fuse and solidify identity, providing continuity over time. It more often constrains rather than changes identity, yet it can support the evolution of identity. It is at the core of identity and serves as an anchor in this process and can provide meaning to identity.
2. Memory can serve to differentiate one group's identity from that of another group through affirming and defining membership of the group. It structures identity.

3. Memory functions to guide further actions of the group. Power is a key variable that influences how memory functions to support identity.

How Identity Supports Memory

As discussed earlier in this text, identity is defined in part in relationship to memory. The relationship between collective memory and identity is present throughout the definitions and related discussions of identity, whether national, cultural, or group. National identity, for example, is defined as a product of history and is constructed in processes of commemoration and symbolism (Korostelina, 2013, p. 293). Foundational to this is the definition of a nation as "a group of people who—whether or not they live in the same land—share a common language, a *common history, a common tradition*, a common religion, a common way of life, a common sense of destiny, a common set *of memories* and aspirations" (Kelman, 1997, p. 169, *italics added*). Although not all aspects are required, as a set, they provide a foundation for unity of the group, and this "consciousness" is identity and is a collective phenomenon (Kelman, 2001, p. 171). Collective memory and identity are not an aggregation of individual member identities and memories and can exist independently in books, oral traditions, and other forms.

Identity at the collective level serves memory in that it influences why, what, and how events are recalled. Identity serves as a filter to determine what is critical to be remembered and why. This relationship is often used to establish the social constructive nature of memory, in that past events may be forgotten because they do not represent the identity of the collective or group (Keightley & Pickering, 2006).

Identity is a type of cultural schema that can serve to guide and frame memory. From a sociological perspective, Schwartz (1997, 2000) and Zerubavel (2003) proposed that the relationship between commemoration and collective identity is constituted through cultural schemas that guide why and how events are chosen for commemoration. Schwartz proposed in addition that these recollections consist of "facts (assertions of varying reliability and generalizability) whose interpretation is constrained by rules of evidence" (Schwartz, 2000). Identity as a type of schema impacts the selection of events by attributing meaning to them (Schwartz, 2000; Zerubavel, 2003). Schwartz (2000) proposed that "collective memory works by subsuming individual experiences under culture schemas that make them comprehensible and, therefore, meaningful" (p. xi).

For example, Schwartz and Kim's (2002) research on Korean and American students' memories of past world events supports the idea that memory processes of storage and retrieval are influenced by a national identity schema that functions as "priming schemata, that powerfully direct and configure memories of their nation's past" (p. 205); they stated that "collective memory and this interpretation is culturally as well as factually molded" (p. 222).

Overall, from a historical, sociological, and material culture perspective, while identity influences the meaning attributed to the past (De Jong, 2009; Krmpotich, 2010), memory is the core of identity and informs the construction of identity.

Conclusion

This dynamic, interdependent social process between collective memory and identity is constituted from interactions between individuals, groups, countries, and other collectives, as well as between past, present (De Jong, 2009), and future. There has been a move away from psychological and social psychological theories of memory and identity to theories that focus on collectives and history as a social process (Hewer & Roberts, 2012). This shift has been spurred by significant political changes in the world and fluctuating national boundaries that impact the histories of collectives and the importance of these histories to the collective identities of majority and minority groups. This multidisciplinary focus has offered the opportunity to free the study of memory from the more static focus of disciplines such as psychology (Haas & Levasseur, 2013).

Given that memory (Adamczyk, 2002) and identity are generally considered to be constructed socially, it is understandable that most scholars assume that the relationship between collective identity and memory is also a dynamic social process formed through the interaction of individuals and groups with their physical environments. The degree to which memory and identity are malleable—and the aspects that are malleable— remain subject to debate across the social sciences. In addition, given that the relationship is a social process and at times contested, the assumptions about the degree to which the process can be controlled or managed vary depending on the perspective taken by the researcher.

References

Adamczyk, A. (2002). On Thanksgiving and collective memory: Constructing the American tradition. *Journal of Historical Sociology*, *15*(3), 343–365. https://doi.org/10.1111/1467-6443.00182.

Albert, S., & Whetten, D. A. (1985). Organizational identity. In L. L. Cummings & B. M. Staw (Eds.), *Research in organizational behavior* (pp. 263–295). Greenwich, CT: JAI Press.

Andersen, C. (2014). More than the sum of our rebellions: Métis histories beyond Batoche. *Ethnohistory (Columbus, Ohio)*, *61*(4), 619–633. https://doi.org/10.1215/00141801-2717795.

Anteby, M., & Molnar, V. (2012). Collective memory meets organizational identity: Remembering to forget in a firm's rhetorical history. *Academy of Management Journal*, *55*(3), 515–540. https://doi.org/10.5465/amj.2010.0245.

Assmann, J., & Czaplicka, J. (1995). Collective memory and cultural identity. *New German Critique, 65*, 125–133. https://doi.org/10.2307/488538.

Avdikos, E. G. (2013). Memory and identity on the Greek-Bulgarian border. *Journal of Balkan & Near Eastern Studies, 15*(4), 396–411. https://doi.org/10.1080/19448953.2013.844586.

Barros, V. F., Ramos, I., & Perez, G. (2015). Information systems and organizational memory: A literature review. *Journal of Information Systems and Technology Management, 12*(1), 45–63. https://doi.org/10.4301/S1807-17752015000100003.

Bigelow, A. (2011). Memory and minority: Making Muslim Indians. *International Review for the History of Religions, 58*(2/3), 375–403.

Bruner, M. L. (2011). Rhetorical studies and national identity construction. *National Identities, 13*(4), 403–414. https://doi.org/10.1080/14608944.2011.629428.

Bullock, A. (1994). Has history ceased to be relevant? *The Historian, 43*(104), 16–19. ISSN: 0265–1076.

Casey, A. (1997). Collective memory in organizations. In P. Shrivastava, A. Huff, & J. Dutton (Series Eds.), J. Walsh & A. Huff (Vol. Eds.), *Organizational learning and strategic management* (Advances in Strategic Management, Vol. 14, pp. 111–151). Greenwich, CT: JAI Press.

Casey, A., & Byington, L. (2013). *Nike: A case study of identity claims in a complex global world*. Presented at the annual conference of the Academy of Management, Lake Buena Vista, FL. https://doi.org/10.5465/ambpp.2013.12456abstract.

Connerton, P. (1989). *How societies remember*. New York, NY: Cambridge University Press. https://doi.org/10.1017/CBO9780511628061.

De Jong, N. (2009). The (Cuban) voice of the (Curaçaoan) people: The making (and taking) of a collective memory. *Journal of Historical Sociology, 22*(3), 351–365. https://doi.org/10.1111/j.1467-6443.2009.01353.x.

Espinoza, A. E., Piper, I., & Fernandez, R. A. (2014). The study of memory sites through a dialogical accompaniment interactive group method: A research note. *Qualitative Research, 14*(6), 712–728. https://doi.org/10.1177/1468794113483301.

Feldman, R. M., & Feldman, S. P. (2006). What links the chain: An essay on organizational remembering as practice. *Organization, 13*(6), 861–887. https://doi.org/10.1177/1350508406068500.

Figlio, K. (2012). A psychoanalytic reflection on collective memory as a psychosocial enclave: Jews, German national identity, and splitting in the German psyche. In *UNESCO* (pp. 166–177). Oxford, UK: Blackwell Publishing Ltd.

Fine, G. A., & Beim, A. (2007). Introduction: Interactionist approaches to collective memory. *Symbolic Interaction, 30*(1), 1–5. https://doi.org/10.1525/si.2007.30.1.1.

Frijda, N. H. (1997). Commemorating. In J. W. Pennebaker, D. Paez, & B. Rime (Eds.), *Collective memory of political events. Social psychological perspectives* (pp. 103–127). Mahwah, NJ: Lawrence Erlbaum Associates.

Gabel, I. (2013). Historical memory and collective identity: West Bank settlers reconstruct the past. Engaging in illegal acts is accepted. *Media Culture & Society, 35*(2), 250–259. https://doi.org/10.1177/0163443712467592.

Gillis, J. R. (1994). Introduction. Memory and identity: The history of a relationship. In J. R. Gillis (Ed.), *Commemorations: The politics of national identity* (pp. 3–24). Princeton, NJ: Princeton University Press.

Gioia, D. A., Schultz, M., & Corley, K. G. (2000). Organizational identity, image, and adaptive instability. *Academy of Management Review*, 25(1), 63–81. https://doi.org/10.5465/amr.2000.2791603.

Greenwood, A., & Bernardi, A. (2014). Understanding the rift, the (still) uneasy bedfellows of history and organization studies. *Organization*, 21(6), 907–932. https://doi.org/10.1177/1350508413514286.

Haas, V., & Levasseur, E. (2013). Rumour as a symptom of collective forgetfulness. *Culture and Psychology*, 19(1), 60–75. https://doi.org/10.1177/1354067X12464986.

Haebich, A. (2011). Forgetting indigenous histories: Cases from the history of Australia's stolen generations. *Journal of Social History*, 44(4), 1033–1046. doi:10.1353/jsh.2011.0042.

Halbwachs, M. (1980). *The collective memory* (F. J. Ditter, Jr. & V. Y. Ditter, Trans.). New York, NY: Harper and Row. (Originally published in 1950)

Halbwachs, M. (1992). *On collective memory*. Chicago, IL: University of Chicago Press.

Hall, S. (1996). The question of cultural identity. In S. Hall, D. Held, D. Hubert, & K. Thompson (Eds.), *Modernity: An introduction to modern societies* (pp. 595–634). Cambridge, UK: Blackwell Publishers.

Hatch, M. J., & Schultz, M. (2017). Toward a theory of using history authentically: Historicizing in the Carlsberg Group. *Administrative Science Quarterly*, 62, 657–697. https://doi.org/10.1177/0001839217692535.

Hewer, C. J., & Roberts, R. (2012). History, culture and cognition: Towards a dynamic model of social memory. *Culture and Psychology*, 18(2), 167–183. https://doi.org/10.1177/1354067X11434836.

Huber, G. (1991). Organizational learning: The contributing processes and the literature. *Organization Science*, 2(1), 88–115. https://doi.org/10.1287/orsc.2.1.88.

Keightley, E., & Pickering, M. (2006). For the record: Popular music and photography as technologies of memory. *European Journal of Cultural Studies*, 9(2), 149–165.

Kelman, H. C. (1997). Nationalism, patriotism, and national identity: Social psychological dimensions. In D. Bar-Tal & E. Staub (Eds.), *Patriotism in the lives of individuals and nations* (pp. 165–189). Chicago, IL: Nelson-Hall.

Kelman, H. C. (2001). The role of national identity in conflict resolution. In R. D. Ashmore, L. Jussim, & D. Wilder (Eds.), *Social identity, intergroup conflict, and conflict reduction* (pp. 187–212). Oxford, UK: Oxford University Press.

Korostelina, K. (2013). Mapping national identities in Ukraine. *Journal of Nationalism and Ethnicity*, 41(2), 293–315. doi: 10.1080/00905992.2012.747498.

Kratochwil, F. (2006). On legitimacy. *International Relations*, 20, 302–308. https://doi.org/10.1177/0047117806066706.

Kreiner, G. E., Hollensbe, E., Sheep, M. L., Smith, B. R., & Kataria, N. (2015). Elasticity and the dialectic tensions of organizational identity: How can we hold together while we are pulling apart? *Academy of Management Journal*, 58(4), 981–1011. https://doi.org/10.5465/amj.2012.0462.

Krmpotich, C. (2010). Remembering and repatriation: The production of kinship, memory, and respect. *Journal of Material Culture*, 15(2), 157–179. https://doi.org/10.1177/1359183510364077.

Lebow, R. N. (2008). The future of memory. *Annals of the American Academy of Political and Social Science, 617*(1), 25–40. https://doi.org/10.1177/000 2716207310817.

Levy, D. (1999). The future of the past: Historiographical disputes and competing memories in Germany and Israel. *History and Theory, 38*(1), 51–66. 10.1111/0018-2656.761999076.

Loveday, V. (2014). Flat-capping it: Memory, nostalgia and value in retroactive male working class identification. *European Journal of Cultural Studies, 17*(6), 721–735. https://doi.org/10.1177/1367549414544117.

McDonald, M. (2010). "Lest we forget": The politics of memory and Australian military intervention. *International Political Sociology, 4*(3), 287–302. https://doi.org/10.1111/j.1749-5687.2010.00106.x.

Mead, G. H. (1934). *Mind, self and society*. Chicago, IL: University of Chicago Press.

Misztal, B. A. (2003). Durkheim on collective memory. *Journal of Classical Sociology, 3*, 123–143. https://doi.org/10.1177/1468795X030032002.

Murray, M. J. (2013). Collective memory in place: The Voortrekker monument and the Hector Pieterson memorial. In *Commemorating and forgetting: Challenges for the New South Africa*. Minneapolis, MN: University of Minnesota Press.

Nissley, N., & Casey, A. (2002). The politics of the exhibition: Viewing corporate museums through the paradigmatic lens of organizational memory. *British Journal of Management, 13*(S2), S35–S44. https://doi.org/10.1111/1467-8551.13.s2.4.

Nora, P. (1996). *Realms of memory*. New York, NY: Columbia University Press.

Olick, J. K. (2007). Collective memory and nonpublic opinion: A historical note on a methodological controversy about a political problem. *Symbolic Interaction, 30*(1), 41–55.

Olick, J. K., & Levy, D. (1997). Collective memory and cultural constraint: Holocaust myth and rationality in German politics. *American Sociological Review, 62*, 921–936.

Olick, J. K., & Robbins, J. (1998). Social memory studies: From "collective memory" to the historical sociology of mnemonic practices. *Annual Review of Sociology, 24*(1), 105–140. https://doi.org/10.1146/annurev.soc.24.1.105.

Olick, J. K., Vinitzky-Seroussi, V., & Levy, D. (Eds.). (2011). *The collective memory reader*. New York, NY: Oxford University Press.

Pennebaker, J. W., & Banasik, B. L. (1997). On the creation and maintenance of collective memories: History as social psychology. In J. W. Pennebaker, D. Paez, & B. Rimé (Eds.), *Collective memory of political events: Social psychological perspectives* (pp. 3–19). Hillsdale, NJ: Lawrence Erlbaum Associates.

Radstone, S. (2000). Introduction. In S. Radstone (Ed.), *Memory and methodology* (pp. 1–22). Oxford and New York, NY: Berg.

Ravasi, D., & Schultz, M. (2006). Responding to organizational identity threats: Exploring the role of organizational culture. *Academy of Management Journal, 49*(3), 433–458. https://doi.org/10.5465/amj.2006.21794663.

Rime, B., Bouchat, P., Klein, O., & Licata, L. (2015). When collective memories of victimhood fade: Generational evolution of intergroup attitudes and political aspirations in Belgium. *European Journal of Social Psychology, 45*(4), 515–532. https://doi.org/10.1002/ejsp.2104.

Rindova, V., Dalpiaz, E., & Ravasi, D. (2011). A cultural quest: A study of organizational use of new cultural resources in strategy formation. *Organization Science*, *222*, 413–431. doi: 10.1287/orsc.1100.0537.

Rowlinson, M., Hassard, J., & Decker, S. (2014). Research strategies for organizational history: A dialogue between historical theory and organization theory. *Academy of Management Review*, *39*(3), 250–274. https://doi.org/10.5465/amr.2012.0203.

Schultz, M., & Hernes, T. (2013). A temporal perspective on organizational identity. *Organization Science*, *24*(1), 1–21. https://doi.org/10.1287/orsc.1110.0731.

Schwartz, B. (1991a). Iconography and collective memory: Lincoln's image in the American mind. *The Sociological Quarterly*, *32*(3), 301–319. https://doi.org/10.1111/j.1533-8525.1991.tb00161.x.

Schwartz, B. (1991b). Social change and collective memory: The democratization of George Washington. *American Sociological Review*, *56*(2), 221–236. https://doi.org/10.2307/2095781.

Schwartz, B. (1997). Collective memory and history. *The Sociological Quarterly*, *38*(3), 469–496. https://doi.org/10.1111/j.1533-8525.1997.tb00488.x.

Schwartz, B. (2000). *Abraham Lincoln and the forge of national memory*. Chicago, IL: University of Chicago Press.

Schwartz, B. (2005). The new Gettysburg Address: Fusing history and memory. *Poetics*, *33*(1), 63–79. https://doi.org/10.1016/j.poetic.2005.01.003.

Schwartz, B. (2010). Culture and collective memory. In J. R. Hall, L. Grindstaff, & M.-C. Lo (Eds.), *Handbook of cultural sociology* (pp. 619–629). Abingdon, UK: Routledge.

Schwartz, B., & Kim, M. (2002). Honor, dignity and collective memory. In K. Cerulo (Ed.), *Culture in mind* (pp. 209–226). London, UK: Routledge.

Suddaby, R., Foster, W. M., & Quinn Trank, C. (2010). Rhetorical history as a source of competitive advantage. *Advances in Strategic Management*, *27*, 147–173. https://doi.org/10.1108/S0742-3322(2010)0000027009.

Suddaby, R., & Greenwood, R. (2005). Rhetorical strategies of legitimacy. *Administrative Science Quarterly*, *50*(1), 35–67. https://doi.org/10.2189/asqu.2005.50.1.35.

Topp, S. (2009). Collective memory: Representation of national socialist "euthanasia." *Korot*, *19*, 11–27.

Wagner-Pacifici, R., & Schwartz, B. (1991). The Vietnam Veterans Memorial: Commemorating a difficult past. *American Journal of Sociology*, *97*, 376–420.

Walsh, J. P., & Ungson, G. R. (1991). Organizational memory. *Academy of Management Review*, *16*(1), 57–91. https://doi.org/10.5465/amr.1991.4278992.

Weber, K., Heinze, K. L., DeSoucey, D. L. (2008). Forage for thought: Mobilizing codes in the movement for grass-fed meat and dairy products. *Administrative Science Quarterly*, *53*(3), 529–567.

Weick, K. (1995). *Sensemaking in organizations*. Thousand Oaks, CA: Sage.

Wertsch, J. V. (2002). *Voices of collective remembering*. Cambridge, UK: Cambridge University Press. https://doi.org/10.1017/CBO9780511613715.

Wertsch, J. V. (2008). Collective memory and narrative templates. *Social Research*, *75*(1), 133–155.

Whetten, D. A. (2006). Albert and Whetten revisited: Strengthening the concept of organizational identity. *Journal of Management Inquiry*, *15*(3), 219–234. https://doi.org/10.1177/1056492606291200.

Whetten, D. A., & Mackey, A. (2002). A social actor conception of organizational identity and its implications for the study of organizational reputation. *Business & Society*, *41*(4), 393–414. https://doi.org/10.1177/0007650302238775.

Wry, T., Lounsbury, M., & Glynn, M. A. (2011). Legitimating nascent collective identities: Coordinating cultural entrepreneurship. *Organization Science*, *22*, 449–463.

Zerubavel, E. (2003). *Time maps: Collective memory and the social shape of the past*. London, UK: University of Chicago Press. https://doi.org/10.7208/chicago/9780226924908.001.0001.

Zundel, M., Holt, R., & Popp, A. (2016). Using history in the creation of organizational identity. *Management & Organizational History*, *11*(2), 211–235. https://doi.org/10.1080/17449359.2015.1124042.

4 Factors That Influence the Relationship Between Collective Identity and Memory

The relationship between collective memory and identity and the factors that influence this relationship have been theorized and researched across the social sciences. The relationship between collective memory and identity as an iterative social process is discussed as a process of identity construction at times and memory construction at other times. In either case, it is explored and described as a dynamic, iterative process and is influenced by power, space, and traditions.

The factors that emerge that influence this relationship and how these factors are conceptualized are largely dependent on the theoretical lens and related assumptions about the constructs of identity and memory and how they are defined. For example, in organizational studies, this relationship has been articulated in work that either takes a social actor perspective of organizational identity or a social constructionist or process perspective. The social actor perspective of identity considers history to be a stabilizing influence on organizational identity while still supporting the temporally continuous features of organizational identity (Albert & Whetten, 1985; Whetten, 2006) through commemoration (Casey & Byington, 2013) and the tension that resides between these components of collective memory (Casey, 2010; Schwartz, 2005). Theorists who define organizational identity from a social constructionist perspective or in terms of a process primarily take a revisionist history perspective (Gioia, Schultz, & Corley, 2000) to explore the relationship and its impact on other organizational phenomena such as strategy, change, or culture. More recently, the idea of a dynamic stability of identity based on authentic interpretation of organizational history or recollections is surfacing in the organizational studies literature (Hatch & Schultz, 2017). Assumptions about temporality (Schultz & Hernes, 2013) are also critical to theorizing about this relationship and the concepts, since both collective memory and identity are defined temporally, including the past, present, and future. This chapter discusses these factors that influence the relationship between memory and identity.

Critical Events

Research on collective memory, particularly in sociology and anthropology and, to a lesser degree, organizational studies (Anteby & Molnar, 2012; Casey, 1997; Hatch & Schultz, 2017; Ravasi & Schultz, 2006; Whetten, 2006), has noted the importance of critical events in a collective's history and how or why these events are recalled during the life of the collective. These events are often considered critical because they most frequently represent a threat to the identity of the collective, and this connection or relationship between the events and identity threat influences the meaning or interpretation of the events as well as how, when, and why they are recalled. They are most often true forks-in-the-road (Whetten, 2006), where the two paths are fundamentally different and represent a different future for the organization or collective. Occasionally the critical events are positive or are interpreted to positively shape the strategic future of an organization (Casey & Byington, 2013) and, therefore, are significant.

The process of remembering together or commemoration of these events in a collective is important, particularly in times of crisis (De Jong, 2009). In sociological research (De Jong, 2009; McDonald, 2010), collective identity is a source of meaning making in this process and provides a foundation for a narrative to be reconstructed or sustained to support and maintain the identity (McDonald, 2010), and at other times to revise the identity. As McDonald (2010) noted, "Traumatic experiences can be seen as shaking existing discourses of community and security, providing opportunities for strategic intervention to give (new) meaning to that experience or to fold it into existing narratives" (p. 289). Commemoration and remembrance are crucial to this process and often are further shaped by political forces (p. 289).

One type of crisis or critical event is when important members of a generation or a community die (McDonald, 2010) or, in the case of organizations, retire (Casey, 1997; Casey & Byington, 2013). These individuals are often among the few to have lived through or directly experienced the organization's history and threats to the organization. When the founders and the original group of "true believers" begin to retire from an organization, it is often a time of turmoil and is perceived as a threat to the future of the organization. Research has shown that often a narrator (Linde, 2000) of some of the important stories of an organization's past becomes the carrier of the memory of the events and what the events mean in terms of the identity of the collective moving forward, even if the individual did not experience the event directly.

Emotions, both negative and positive, are factors in why these critical events are recalled. Negative events are recalled because they represent threats to the identity of the collective or the survival of the collective.

A negative emotion about the past "embodies a contradiction between the desire to forget and the need to remember" (Murray, Zedeno, Hollenback, Grinnell, & Breast, 2011, p. 470). Murray et al.'s ethnography of the Mandan, Hidatsa, and Arikara people described how they negotiated the identity of a lake and its meaning to them and their history in relationship to drastic changes in the present. Commemorating, or coremembering or remembering together, as a component of collective memory involves rituals that facilitate "order and continuity" and are connected with emotionally significant events that affirm and sustain "the identity of one's group and redefining membership with that group" (Frijda, 1997, p. 109).

In organizational studies, positive emotions have also emerged as a factor in the relationship between identity and memory. Organizational identity claims are by default statements about the positive characteristics of an organization, and in some research (Casey, 1997; Casey & Byington, 2013) those events viewed as the most critical or significant in an organization's history are connected to one salient identity claim or a set of claims. In Casey and Byington's (2013) case study of Nike, these events also positively changed the trajectory of the organization, such as the first signing of a famous athlete to Nike marketing campaigns. These events are both recalled in organizational histories such as timelines on company websites and commemorated in stories told in routine meetings or orientation programs for new employees.

Individuals and Social Interaction

The individual member of a collective also emerges as an important factor in the relationship between memory and identity. From a sociological perspective, Schwartz (2010) noted that "collective memory cannot be reduced to the individual orientations that constitute it, but it is realized in these orientations." These "individual orientations" can then in turn shape how memory or identity is considered and further interpreted. Collective remembering is constituted by the "variant individual expressions of culturally induced beliefs, feelings and moral judgements about the past" (Schwartz, 2010, p. 620). Several elements affect how individuals might impact this process, including the individual's power, personal history, role, and current experiences, as well as the sensory and emotional aspects of these experiences.

Power surfaces as the primary factor in these discussions related to the influence of individuals on collective identity. Individuals who hold dominant roles in a group frequently contribute to shaping the narrative of the past. An example is in recollections of historical figures such as Lincoln (Schwartz, 2000, 2010), when interactions with others who are also interpreting these narratives are influenced by their own personal histories and current events as well as those of the group. The relationship between collective memory and identity is a meaning-making process in social groups and is at the same time influenced by the transmission processes within those groups or cohorts of individuals (Edwards & Middleton, 1986; Haas & Levasseur, 2013). Collective memory and identity viewed as a dynamic social process (Espinoza, Piper, & Fernandez, 2014) articulates the relationship between these ideas as influenced in part by the tensions between the interpretations of the different groups and individuals within the collective and at times through dominance and power (De Jong, 2009). The social transmission shapes the content of memory, as it is "molded" by the group based on their current experiences (Rime, Bouchat, Klein, & Licata, 2015, p. 516) as well as the identity of the collective.

These factors of emotions, personal histories, and current experiences of individual actors appeared in Moulton's (2015) anthropological study of postdisaster identity work following the devastating tornado in Missouri in 2011. Building upon the sociological foundation of Halbwachs (1992) as well as social memory (Nora, 1996), Moulton found that individuals' memory of the event was influenced by sensory and emotional aspects as they constructed narratives of what they experienced. For example, in recollections of a tornado, they recalled the "tornado smell." Moulton also noted the role of social interaction in the collective memory process as the personal history of the survivors' stories of the event and the community's history interacted to create narratives in which recurring themes about the event emerged. These narratives became part of memorials and monuments. This "memory, which is recalled, performed, and even inscribed in the landscape through monuments and memorials, becomes an integral part of the local identity, capable of influencing the recovery process" (Moulton, 2015, p. 319). This collective identity helped to unite people, and the "shared experience becomes the cornerstone of a new identity" that is recreated and "mediated through commemoration and narration of events" (Moulton, 2015, p. 323).

The interpretations and relative meanings that surface in the process of collective memory and identity often become narratives that are recalled in historical accounts on memorials or in books. This process is influenced by the identity of the collective and also the work of tensions and diverse viewpoints of individuals that surface "and configure fields of meanings in these given social contexts" (Espinoza et al., 2014, p. 717). The telling and retelling of the event shapes what is remembered, and the themes that emerge became part of the history of the event, which further shapes the identity of the collective. Diverse perspectives and meanings of memories and events become intertwined in these recollections.

Generational Cohorts

Acknowledging the important role of social interaction in the relationships between collective memory and identity in social sciences research, a substantial stream of research has studied cohorts of individuals, particularly generational cohorts. This work stems in part from early sociological work on collective memory that studied generational cohorts and their memories of critical events. This work has continued in other disciplines such as anthropology (High, 2009) and organizational studies (Lippmann & Aldrich, 2016). Overall, several themes emerged from this research, including that collective memory can strengthen the social identity of a group (Ma & Kim, 2015) by supporting similar interpretations (Ester, Vinken, & Diepstraten, 2002; Rime et al., 2015) of the past events; that a generational group's memory can be used to further differentiate one generation from another; that different types of social identity impact collective memory as well as wider sets or networks of identity; and that autobiographical memory has interrelationships with social or collective memory (Cole, 2001; High, 2009). Two factors that appear to interact with the influence of generations are power and age or life stage.

The research on generations in the context of identity and memory is set in the debates about what constitutes a generation, particularly in sociology, and how cohorts within them are defined. Olick (1999) noted that some define a generation "not as an objective time period but as subjectively defined cohorts; a generation exists if and only if a number of birth cohorts share a historical event that creates a community of perception" (Olick, 1999, p. 339). This view is supported by political science theory that differentiates between political generations and cohorts, with the latter being a group of individuals who are close in age and "who share a particular set of social and historical experiences" (Braungart & Braungart, 1986, p. 215, as cited in Ma & Kim, 2015) and that a collective identity of this cohort can emerge from the experiences and recollections of a historical traumatic event (Eyerman & Turner, 1998). In sociology, Ma and Kim (2015) studied generational cohort differences and collective memory, grounding their work in Mannheim's sociological studies of generations. They found that a regional identity, in addition to a political or cohort identity, intersected with memory of past events. In interpreting their findings, they noted that "some of the important functions of collective memory are to strengthen the cohesion of social groups and to consolidate their identities" (Ma & Kim, 2015, p. 82).

In organizational studies, Lippmann and Aldrich (2016) proposed "generational units," drawing from Mannheim's concept of a generational unit, and defined them as people who shape collective memories; these are "meaningful collectives that move through time with high degrees of self awareness" (pp. 658–659) and who share a common identity that is often shaped by historical events and a shared social space. Yet these researchers share the concern when sweeping homogeneity is assumed across large generational units without attending to geographical and other demographics.

A generational cohort's influence on what past events are recalled and how they are interpreted is also supported by the work of Rime et al. (2015) and Ester et al. (2002). Rime et al. (2015), drawing from the sociological literature on collective memory (Halbwachs, 1950/1980; Mannheim, 1928/1952) as well as from social psychology, studied how intergenerational memories might shift and also investigated the potential influence of the regional context on these memories. They drew primarily from Mannheim's (1928/1952) definition of generation, which is based on a group of individuals who are similar in age and experience a significant social or historical event. They also compared those who were in their formative years, i.e., 17 to 25, when the event happened with others. In their study, they compared three generations of Dutch-speaking and French-speaking Belgian citizens on a number of variables that assessed collective memories and attitudes toward intergroup conflict. They based their hypotheses on the changing conditions of economic, political, and social conditions of these groups over time. They thought the collective memories of perceived victimhood would not be as relevant to the newer generations, particularly the younger Belgian population. They found that which events from a country's history were recollected was not dissimilar across the generations and national culture origins, but the interpretations, and particularly the attributions related to these memories, varied by generation and, at time, geographical region. The authors speculated that collective memories—i.e., how and which events were recalled and interpreted—might change if the social groups with which individuals identified changed.

As different generations may interpret the same events in diverse ways, the interaction between generations as they recollect the past also impacts the relationship between memory and identity. Drawing upon the seminal works of anthropologist Paul Connerton and the sociological theories of Halbwachs and Durkheim, High's (2009) study of generational memory of violence and struggles in Ecuador found that narratives of the past are part of a wider interconnected set of embedded identities and that generations use these narratives to differentiate themselves from other generations. High's study suggested that "memory is not simply the transmission of historical knowledge from one generation to the next" (p. 732) but also represents different sets of people and their identities, including gender. There may be differences in interpretation of the different forms of historical representations of the past within a generation based on gender or role. High's research highlights the "dynamic multiplicity" (p. 733) of social memory as it intersects with social identities of individuals such as race and gender.

Espinoza et al. (2014) also studied generational interactions and differences in memory sites related to violent events that occurred during the military dictatorship in Chile. In this research, they focused on the different memories these generations constructed as they interacted with a memory site. Through the interactions of individuals with the sites and each other, the memories became "anchored, situated" and had "roots in those places" (Espinoza et al., 2014, p. 716); these social memories became embodied not just in the physical space but in the human body itself. Memories are both intersubjective and embodied. This dynamic collective memory process is influenced by the "social and political contexts in which it is produced, to the places involved and to the collective identities of the actors" (Espinoza et al., 2014, p. 714), particularly their "generational belonging" (p. 714).

Linde's (2000) anthropological research on memory and identity in a corporation described the process of narrative induction across generations of employees in a corporation. She articulated how this process informs how collective memory emerges and evolves over time through the interaction of individuals and how this memory further supports and sustain the organization's identity. Based on her ethnographic study, Linde identified three phases in the narrative induction process: how a person adopts another's story as central to her own; how this shapes the individual's story; and how a person's story begins to be told and shared by others in an organization (Linde, 2000, p. 608). She asserted that non-participant narratives or stories told by individuals who were not part of an event are a tool used to sustain collective memory and socialize new organizational members, inducting them into the narrative (Linde, 2000, p. 608). This is a process of social construction, and identity construction is dependent upon stories and memory of past events, particularly those that recall the founding of the organization and its early days and how the business grew, as told by the founder and the early members. Key organizational members suggested that "the company's past could be used to understand the present and to predict the future: the company could be relied on to change in a way that would preserve its essential identity and its concern for the welfare of its agents" (p. 617).

Physical Space and Its Influence on Collective Memory and Identity

Physical space is also a critical factor in the relationship between collective memory and identity. Halbwachs's (1950/1980) work described the role of physical space as part of the social frameworks of memory. This space contains and often displays the physical evidence of history and memory and can become a location for a group or collective to remember together either people or critical events and how they represent "who they are" as a group (Espinoza et al., 2014). As Hass and Levasseur (2013) emphasized, space "bears within itself the traces of its history" (p. 70) as a "permanent reference, a source of stability and a symbol of the group" to allow individuals "to remain in a common universe with which they identify" (p. 70).

Most scholars portray the complex relationship between memory and identity and physical space as influenced by factors such as the individuals within the groups (White, 2006); time, i.e., the present and the future (Murray et al., 2011); emotions; power, often represented in political struggles and change (White, 2006); the meaning and emotions attached to these interactions (White, 2006); or an interaction of a combination of these factors. These meanings attached to elements of the physical space may be multivalent and multivocal if there are diverse identities with a group (Paabo, 2014; White, 2006). The physical space facilitates meaning making (Paabo, 2014) and interpretation of "who they are" as a collective. These sites and the people and events in history that are commemorated at these sites are used for meaning making to create and re-create and at times reinterpret the identity of the collective (Paabo, 2014).

These spaces can be geographic, i.e., regions or territories and urban landscapes (Hall, 2006), in addition to the more traditional monuments or statues that occupy a physical site in a community (Hall, 2006; Paabo, 2014), and may include artifacts from critical events in the collective's past. These spaces become sites of memory and identity through commemoration and history. Stories of historic events or key individuals in a collective's past may be memorialized in figures and plaques. All facets of these physical spaces, including the selection of the individuals and events to be memorialized, are part of the process of collective memory and identity and involve many of the factors discussed thus far in this chapter. Individuals in groups or other types of collectives are representatives of these collectives and "use the environment in order to conduct their remembering and commemoration activities" (Schleifman, 2001, p. 6, as cited in Paabo, 2014).

Collective identity shapes and is shaped by these physical sites and locations, and this process is often inseparable from the politics and economics of the area. Some of this research theorizes that these spaces and landscapes are the production of power dynamics by privileging some over others and "rediscovering the past in different ways" (Hall, 2006, p. 190).

Multiple meanings may also be attached to these monuments and spaces in part due to the identity of the collectives involved and the power dynamics between these collectives. In societies, this "contested nature of public memorialization," particularly in geographical areas that are rapidly changing, such as Europe, can be analyzed from the perspective of political identity and public memory. As political changes emerge, statues and other physical representations of people and critical events "have the potential to act as a nexus of identity formation" (Foxall, 2013, p. 177). Powerful individuals in societies can develop and structure public spaces and memorials to create new political visions and meaning. This is represented in Light and Young's (2010) research on the relationship between political identity, public memory, and urban space in Bucharest from 1906 to 2009.

Time is also a factor that is intertwined with the relationship between physical space, identity, and memory, particularly in the research related to national identity (Smith, 1999) and memory. In master narratives of countries, time and space mark the nation's boundaries and historical space. It is not only a physical landscape developed and constructed by a certain sociocultural group (Kapralski, 2001) but also a space for commemoration where critical historical events are remembered. Historical space can be framed by the national borders of the contemporary nation, but usually it has a broader meaning and use. Both space and time determine the history and landmarks and artifacts that define a nation.

Artifacts from the past, as part of this physical space, are also used to construct the identity of a collective (Lowenthal, 1985; Nora, 1989). This process is influenced by the intersection of the events from the past, the current setting, and the future, and these intersections are frequently impacted by power. Two studies from anthropology illuminate this relationship. For example, Murray et al. (2011) studied the heritage connected to Lake Sakakawea and how "physical space is embedded in processes of remembering and forgetting and how the spatial and temporal dimensions of memory can be renetworked to accommodate uninvited and inevitable change" (p. 480). These processes in turn influenced many different groups of people connected to this lake over time. Murray et al. (2011) noted that conceptualizing the past, in this case heritage, underscores the relationship between contemporary needs, perceptions, and identity and how these may shape how the "past is defined and managed" (p. 469). Fewster (2007) agreed with this recursive relationship between artifacts as representative of material culture, identity, and memory. She cited Appadurai (1986, p. 3) in saying that "commodities, like persons, have social lives," and they create each other. In Fewster's research, physical spaces with their own agency played a critical role in shaping the relationship between identity and memory, but the human agent played the "central role in enacting the dialectic between structure and agency, albeit through the medium of material culture" (p. 107).

Physical space such as a lake (Murray et al., 2011) and artifacts such as monuments (Marschall, 2012) and memorial sites, as well as routines or rituals (Shore, 2008) and other facets of a material culture (Fewster, 2007), have been proposed as types of memory that are critical in the processes of remembering and forgetting (Murray et al., 2011). These relationships are most often linked to power differentials, as objects like physical memorial sites can be more controlled and are often influenced by powerful stakeholders. Marschall (2012), in commenting on physical memory markers that are often created and managed by a country's government, questioned whether these monuments can create space for debates about the past or if they are mainly trying to accomplish outcomes desired by the ruling parties (p. 201). Foxall's (2013) research shed additional light on this question in researching the role of geography and monuments in the creation of collective memory. He emphasized the role of the individual in creating memory as a country's residents tell stories about statues. His research also surfaced the role of emotions, collective and individual, related to the events and their role in shaping what was recalled about the monuments or statues. The relationship between history and commemoration is reflected in sites of memory such as memorial spaces and how these memorials are used for recollection through interaction between narratives of different collectives and related identities (Zederman, 2014), as well as official accounts of the past (Welch & Wittlinger, 2011).

Power

Although power has surfaced in the relationship between identity and memory, as described above, particularly as part of commemoration of physical space, power also emerges as a factor in other processes related to identity and memory. Overall, the relationship between collective memory and identity has been described as a dynamic interdependent social process influenced by power (Cipolla, 2008; Gillis, 1994). Memory is the core of identity and informs the construction of identity, while identity influences the meaning attributed to the past (De Jong, 2009; Krmpotich, 2010). In this work, power and political influences shape what is recalled, as well as when, how, and why the memories are recalled.

In anthropology and sociology, power is most often framed with particular focus on the power differentials between individuals and groups across social, political (Ciubrinskas, 2009; McDonald, 2010), and other institutions. In the national identity and memory literature, power and its impact on the relationship is often described in terms of oppression that results in destruction and violence in efforts to destroy the collective memory and identity of one group through the construction of another's. It is a process of "positioning more 'effectively' one's own narrative" or identity while the memory and identity of others are "marginalized, excluded or destroyed" (Gur-Ze'ev & Pappé, 2003, p. 93). The groups who are marginalized are often those in the minority in a population, particularly in a society, nation, or culture. Power that emerges as oppression in the collective memory-identity process often results in violence, most notably during significant cultural changes, wars, or shifts in governments, and at times is related to a traumatic past.

This violence can be both direct and symbolic "as collective memories are produced, reproduced, disseminated and consumed within concrete historical power relations" (Gur-Ze'ev & Pappé, 2003, p. 93). Collective memories can be positioned to narrate a group's interests, goals, and identity, while marginalizing or destroying those of others. Those memories and identities of minority groups can be marginalized by "one monolithic, hegemonic legend," with exclusions to this legend frequently based on gender and race (McDonald, 2010, p. 291). McDonald (2010) spoke to the role of "memory politics," particularly in regard to traumatic experiences, and "how power and use of both practices of remembrance and broader discourses of the past" (especially a traumatic past) play an important role.

The power differentials that surfaced in the relationship between identity and memory often emerge during substantial cultural change, and the influence can be subtle and involve many different groups or hierarchies. For example, in empirical research in anthropology, power differentials surfaced in McEwan's (2003) study of social memory and identity in postapartheid South Africa. The power differential and its influence on what was being remembered about the past and how it was told emerged between social scientists who were constructing the history of a group and the local rural voices that composed the group. McEwan examined the process of establishing the collective memory and historical truth of black women who have been "marginalized by colonialism and apartheid and excluded from dominant accounts of history" (p. 740). Using a theoretical lens of postcolonialism, McEwan found that social scientists and scholars had power in this process because they were reconstructing the memory of the past without the input of local rural voices, particularly those of black women. The histories constructed by social scientists studying these groups influenced what was remembered and why; in the process, familiar home landscapes lost their meaning and connections with the present.

Although discussions of the role of power and political influence on the relationship between memory and identity frequently highlight the oppression of minorities and other groups, some research highlights the power of these alternative memories in changing the "official" memory of a society created through dominant voices. For example, from a historical perspective, Bigelow's (2011) work on the Muslim integration into the new India showed the impact of the minority group on collective memory and noted the importance of the social location of the rememberers as well as the individuals' recollections for the collective identity of groups (p. 376). This study highlights the importance of the minority groups' memories that surfaced in the collective memory process. These memories were characterized as "subversive and discarded cultural memories," yet they were part of the collective memory work and demonstrated the "simultaneity of multiple collectivities and the power imbalances" (Bigelow, 2011, p. 379). This research also emphasizes the resilience of minority groups and their interpretations of the past in preserving aspects of their identities as well as contributing to the memory and identity of the collective.

These multiple memory systems are not merely suppressed elements of cultural memory but are active parts of a dynamic equilibrium of

shifting memories that allow space and voice to all. In this way everyone finds his or her way to a stake in the process of memory making
and identity construction.

(Bigelow, 2011, p. 376)

Bigelow's research points out the interplay of simultaneous memory systems and how different memories framed by identities can coexist even
within a stable collective memory system (p. 376).

Time

An ongoing theme in theorizing about the relationship between collective
memory and identity in the social sciences is time and the intersection of
the past, present, and future (De Jong, 2009). In his seminal work, Halbwachs described collective memory as a social process that intersects
with identity, time, and space (Espinoza et al., 2014). Collective memory by definition is the memory about critical events from the past, and
this memory process enhances the construction of traditions and collectives' identity (Espinoza et al., 2014; Halbwachs, 1950/1980) both
in the present and the future. At other times, theorists have suggested
that the present influences how we reconstruct the past, as we may bring
the past forward to meet the needs of the present (Rime et al., 2015).
These needs are in part determined by the political context in which the
groups live and, to the focus of this book, the identity of the collective.
The literature on the relationship between identity and memory suggests that as these needs of the present change, the memories of the past
may not be sustained, particularly if the political context changes (Rime
et al., 2015). As noted earlier in this text, the relationship between present needs and memories of the past is one of the significant debates in
the literature on collective memory.

Although the importance of the past and the present in the relationship between identity and memory has been highlighted, there is little
understanding of their dynamic relationship. Most research has focused
on how the past affects present recollections (Rime et al., 2015), and
less attention has been given to how current factors influence the reconstruction of the past (Rime et al., 2015) and the importance for pro-
jections about the future. Anthropologists (Aydarova, 2015) who have
studied the interaction of the past, present, and future in forming collective memory have frequently drawn from the theoretical work of
Bakhtin (1986) on historical becoming. Bakhtin suggested that human
development is social and that the space for emergence is on the border or interaction between two epochs at the intersection of the past,
present, and future. His work is helpful to theorize about the effects of
the past on the interpretations of the present and the future (Aydarova,
2015, p. 149).

Murray (2013) and others noted that the collective memory process is not important because of what it tells us about specific historical events but because of what it highlights in terms of the identity of the collective and its identification with a social group. The commemoration process connects us with the past, but the "symbolic power of commemoration" offers insights into what we consider important in the present in relationship to who we are as a collective. The knowledge of our identity that we bring to this process "makes them [these memories] historically significant, transforming a chance occurrence that happened in the past into a transcendental moment—an iconic signifier—for an entire historical period" (Murray, 2013, pp. 103–104).

Similarly, Paabo (2014) offered that to create and sustain national identities, collectives such as nations must construct a narrative that assumes and assures continuity across time. Narratives, particularly of events from the past, construct a "comprehensive understanding of a nation by defining its origins, main identity markers, and the image of the national Self" (Paabo, 2014, p. 187). Memory and identity are also linked to anticipations of and expectations for the future, and in this constellation present and future are linked (Feindt, Krawatzek, Mehler, Pestel, & Trimcev, 2014, p. 29). Memory and identity may be revised to meet the needs of the present, yet a collective's identity may reflect a sense of continuity over time and space (Gillis, 1994, p. 3).

Summary

Although this section has presented separate discussions of each factor that impacts the relationship of identity and memory, the factors are interconnected and interact with each other; they do not exist in isolation. Whether it's an organization or a nation, collective identity and memory are intertwined and are influenced by time (past, present, and future), power dynamics, the individual, agency and interactions between groups, and the location or physical space in which the collective is located. The artifacts are called upon by the group to symbolize aspects of who they were, who they are, and who they seek to be in the future. The material artifacts themselves have a role in these processes. Key members of the collective, whether a founder of an organization, a hierarchical leader in power in a nation or an organization, or an influential member of the group, influence the relationship between identity and memory. These are processes that occur over time, and the primary debate remains the degree to which identity and memory evolve over time, representing stability as well as change.

References

Albert, S., & Whetten, D. A. (1985). Organizational identity. In L. L. Cummings & B. M. Staw (Eds.), *Research in organizational behavior* (pp. 263–295). Greenwich, CT: JAI Press.

Anteby, M., & Molnar, V. (2012). Collective memory meets organizational identity: Remembering to forget in a firm's rhetorical history. *Academy of Management Journal, 55*(3), 515–540. https://doi.org/10.5465/amj.2010. 0245.

Appadurai, A. (1986). Theory in anthropology: Center and periphery. *Comparative Studies in Society and History, 28*(1), 356–361.

Aydarova, O. (2015). Glories of the Soviet past or dim visions of the future: Russian teacher education as the site of historical becoming. *Anthropology and Education Quarterly, 46*(2), 147–166. doi: 10.1111/aeq.12096.

Bakhtin, M. (1986). *Speech genres and other late essays*. Austin, TX: University of Texas Press.

Bigelow, A. (2011). Memory and minority: Making Muslim Indians. *International Review for the History of Religions, 58*(2/3), 375–403.

Casey, A. (1997). Collective memory in organizations. In P. Shrivastava, A. Huff, & J. Dutton (Series Eds.), J. Walsh & A. Huff (Vol. Eds.), *Organizational learning and strategic management* (Advances in Strategic Management, Vol. 14, pp. 111–151). Greenwich, CT: JAI Press.

Casey, A. (2010). *The role of collective memory in organizational identity*. Presented at the annual conference of the Academy of Management, Montreal, Quebec, Canada.

Casey, A., & Byington, L. (2013). *Nike: A case study of identity claims in a complex global world*. Presented at the annual conference of the Academy of Management, Lake Buena Vista, FL. https://doi.org/10.5465/ambpp.2013. 12456abstract.

Cipolla, C. (2008). Signs of identity, signs of memory. *Archaeological Dialogues, 15*(2), 196–215. https://doi.org/10.1017/S1380203808002675.

Ciubrinskas, V. (2009). Reclaiming European heritages of transatlantic migration: The politics of identity of East European immigrants to the USA. *Anthropological Journal on European Cultures, 18*(2), 50–68.

Cole, J. (2001). *Forget colonialism? Sacrifice and the art of memory in Madagascar*. Berkeley, CA: University of California Press.

De Jong, N. (2009). The (Cuban) voice of the (Curaçaoan) people: The making (and taking) of a collective memory. *Journal of Historical Sociology, 22*(3), 351–365. https://doi.org/10.1111/j.1467-6443.2009.01353.x.

Edwards, D., & Middleton, D. (1986). Joint remembering: Constructing an account of shared experience through conversational discourse. *Discourse Processes, 9*, 423–459. http://dx.doi.org/10.1080/01638538609544651.

Espinoza, A. E., Piper, I., & Fernandez, R. A. (2014). The study of memory sites through a dialogical accompaniment interactive group method: A research note. *Qualitative Research, 14*(6), 712–728. https://doi.org/10.1177/1468794 113483301.

Ester, P., Vinken, H., & Diepstraten, L. (2002). Reminiscences of an extreme century: Intergenerational differences in time heuristics: Dutch people's collective memories of the 20th century. *Time and Society, 11*, 39–66.

Eyerman, R., & Turner, B. S. (1998). Outline of a theory of generations. *European Journal of Social Theory, 1*(1), 91–106. https://doi.org/10.1177/136843 198001001007.

Feindt, G. R., Krawatzek, F., Mehler, D. A., Pestel, F., & Trimcev, R. (2014). Entangled memory: Toward a third wave in memory studies. *History and Theory, 53*(1), 24–44. https://doi.org/10.1111/hith.10693.

Fewster, K. (2007). An ethnoarchaeological case study from central Spain. *Journal of Mediterranean Archaeology, 20*(1), 89–114.

Foxall, A. (2013). A contested landscape: Monuments, public memory, and post-Soviet identity in Stavropol' Russia. *Communist and Post-Communist Studies, 46*, 167–178. http://dx.doi.org/10.1016/j.postcomstud.2012.12.012.

Frijda, N. H. (1997). Commemorating. In J. W. Pennebaker, D. Paez, & B. Rime (Eds.), *Collective memory of political events. Social psychological perspectives* (pp. 103–127). Mahwah, NJ: Lawrence Erlbaum Associates.

Gur-Ze'ev, I., & Pappé, I. (2003). Beyond the destruction of the other's collective memory: Blueprints for a Palestinian/Israeli dialogue. *Theory, Culture & Society, 20*(1), 93–108.

Gillis, J. R. (1994). Introduction. Memory and identity: The history of a relationship. In J. R. Gillis (Ed.), *Commemorations: The politics of national identity* (pp. 3–24). Princeton, NJ: Princeton University Press.

Gioia, D. A., Schultz, M., & Corley, K. G. (2000). Organizational identity, image, and adaptive instability. *Academy of Management Review, 25*(1), 63–81. https://doi.org/10.5465/amr.2000.2791603.

Haas, V., & Levasseur, E. (2013). Rumour as a symptom of collective forgetfulness. *Culture and Psychology, 19*(1), 60–75. https://doi.org/10.1177/1354067X12464986.

Halbwachs, M. (1980). *The collective memory* (F. J. Ditter, Jr. & V. Y. Ditter, Trans.). New York, NY: Harper and Row. (Originally published in 1950)

Halbwachs, M. (1992). *On collective memory*. Chicago, IL: University of Chicago Press.

Hall, M. (2006). Identity, memory and countermemory: The archaeology of an urban landscape. *Journal of Material Culture, 11*(1–2), 189–209. https://doi.org/10.1177/1359183506063021.

Hatch, M. J., & Schultz, M. (2017). Toward a theory of using history authentically: Historicizing in the Carlsberg Group. *Administrative Science Quarterly, 62*, 657–697. https://doi.org/10.1177/0001839217692535.

High, C. (2009). Remembering the *auca*: Violence and generational memory in the Amazonian Ecuador. *Journal of the Royal Anthropological Institute, 15*(4), 719–736. https://doi.org/10.1111/j.1467-9655.2009.01581.x.

Kapralski, S. (2001). Battlefields of memory: Landscape and identity in Polish-Jewish relations. *History and Memory, 13*, 35–58.

Krmpotich, C. (2010). Remembering and repatriation: The production of kinship, memory, and respect. *Journal of Material Culture, 15*(2), 157–179. https://doi.org/10.1177/1359183510364077.

Light, D., & Young, C. (2010). Political identity, public memory and urban space: A case study of Parcul Carol 1, Bucharest from 1906 to the present. *Europe-Asia Studies, 62*(9), 1453–1478. https://doi.org/10.1080/09668136.2010.515792.

Linde, C. (2000). The acquisition of a speaker by a story: How history becomes memory and identity. *Ethos (Berkeley, Calif.), 28*(4), 608–632. https://doi.org/10.1525/eth.2000.28.4.608.

Lippmann, S., & Aldrich, H. E. (2016). A rolling stone gathers momentum: Generational units, collective memory, and entrepreneurship. *Academy of Management Review, 41*(4), 658–675. https://doi.org/10.5465/amr.2014.0139.

Lowenthal, D. (1985). *The past is a foreign country*. Cambridge, UK: Cambridge University Press.

Ma, K. H., & Kim, H. K. (2015). Collective memory and the formation of the "unconscious" political generation: Focusing on the former period baby boomers in Korea. *Development and Society*, 44(1), 77–116. https://doi.org/10.21588/dns.2015.44.1.004.

Mannheim, K. (1952). The problem of generations. In P. Kecskemeti (Ed.), *Karl Mannheim: Essays*. London, UK: Routledge. (Originally published in 1927)

Marschall, S. (2012). Memory and identity in South Africa: Contradictions and ambiguities in the process of post-apartheid memorialization. *Visual Anthropology*, 25(3), 189–204. https://doi.org/10.1080/08949468.2012.665335.

McDonald, M. (2010). "Lest we forget": The politics of memory and Australian military intervention. *International Political Sociology*, 4(3), 287–302. https://doi.org/10.1111/j.1749-5687.2010.00106.x.

McEwan, C. (2003). Building a postcolonial archive? Gender, collective memory and citizenship in post-apartheid South Africa. *Journal of South African Studies*, 29, 739–757.

Moulton, S. M. (2015). How to remember: The interplay of memory and identity formation in post-disaster communities. *Human Organization*, 74(4), 319–328. https://doi.org/10.17730/0018-7259-74.4.319.

Murray, M. J. (2013). Collective memory in place: The Voortrekker monument and the Hector Pieterson memorial. In *Commemorating and forgetting: Challenges for the New South Africa*. Minneapolis, MN: University of Minnesota Press.

Murray, W. F., Zedeño, M. N., Hollenback, K. L., Grinnell, C., & Breast, E. C. (2011). The remaking of Lake Sakakawea: Locating cultural viability in negative heritage on the Missouri River. *American Ethnologist*, 38(3), 468–483. https://doi.org/10.1111/j.1548-1425.2011.01317.x.

Nora, P. (1989). Between memory and history: Les lieux de memoire. *Representations (Berkeley, Calif.)*, 26(Spring), 7–24. https://doi.org/10.2307/29 28520.

Nora, P. (1996). *Realms of memory*. New York, NY: Columbia University Press.

Olick, J. K. (1999). Collective memory: The two cultures. *Sociological Theory*, 17, 333–348.

Paabo, H. (2014). Constructing historical space: Estonia's transition from the Russian civilization to the Baltic Sea region. *Journal of Baltic Studies*, 45(2), 187–205. https://doi.org/10.1080/01629778.2013.846929.

Ravasi, D., & Schultz, M. (2006). Responding to organizational identity threats: Exploring the role of organizational culture. *Academy of Management Journal*, 49(3), 433–458. https://doi.org/10.5465/amj.2006.21794663.

Rime, B., Bouchat, P., Klein, O., & Licata, L. (2015). When collective memories of victimhood fade: Generational evolution of intergroup attitudes and political aspirations in Belgium. *European Journal of Social Psychology*, 45(4), 515–532. https://doi.org/10.1002/ejsp.2104.

Schwartz, B. (2000). *Abraham Lincoln and the forge of national memory*. Chicago, IL: University of Chicago Press.

Schwartz, B. (2005). The new Gettysburg Address: Fusing history and memory. *Poetics*, 33(1), 63–79. https://doi.org/10.1016/j.poetic.2005.01.003.

Schwartz, B. (2010). Culture and collective memory. In J. R. Hall, L. Grindstaff, & M.-C. Lo (Eds.), *Handbook of cultural sociology* (pp. 619–629). Abingdon, UK: Routledge.

Shore, B. (2008). Spiritual/work, memory/work: Revival and recollection at Salem camp meeting. *Ethos*, *36*(1), 98–119. doi: 10.1111/j.1548–1352.2 008.00006.x.

Schultz, M., & Hernes, T. (2013). A temporal perspective on organizational identity. *Organization Science*, *24*(1), 1–21. https://doi.org/10.1287/orsc.1110.0731.

Smith, A. D. (1999). *Myth and memories of the nation*. Oxford, UK: Oxford University Press.

Welch, S., & Wittlinger, R. (2011). The resilience of the nation state: Cosmopolitanism, Holocaust memory and German identity. *German Politics & Society*, *29*(3), 38–54. https://doi.org/10.3167/gps.2011.290303.

Whetten, D. A. (2006). Albert and Whetten revisited: Strengthening the concept of organizational identity. *Journal of Management Inquiry*, *15*(3), 219–234. https://doi.org/10.1177/1056492606291200.

White, G. (2006). Epilogue: Memory moments. *Ethos*, *34*(2), 325–341.

Zederman, M. (2014). Memories of the Paris commune in Belleville since the 1980s: Folklorization and new forms of mobilization in a transforming quartier. *History & Memory*, *26*(1), 109–135. https://doi.org/10.2979/histmemo.26.1.109.

Part III

Theoretical Framework and Implications

5 Multidisciplinary Theoretical Framework and Implications for Theory and Research

This chapter develops a theoretical framework on the relationship between organizational identity and organizational memory, in particular history and commemoration. It takes a more targeted approach to both topics in that it explores the relationship between the two concepts, drawing on the wide range of social science theory and research reviewed in this text. Collective memory is the primary lens to address organizational memory, although the relevant theory and research related to memory of collectives such as nations or cultural groups are also incorporated. Organizational identity is the primary focus for the work on identity, although on occasion the identity of nations or cultural groups is also considered. The emphasis is on the relationship between these concepts at the collective level of analysis, with acknowledgment of the factors that influence this relationship as well as the micro-level processes that contribute to the collective level. Through the analysis and integration of the literature, this framework provides a foundation for future theorizing and empirical work on organizational identity and memory and its relationship to practice.

The literature on organizational memory and organizational identity has developed independently and at times in separate disciplines. Scholars have debated whether organizational identity is mutable or enduring. In this debate, organizational history, a form of organizational memory, has been a key factor, but neither side of the debate has drawn extensively on the well-developed literature on collective memory to understand this relationship and its impact on organizational identity. Organizational memory, defined in this chapter as commemoration and history, has been connected to different forms of identity—national (Schwartz & Kim, 2002), group (Cuc, Ozuru, Manier, & Hirst, 2006), and organizational (Anteby & Molnar, 2012; Casey, 1997; Hatch & Schultz, 2017; Ravasi & Schultz, 2006; Schultz & Hernes, 2013)—but this relationship and its impact on organizational processes has only recently (Hatch & Schultz, 2017; Schultz & Hernes, 2013) been empirically studied.

The relationship between organizational identity and memory is critical to theory and practice. From a theoretical perspective, a deeper understanding of this relationship will support future theorizing in organization memory, which has been largely devoid of theory. This multidisciplinary analysis offers theories from social sciences, in particular sociology and anthropology, to strengthen organizational memory theorizing, and the additional understanding of the relationship offers explanatory power in organizational memory and forgetting research. This relationship also offers further explanatory power for theory and research on organizational identity, in that it surfaces why and how organizational identity emerges and offers insight into the discussions of the enduring nature of the concept as well as the work that considers organizational identity as an ongoing process rather than an outcome or a set of characteristics (Anteby & Molnar, 2012; Hatch & Schultz, 2017; Kreiner, Hollensbe, Sheep, Smith, & Kataria, 2015).

From a practice perspective, this analysis of the relationship between organizational memory and identity offers insight into how organizational memory and identity emerge and might be used, the role of the relationship in organizational learning and change, and how it can support individual-level processes such as organizational identification, commitment, and engagement. The implications for practice are discussed in more depth in Chapter 6.

This chapter is organized into four main sections. First, definitions of terms and delineation of definitional boundaries are presented. The theoretical framework is then described, including the process-based relationship between organizational memory and identity in the context of time and space. The third section identifies and explores the factors that influence both the processes of organizational memory and identity as well as the relationship between the two constructs. The chapter closes with implications for future research.

Definitions of Terms

Organizational Memory

In this theoretical framework, organizational memory is defined through the lens of collective memory. In reviewing work on memory across the disciplines represented in this text, the theories and related definitions of collective memory from sociology, anthropology, and history were the most robust. In these disciplines, memory is broadly defined as shared representations and interpretations of the past of a group or collective. The definition of organizational memory in the early organizational studies literature, including information systems, took a more positivist view, and generally the theoretical underpinnings for the concept of organizational memory were not explored. For example, Walsh and Ungson (1991) referred to organizational memory as shared interpretations of the past and categorized memory into storage bins of information or knowledge. This metaphor of organizational memory has dominated the theorizing related to memory in organizational studies since that time (Anderson & Sun, 2010; Casey & Olivera, 2003). This metaphor also resides in much of the theory and research on organizational learning (Argote, 2013; Argote & Miron-Spektor, 2011) and related work on knowledge management and information systems, with organizational memory defined as stocks of knowledge (Barros, Ramos, & Perez, 2015; Lin, 2015) that can be stored and transferred. Only recently with the historical turn in organizational studies (Rowlinson, Hassard, & Decker, 2014) and a focus on organizational history (Godfrey, Hassard, O'Connor, Rowlinson, & Ruef, 2016) has organizational memory been explored in more depth, drawing upon sociological, anthropological, and historical theories of memory.

Collective memory is defined as "representations of the past in the minds of members of a community that contribute to the community's sense of identity" (Manier & Hirst, 2008, p. 253, as cited in Rime, Bouchat, Klein, & Licata, 2015). The most referenced components of collective memory are commemoration, or remembering together, and history (Schwartz, 2000, 2005). Delugan (2013, p. 978) defined history in terms of the "official representations about the past" that are critical to asserting a collective's legitimacy, while memory or remembering is more often distinctive of a group or collective but might have some elements in common with the official history of an organization or a nation. Schwartz (2000, 2005) also distinguished between commemoration and history and acknowledged the tension between them. History presents a balanced view of the past, taking into consideration the multiple motivations and rationales, and is more factual, while commemoration or coremembering or recollecting together presents a narrative of why something happened (Wertsch, 2008). Collective remembering is more of an "identity project in the present—remembering in service of constructing a preferred image of a group—and is resistant to change even in the face of contradictory evidence" (Wertsch, 2008, p. 60).

The move away from theorizing about the memory of a group in terms of psychological theories focused on individual memory has shifted much of the theorizing in the social sciences to the assumption that memory is a dynamic social process (Adamczyk, 2002; Cipolla, 2008; Hewer & Roberts, 2012) and to social constructionist perspectives on the process (Lebow, 2008), with a focus on the memory and identity of the collective. The idea that memory(ies) may be malleable to some degree, albeit slowly, is also supported by the increasing number of academic and popular counterfactual histories (Lebow, 2008, p. 30). Commemoration, heritage, and identity are connected through the process and impacted by emotion or affect, power dynamics, physical space, time, and individuals.

In empirical studies of collective memory, some studies (Espinoza, Piper, & Fernandez, 2014) found differences in the recollection and interpretation of past events depending on whether the events being recalled were experienced firsthand. Yet in other studies, there were only minimal differences in recollections of past events and the meaning attributed to these events, depending on whether the memories were episodic, or personally experienced, or semantic, recalled by others and then retold, i.e., a nonparticipant narrative (Casey, 1997; Linde, 2000). The accuracy in the details of events that are recalled is not as important as which events are recalled, the interpretation of these events, and why they are important. The latter tells us more about the "identity and identification of contemporary social groups" (Murray, 2013, p. 103).

The renewed interest in memory and identity in anthropology has been attributed to "decolonization," and the emphasis has been on surfacing the multiple voices and memories of collectives that emerge (Berliner, 2005; Haukanes & Trnka, 2013). Feindt, Krawatzek, Mehler, Pestel, and Trimcev (2014) discussed memories as symbols with meanings that emerge through collective remembering. These meanings may shift depending on how and when the memories are recalled, and there may be multiple, competing interpretations in a collective, some visible and others not. Feindt et al. (2014) referred to this as the "plurality of memory at any given moment" (p. 32) and noted that this little-explored area of Halbwachs's work is an important area for future research.

In recent work in organizational studies, organizational history has been framed as a process of historicizing (Hatch & Schultz, 2017) and connected to organizational identity. In taking a process or temporal view of organizational identity and history, Hatch and Schultz (2017) expanded on the micro-level activities in which organizational actors use historical artifacts to develop organizational identity at different points in the life of an organization. Similar to Schwartz (2000, 2005) and Delugan (2013), they acknowledged that identity and memory are constrained to some degree by history and the authenticity of the history.

Organizational Identity

The seminal definition of organizational identity by Albert and Whetten (1985) has been the cornerstone for theory and research on this concept in organizational studies. Organizational identity is defined as features of an organization that are core and enduring or temporally continuous and set the organization apart from others in a similar category (Albert & Whetten, 1985; Corley et al., 2006). Organizational identity answers the question, "Who are we as an organization?" (Whetten & Mackey, 2002). Identity rarely surfaces in routine activities in organizations; it becomes conscious and matters during crises or when decisions need to be made that will profoundly affect the organization (Albert & Whetten, 1985).

Whetten (2006) further articulated three components of organizational identity. First, the definitional component of organizational identity is represented by the central, distinct, and enduring (CED) features of an organization. History—in particular, the founding commitments of an organization—is the foundation for the identity claims that endure over time. These commitments are commemorated in recollections of critical events in the organization's history (Casey, 1997) and also surface in statements about the organization from organizational members. Whetten (2006) referred to the recollections of critical events as the phenomenological component of organizational identity, while the organizational members' view of organizational identity is the ideational component. Although the examples or stories used to exemplify these commitments may change, the claims or commitments themselves and the labels (Gioia, Patvardhan, Hamilton, & Corley, 2013) used to describe them often remain the same (Casey, 2010; Casey & Byington, 2013).

Those who take a social constructionist approach, in particular recent work by Kreiner et al. (2015), tend to rely on social psychological theories such as that of Breakwell (2010) because much of the theorizing and empirical study is focused on individuals' actions in organizations. Researchers who take a social actor perspective (Foreman & Whetten, 2002; Whetten, 2006; Whetten & Mackey, 2002) draw more from organizational theories such as institutional theory and sociological theories of collective memory (Casey, 1997).

Researchers who define organizational identity from a social constructionist perspective ask and answer the question "who are we as an organization" from the perspective of the shared interpretations of organizational members (Hogg & Terry, 2001; Kreiner et al., 2015). The social constructionist perspective defines organizational identity as "shared emergent beliefs" or "identity understandings" (Ravasi & Schultz, 2006, p. 436) about what is core and distinct about the organization. Most social constructionist views recognize the influence of official organizational identity claims but emphasize the critical role of members' interpretations of these claims (Gioia, Patvardhan, Hamilton, & Corley, 2013).

The maturation of the work on organizational identity is providing a promising reconceptualization of organizational identity for future theory and research and its link to collective memory through its focus on time and how the past is brought forward to articulate organizational identity. As noted above, most perspectives and definitions of organizational identity reference history, founders, tradition, and legacy at different times, yet the role of collective memory is underdeveloped. More recent work (Hatch & Schultz, 2017; Schultz & Hernes, 2013) is beginning to expand and draw on the rich theories and empirical work on collective memory from a variety of theoretical foundations and is using it to explore organizations through micro, meso, and macro dynamics.

This chapter defines organizational identity from the seminal definition, with the idea that claims about what is core and distinctive are temporally continuous. It acknowledges that identity is malleable to a limited degree through the actions and beliefs of the members in the organization, yet this evolution is temporally continuous and is in reference to the claims that are made by the organization as a social actor. This chapter proposes that identity is a dynamic process of identity construction, building from work by Cipolla (2008) and Hall (1996). Cipolla (2008) asserted that identity is a dynamic process of construction in the context of time and space. Hall (1996) noted that collective identity is linked to culture, is "historically, not biologically defined" (p. 598), and evolves over time. In general in the social sciences, there has been a move away from psychological theories of memory and identity to theories that focus on collectives and the social process (Hewer & Roberts, 2012).

Theoretical Assumptions About the Relationship Between Organizational Identity and Memory

Based on the definitions of organizational memory and identity presented above, this section proposes several assumptions about the relationship between the two constructs:

1. There is a dynamic or bidirectional relationship between identity and memory.
2. The relationship and the concepts are processes.
3. The relationship is socially constructed and evolves over time. Perceptions of identity and memory are malleable, but this malleability is limited in that collectives have unique histories that differentiate them from other collectives and may be recorded in artifacts and other documents. This process evolves over time, with the past interacting with the present and considerations of the future.
4. The process is one of dynamic equilibrium, with a tension between history and memory.
5. This relationship involves making meaning—about who we are through our past and about the past and recollections of the past depending on who we are.
6. The process is multilevel and multivocal, impacted by the individual and different groups within the collective.
7. It is a process of relationships that can be influenced but not managed or controlled.

Nature of the Dynamic Relationship

In this relationship, organizational identity is framed as an evolving "outcome" of the process of collective memory. By definition, identity is a collective's evolving conception of its "enduring characteristics and basic values; its strengths and weaknesses; its hopes and fears; its reputation and conditions of existence; its institutions and traditions; and its past history, current purposes, and future prospects" (Kelman, 1997, p. 171 as cited in Kelman, 2001). It is a constructed process with memory processes such as commemoration of past events and symbolization (Hatch, 2010; Hatch & Schultz, 2017) as part of organizational culture. Identity is created and exhibited through the interplay of aspects of culture including structures, physical space such as monuments and memorials, for example, and traditions framed in institutions such as industries or religions (Bruner, 2011, p. 403). Memory and identity are considered to be interdependent, social constructions of reality (De Jong, 2009). Linde proposed that memory is "key to identity, and to the acquisition of identity" (Linde, 2000, p. 608).

Identity is intimately bound to and entwined with aspects of collective memory in this process. Identity is weakened when parts of collective memory are forgotten (Greenwood & Bernardi, 2014, citing Bullock, 1994). Paabo (2014), in referring to nations, asserted the importance of a narrative that "constructs a comprehensive understanding of a nation by defining its origins, main identity markers, and the image of the national Self" (p. 187). At other times, memory may be reconfigured or changed as an outcome of identity dynamics. As noted by Gillis (1994), memory and identity are interdependent "constructions of reality" under ongoing revision in accordance with present needs, with group identity reflecting "a sense of sameness over time and space . . . sustained by remembering; and what is remembered is defined by the assumed identity"(p. 3) and constrained by the past of its history.

At times, collectives may reconfigure the past (Avdikos, 2013, p. 397) to meet the needs of the present. This interdependent process of memory and identity can be influenced by current issues (De Jong, 2009; Gillis, 1994, p. 3) as well as history. It is a process, and, at the collective level, there may be conflicts or "contested recollections of the past" as "different events represent different symbols" (Levy, 1999). Yet the group identity reflects "a sense of sameness over time and space, [as] sustained by remembering; and what is remembered is defined by the assumed identity" (Gillis, 1994, p. 3). Conflicting recollections of past events often stem from power differentials of groups or individuals within the collective.

In this dynamic relationship, memory serves several functions. It serves as a foundation for collective identity and its ongoing formation (Manier & Hirst, 2008, as cited in Rime et al., 2015). It does this through serving the differentiation function of organizational identity, in that memory, or the past of a collective, serves to differentiate (Assmann & Czaplicka, 1995; Haas & Levasseur, 2013) one collective from another because its history and memory are different than those of other collectives. Memory also serves to structure the identity of a collective (Gabel, 2013, p. 255). It "inscribes itself materially in the present as narrative, place, memorial" (Murray, 2013, p. 103). This "memory, which is recalled, performed, and even inscribed in the landscape through monuments and memorials, becomes an integral part of the local identity" (Moulton, 2013, p. 319) and becomes part of the collective identity. This identity helps unite people, and the "shared experience becomes the cornerstone of a new identity" that is recreated and "mediated through commemoration and narration of events" (Moulton, 2013, p. 323).

Factors Influencing the Relationship Between Organizational Memory and Identity

Emotion is a critical factor in the dynamic relationship between identity and memory. It surfaces when collectives protect their memories when they are "content" with their identity (Lebow, 2008, p. 142) and "defend their memories with a particular vengeance" (p. 29) when their identity is threatened. Schematic templates "mold the deep collective memory" and "have deeply held emotional resonance and are a fundamental part of the identity claims of a group" (Wertsch, 2008, p. 142). Emotions and cognition are fundamental in how we recall and retell the past, particularly when it includes events that are critical to the identity of the collective (Hatch & Schultz, 2017; Howard-Grenville, Metzger, & Meyer, 2013; Schultz & Hernes, 2013; Wertsch, 2008). Commemoration and heritage are connected through the process and impacted by emotion. The role of emotions in this dynamic process has not been studied extensively in the organizational studies literature.

Time—i.e., the relationship between past, present, and future—is core to the definitions of memory and identity in this framework and the relationship between the two processes. The concepts are both framed within and over time, i.e., organizational identity is defined as temporally continuous (Albert & Whetten, 1985). Critical events such as a decision that profoundly affects the direction of an organization become markers in history, are often the foundation of stories that are told in the organization, and are frequently preserved in recorded organizational histories. The "central and distinguishing features" of the organization are preserved in the components of collective memory, i.e., commemoration and history; they are "historical frames of reference" (Whetten, 2006, p. 223). Organizational memory is shared recollections of a past that impacts the present and the future of the organization. Others have noted that memory gives meaning to the present because it is the "means by which we remember who we are" and as such "provides the very core of identity" (De Jong, 2009, p. 362). Memory is core to the construction of identity (Lowenthal, 1985), yet it is "always interacting with the present" (Lowenthal, 1985, p. 248, as cited in Fewster, 2007, p. 90). Time has been a relatively undertheorized and empirically studied factor in the relationship between organizational memory and identity.

Physical space or context also impacts the dynamic relationship between identity and memory (Paabo, 2014; Smith, 1999). The memory and related meaning of events continue to emerge and change over time through social interactions and activities around and including physical entities such as memorial sites (Allen & Brown, 2016; Espinoza et al., 2014). The relationship between collective memory and identity surfaces in physical space through processes such as commemoration and coremembering, or remembering together (Schwartz, 2000, 2005). The physical space becomes a narrated space associated with historical milestones (Kapralski, 2001). Researchers have theorized about commemoration in many ways, including narratives or stories that are coremembered through physical space and material objects such as monuments and museums or events that took place in places that are recalled in a shared story. As Allen and Brown (2016) noted in their study of the Hyde Park memorial, material objects such as memorials "are attempts to preserve a contemporary account of a past event" (p. 11). Yet there are often conflicting views regarding how the memorial should be constructed, differing accounts of the event itself, and differences of opinion regarding which communities are the benefactors and if the memorial and the process of remembering sustain the values of that community and its identity. Physical space has not been explored in depth in organizational studies of organizational identity and memory and, in particular, the relationship between the two.

Power and power dynamics are also critical factors in the relationship between organizational identity and memory. Power surfaces in many forms, including in the contested recollections of past events and the meaning of these events. The differences are connected to the disputed nature of "who we are," particularly in times of crisis or significant change. Conflicts over who we are as a collective are represented in contested stories of events as they are recalled, and the events are used as symbols and in meaning making about the present and the past (Levy, 1999) and who we are and have been.

There are also interactions between factors such as physical space and power as they influence the relationship between memory and identity. Physical spaces such as landscapes can shape the identity of collectives who interact with them (Hall, 2006), in that key elements in these landscapes such as buildings, monuments, or memorials are the "production of power dynamics by privileging some over others" (Hall, 2006, p. 190). In organizations, power dynamics can be evident when artifacts such as pictures or other depictions of founders or key events in an organization's history change following a merger or acquisition, for example. The acquiring organization's story may be "privileged" over that of the acquired organization, and the retelling of the acquisition story in plaques or other markers may be influenced by which individuals in the organization are charged with creating the markers and the narrative.

Another example is how people are memorialized in physical spaces following the death of these significant stakeholders (Bell & Taylor, 2016). Formalized commemoration can be controlled by power dynamics that frame who or what is mourned and how (Bell & Taylor, 2016).

Other forms of commemoration such as stories told in more informal spaces may be more multivocal, and the stories of historical events recalled in these spaces may have different meanings assigned to them depending on the individuals participating in the recollections and their own histories in the organization. Heritage or memory theorized in terms of oral and performative traditions such as storytelling (Marschall, 2012) may offer more understanding of the dynamics of power and its influence on organizational identity and memory in addition to physical spaces that may be more controlled by those in power. Memories are symbols with meanings that emerge through collective remembering (Feindt et al., 2014, p. 40). These meanings may evolve; there may be multiple, competing interpretations at one time in a collective, but not all may be visible. This represents the "plurality of memory" (Feindt et al., 2014, p. 32) that exists in collectives and may impact the relationship between memory and identity. This is an important area for future research.

The power dynamics in these processes of remembering (Cipolla, 2008; De Jong, 2009) as well as forgetting (Mena, Rintamaki, Fleming, & Spicer, 2016) can shape identity processes of organizations (Rodgers, Petersen, & Sanderson, 2016) and other types of collectives and are often attributed to managerial or dominant voices (McDonald, 2010; Keightley & Pickering, 2006). This has been studied in relationship to organizational identity work (Hatch & Schultz, 2017; Kreiner et al., 2015) and in the relationship between organizational identity and memory (Hatch & Schultz, 2017) and is an important area for future research.

Microfoundations of collective processes such as the relationship between organizational identity and memory are also crucial to our understanding of these processes. In this theoretical framework, the microprocesses are factors that create and influence the relationship. For example, the histories and experiences of individual members of organizations play a role in how and why past events in an organization's history are recalled. These episodic memories or recollections of firsthand experiences often are recalled because of the emotion attached to these memories and the threat to an organization's identity and the individual's identification with that organization. In addition, individuals' perceptions and hopes for the future are key to the intersection of past, present, and future as well as how they perceive themselves and their own identity, professional or otherwise. In addition, it is the social interaction during recollections of events in the context of physical spaces such as memorial services or monuments that also creates and recreates the relationship between identity and memory. The individual agents or actors and their attributes, histories, experiences, and emotions, as well as the interactions of these agents, are key in creating and recreating the dynamic relationship between identity and memory. This focus on individuals and their interactions is beginning to surface in studies of identity work (Kreiner et al., 2015) as well as research on organizational history (Hatch & Schultz, 2017).

Implications for Research

As noted earlier, organizational memory as a concept has been under-theorized and underresearched (Anderson & Sun, 2010; Casey & Olivera, 2003) despite the well-cited seminal work of Walsh and Ungson (1991). The research on organizational memory since this work has primarily taken two tracks, depending on the theoretical foundations and related definitions of the concept. Research on organizational memory drawing from the sociological foundations of collective memory (Casey, 1997), history, and commemoration (Schwartz, 2000, 2005) has most frequently employed case study designs using primarily qualitative methods such as interviews, document analysis, and observation. Memory has been operationalized in terms of stories of significant events or interpretations or narratives about an organization's history. Since the mid-2000s, several studies have taken this approach to organizational memory and have investigated the relationship between organizational memory and identity.

Research on organizational memory that draws from theories of knowledge and learning has either focused on memory as a knowledge process or viewed knowledge from the perspective of a repository, i.e., stocks of knowledge. The research on memory as a knowledge process has tended to use case study designs and qualitative methods and has been incorporated into organizational learning research. For the most part, the relationship between organizational memory and identity has not been addressed in this research. Research on organizational memory as a knowledge repository has frequently employed both case study designs and quantitative studies, conceptualizing memory as a variable that impacts organizational performance, innovation, and other outcomes. This research has often been part of studies of knowledge management and transfer. In this research, the relationship between organizational memory and identity has not been addressed, yet it offers fruitful ground for future work.

There has been extensive theory and research on organizational identity in the organizational studies literature since the seminal work of Albert and Whetten (1985). In addition, the concept has been researched in other disciplines, such as higher education. Although there has been a division between theorists who take a social constructionist perspective on organizational identity and those who have maintained the original social actor perspective, most research has taken a qualitative approach to the study of the concept, with case study designs employing interviews, observation, and document review. The relationship of organizational memory and identity has been researched primarily taking a social constructionist perspective on organizational identity and memory, with memory defined as history and commemoration, and taking into account some of the variables that impact this relationship, including power dynamics, physical space or context, and time.

Many of the studies of organizational identity and memory have also taken a process view. A common denominator of process-based studies is time. These studies require a prolonged engagement of the researcher to explore and describe in depth the social interactions that comprise or constitute the processes. Case studies and comparative case studies will continue to serve as valuable research strategies to study the relationship. Representing this research beyond boxes and quadrants will continue to be an opportunity to creatively depict the dynamics of processes involving such factors as language, symbols, meaning making, and emotion across multiple levels of analysis and taking into account multiple voices and cultures. Memory and identity and the related processes are constituted by language. Identity and memory are symbols with meanings that emerge through collective remembering and language used in the process. These meanings may shift depending on how and when the memories are recalled, and there may be multiple, competing interpretations at one time in a collective, but not all may be equally visible. This is often referred to as the "plurality of memory at any given moment" (Feindt et al., 2014, p. 32) and is a little explored area of Halbwachs's work.

Recent work aligning with process theory studies (Hatch & Schultz, 2017) has proposed history in organizations as a process, i.e., historicizing, where organizational actors link their past with their present and the future. In their model, Hatch and Schultz (2017) theorized how microprocesses enable "actors to rediscover historical material and renew it for possible future use" (p. 35). This process "keeps history alive by transporting it from past to future while expanding its material manifestation and meaning in the present" (p. 35). In their work, historicizing was more than simply reconfiguring and manipulating the past to meet present and future needs. Rather, history itself had agency: Organizational actors in their study responded to critical artifacts with "immediacy, intensity, and emotionality," indicating "that history inspired its own use and therefore possesses agency" (p. 36). Authenticity played a critical role, as the authors concluded that "manipulating history risks failure because it undermines the immediacy, intensity and emotionality that history inspires in others and thereby denies its agency" (p. 36).

In the organizational identity literature, there is limited empirical work taking a social actor perspective on identity. There is an opportunity to pursue this perspective taking an institutional theory approach to explore the relationship with variables such as corporate social responsibility over time.

Over the past 20-plus years, much of the theory and research on organizational identity has focused on further explicating the concept, particularly in terms of whether it endures or changes over time. The antecedents and outcomes of organizational identity have also been studied. More recently, since it has been studied in other disciplines, organizational identity has been used to explain other concepts such as corporate social responsibility and leadership. The relationship between organizational identity and aspects of collective memory such as history and commemoration has great potential to expand and provide more in-depth theorizing about organizational identity.

References

Adamczyk, A. (2002). On Thanksgiving and collective memory: Constructing the American tradition. *Journal of Historical Sociology*, *15*(3), 343–365. https://doi.org/10.1111/1467-6443.00182.

Albert, S., & Whetten, D. A. (1985). Organizational identity. In L. L. Cummings & B. M. Staw (Eds.), *Research in organizational behavior* (pp. 263–295). Greenwich, CT: JAI Press.

Allen, M., & Brown, S. D. (2016). Memorial meshwork: The making of the commemorative space of the Hyde Park 7/7 Memorial. *Organization*, *23*(1), 10–28. https://doi.org/10.1177/1350508415605103.

Anderson, M., & Sun, P. Y. T. (2010). What have scholars retrieved from Walsh and Ungson (1991). A citation context study. *Management Learning*, *41*(2), 131–145. https://doi.org/10.1177/1350507609341091.

Anteby, M., & Molnar, V. (2012). Collective memory meets organizational identity: Remembering to forget in a firm's rhetorical history. *Academy of Management Journal*, *55*(3), 515–540. https://doi.org/10.5465/amj.2010.0245

Argote, L. (2013). *Organizational learning: Creating, retaining and transferring knowledge* (2nd ed.). New York, NY: Springer. https://doi.org/10.1007/978-1-4614-5251-5.

Argote, L., & Miron-Spektor, E. (2011). Organizational learning: From experience to knowledge. *Organization Science*, *22*(5), 1123–1137. https://doi.org/10.1287/orsc.1100.0621.

Assmann, J., & Czaplicka, J. (1995). Collective memory and cultural identity. *New German Critique*, *65*, 125–133. https://doi.org/10.2307/488538.

Avdikos, E. G. (2013). Memory and identity on the Greek-Bulgarian border. *Journal of Balkan & Near Eastern Studies*, *15*(4), 396–411. https://doi.org/10.1080/19448953.2013.844586.

Barros, V. F., Ramos, I., & Perez, G. (2015). Information systems and organizational memory: A literature review. *Journal of Information Systems and Technology Management*, *12*(1), 45–63. https://doi.org/10.4301/S1807-1775201 5000100003.

Bell, E., & Taylor, S. (2016). Vernacular mourning and corporate memorialization in framing the death of Steve Jobs. *Organization*, *23*(1), 114–132. https://doi.org/10.1177/1350508415605109.

Berliner, D. (2005). The abuses of memory: Reflections on the memory boom in anthropology. *Anthropological Quarterly*, *78*(1), 197–211. https://doi.org/10.1353/anq.2005.0001.

Breakwell, G. M. (2010). Resisting representations and identity processes. *Papers on Social Representations, 19*, 6.1–6.11. Retrieved from www.psych.lse.ac.uk/Psr/PSR2010/19_06Breakwell.pdf

Bruner, M. L. (2011). Rhetorical studies and national identity construction. *National Identities, 13*(4), 403–414. https://doi.org/10.1080/14608944.2011.629428.

Casey, A. (1997). Collective memory in organizations. In P. Shrivastava, A. Huff, & J. Dutton (Series Eds.), J. Walsh & A. Huff (Vol. Eds.), *Organizational learning and strategic management* (Advances in Strategic Management, Vol. 14, pp. 111–151). Greenwich, CT: JAI Press.

Casey, A. (2010). *The role of collective memory in organizational identity*. Presented at the annual conference of the Academy of Management, Montreal, Quebec, Canada.

Casey, A., & Byington, L. (2013). *Nike: A case study of identity claims in a complex global world*. Presented at the annual conference of the Academy of Management, Lake Buena Vista, FL. https://doi.org/10.5465/ambpp.2013.12456abstract.

Casey, A., & Olivera, F. (2003). *Organizational memory remembered: A look back and future directions*. Paper presented at the annual meeting of the Academy of Management, Seattle, WA.

Cipolla, C. (2008). Signs of identity, signs of memory. *Archaeological Dialogues, 15*(2), 196–215. https://doi.org/10.1017/S1380203808002675.

Corley, K. G., Harquail, C. V., Pratt, M. G., Glynn, M. A., Fiol, C. M., & Hatch, M. J. (2006). Guiding organizational identity through aged adolescence. *Journal of Management Inquiry, 15*(2), 85–99. https://doi.org/10.1177/1056492605285930.

Cuc, A., Ozuru, Y., Manier, D., & Hirst, W. (2006). On the formation of collective memories: The role of a dominant narrator. *Memory & Cognition, 34*(4), 752–762. https://doi.org/10.3758/BF03193423.

De Jong, N. (2009). The (Cuban) voice of the (Curaçaoan) people: The making (and taking) of a collective memory. *Journal of Historical Sociology, 22*(3), 351–365. https://doi.org/10.1111/j.1467-6443.2009.01353.x.

DeLugan, R. M. (2013). Commemorating from the margins of the nation: El Salvador 1932, indigeneity and transnational belonging. *Anthropological Quarterly, 86*(4), 965–994. https://doi.org/10.1353/anq.2013.0046.

Espinoza, A. E., Piper, I., & Fernandez, R. A. (2014). The study of memory sites through a dialogical accompaniment interactive group method: A research note. *Qualitative Research, 14*(6), 712–728. https://doi.org/10.1177/1468794113483301.

Feindt, G. R., Krawatzek, F., Mehler, D. A., Pestel, F., & Trimcev, R. (2014). Entangled memory: Toward a third wave in memory studies. *History and Theory, 53*(1), 24–44. https://doi.org/10.1111/hith.10693.

Fewster, K. (2007). An ethnoarchaeological case study from central Spain. *Journal of Mediterranean Archaeology, 20*(1), 89–114.

Foreman, P., & Whetten, D. A. (2002). Members' identification with multiple-identity organizations. *Organization Science, 13*(6), 618–635. https://doi.org/10.1287/orsc.13.6.618.493.

Gabel, I. (2013). Historical memory and collective identity: West Bank settlers reconstruct the past. Engaging in illegal acts is accepted. *Media Culture & Society, 35*(2), 250–259. https://doi.org/10.1177/0163443712467592.

Gillis, J. R. (1994). Introduction. Memory and identity: The history of a relationship. In J. R. Gillis (Ed.), *Commemorations: The politics of national identity* (pp. 3–24). Princeton, NJ: Princeton University Press.

Gioia, D., Patvardhan, S., Hamilton, A., & Corley, K. (2013). Organizational identity formation and change. *The Academy of Management Annals, 7*(1), 123–193. https://doi.org/10.5465/19416520.2013.762225.

Godfrey, P. C., Hassard, J., O'Connor, E., Rowlinson, M., & Ruef, M. (2016). What is organizational history? Toward a creative synthesis of history and organizational studies. *Academy of Management Review, 41*(4), 590–608. https://doi.org/10.5465/amr.2016.0040.

Greenwood, A., & Bernardi, A. (2014). Understanding the rift, the (still) uneasy bedfellows of history and organization studies. *Organization, 21*(6), 907–932. https://doi.org/10.1177/1350508413514286.

Haas, V., & Levasseur, E. (2013). Rumour as a symptom of collective forgetfulness. *Culture and Psychology, 19*(1), 60–75. https://doi.org/10.1177/135 4067X12464986.

Hall, S. (1996). The question of cultural identity. In S. Hall, D. Held, D. Hubert, & K. Thompson (Eds.), *Modernity: An introduction to modern societies* (pp. 595–634). Cambridge, UK: Blackwell Publishers.

Hall, M. (2006). Identity, memory and countermemory: The archaeology of an urban landscape. *Journal of Material Culture, 11*(1–2), 189–209. https://doi.org/10.1177/1359183506063021.

Hatch, M. J. (2010). Material and meaning in the dynamics of organizational culture and identity with implications for leadership of organizational change. In N. Ashkanasy, C. Wilderom, & M. Peterson (Eds.), *The handbook of organizational culture and climate* (2nd ed., pp. 341–348). Thousand Oaks, CA: Sage.

Hatch, M. J., & Schultz, M. (2017). Toward a theory of using history authentically: Historicizing in the Carlsberg Group. *Administrative Science Quarterly, 62*, 657–697. https://doi.org/10.1177/0001839217692535.

Haukanes, H., & Trnka, S. (2013). Memory, imagination, and belonging across generations: Perspectives from postsocialist Europe and beyond. *Focaal— Journal of Global and Historical Anthropology, 66*, 3–13.

Hewer, C. J., & Roberts, R. (2012). History, culture and cognition: Towards a dynamic model of social memory. *Culture and Psychology, 18*(2), 167–183. https://doi.org/10.1177/1354067X11434836.

Hogg, M. A., & Terry, D. J. (2001). *Social identity process in organizational identity*. Philadelphia, PA: Psychology Press.

Howard-Grenville, J., Metzger, M. L., & Meyer, A. D. (2013). Rekindling the flame: Processes of identity resurrection. *Academy of Management Journal, 56*(1), 113–136. https://doi.org/10.5465/amj.2010.0778.

Kapralski, S. (2001). Battlefields of memory: Landscape and identity in Polish-Jewish relations. *History and Memory, 13*, 35–58.

Keightley, E., & Pickering, M. (2006). For the record: Popular music and photography as technologies of memory. *European Journal of Cultural Studies, 9*(2), 149–165.

Kelman, H. C. (2001). The role of national identity in conflict resolution. In R. D. Ashmore, L. Jussim, & D. Wilder (Eds.), *Social identity, intergroup conflict, and conflict reduction* (pp. 187–212). Oxford, UK: Oxford University Press.

Kreiner, G. E., Hollensbe, E., Sheep, M. L., Smith, B. R., & Kataria, N. (2015). Elasticity and the dialectic tensions of organizational identity: How can we hold together while we are pulling apart? *Academy of Management Journal,* 58(4), 981–1011. https://doi.org/10.5465/amj.2012.0462.

Lebow, R. N. (2008). The future of memory. *Annals of the American Academy of Political and Social Science, 617*(1), 25–40. https://doi.org/10.1177/00027 16207310817.

Levy, D. (1999). The future of the past: Historiographical disputes and competing memories in Germany and Israel. *History and Theory, 38*(1), 51–66. 10.1111/0018-2656.761999076.

Lin, H.-F. (2015). Linking knowledge management orientation to balanced scorecard outcomes. *Journal of Knowledge Management, 19*(6), 1224–1249. https://doi.org/10.1108/JKM-04-2015-0132.

Linde, C. (2000). The acquisition of a speaker by a story: How history becomes memory and identity. *Ethos (Berkeley, Calif.), 28*(4), 608–632. https://doi.org/10.1525/eth.2000.28.4.608.

Lowenthal, D. (1985). *The past is a foreign country.* Cambridge, UK: Cambridge University Press.

Marschall, S. (2012). Memory and identity in South Africa: Contradictions and ambiguities in the process of post-apartheid memorialization. *Visual Anthropology, 25*(3), 189–204. https://doi.org/10.1080/08949468.2012.665335.

McDonald, M. (2010). "Lest we forget": The politics of memory and Australian military intervention. *International Political Sociology, 4*(3), 287–302. https://doi.org/10.1111/j.1749-5687.2010.00106.x.

Mena, S., Rintamaki, J., Fleming, P., & Spicer, A. (2016). On the forgetting of corporate irresponsibility. *Academy of Management Review, 41*(4), 720–738. https://doi.org/10.5465/amr.2014.0208.

Murray, M. J. (2013). Collective memory in place: The Voortrekker monument and the Hector Pieterson memorial. In *Commemorating and forgetting: Challenges for the New South Africa.* Minneapolis, MN: University of Minnesota Press.

Paabo, H. (2014). Constructing historical space: Estonia's transition from the Russian civilization to the Baltic Sea region. *Journal of Baltic Studies, 45*(2), 187–205. https://doi.org/10.1080/01629778.2013.846929.

Ravasi, D., & Schultz, M. (2006). Responding to organizational identity threats: Exploring the role of organizational culture. *Academy of Management Journal, 49*(3), 433–458. https://doi.org/10.5465/amj.2006.21794663.

Rime, B., Bouchat, P., Klein, O., & Licata, L. (2015). When collective memories of victimhood fade: Generational evolution of intergroup attitudes and political aspirations in Belgium. *European Journal of Social Psychology, 45*(4), 515–532. https://doi.org/10.1002/ejsp.2104.

Rodgers, D. M., Petersen, J., & Sanderson, J. (2016). Commemorating alternative organizations and marginalized spaces: The case of forgotten Finntowns. *Organizations, 23*(1), 90–113. doi: 10.1177/1350508415605110.

Rowlinson, M., Hassard, J., & Decker, S. (2014). Research strategies for organizational history: A dialogue between historical theory and organization theory. *Academy of Management Review, 39*(3), 250–274. https://doi.org/10.5465/amr.2012.0203.

Schultz, M., & Hernes, T. (2013). A temporal perspective on organizational identity. *Organization Science, 24*(1), 1–21. https://doi.org/10.1287/orsc.1110.0731.

Schwartz, B. (2000). *Abraham Lincoln and the forge of national memory.* Chicago, IL: University of Chicago Press.

Schwartz, B. (2005). The new Gettysburg Address: Fusing history and memory. *Poetics, 33*(1), 63–79. https://doi.org/10.1016/j.poetic.2005.01.003.

Schwartz, B., & Kim, M. (2002). Honor, dignity and collective memory. In K. Cerulo (Ed.), *Culture in mind* (pp. 209–226). London, UK: Routledge.

Smith, A. D. (1999). *Myth and memories of the nation.* Oxford, UK: Oxford University Press.

Walsh, J. P., & Ungson, G. R. (1991). Organizational memory. *Academy of Management Review, 16*(1), 57–91. https://doi.org/10.5465/amr.1991.4278992.

Wertsch, J. (2008). Collective memory and narrative templates. *Social Research, 75*(1), 133–155.

Wertsch, J. V. (2008). Blank spots in collective memory: A case study of Russia. *Annals of the American Academy of Political and Social Science, 617,* 58–71.

Whetten, D. A. (2006). Albert and Whetten revisited: Strengthening the concept of organizational identity. *Journal of Management Inquiry, 15*(3), 219–234. https://doi.org/10.1177/1056492606291200.

Whetten, D. A., & Mackey, A. (2002). A social actor conception of organizational identity and its implications for the study of organizational reputation. *Business & Society, 41*(4), 393–414. https://doi.org/10.1177/0007650302238775.

6 Implications for Practice

Based on the theoretical and empirical work integrated across the disciplines reviewed in this text, this chapter discusses how organizations use the relationship between organizational memory and identity and how managers and leaders can better understand and enhance how they incorporate this relationship into their practice. Recent examples of organizational history and commemorative practices from corporations and nonprofits are discussed in the context of how organizational identity and memory surface, along with how these practices could be further enhanced through theory and research.

The relationship between organizational memory and identity is critical to organizations from two primary perspectives. First, from a communications perspective, how organizations project who they are in relationship to who they have been and who they will be in the future is key to building loyalty to their products and services and building relationship with their communities, both internal stakeholders such as staff and external environments from local to worldwide. This communication is vital in an increasingly virtual world, where a firm is known via websites and other online repositories and through social media. Through these venues, what others communicate about the organization is crucial to organizations; this communication can be initiated from people from different cultures and countries, and they can understand the firm's identity and history in different ways. Communication is especially important during major change or significant events in the organization, such as the death of a founder or a major merger or acquisition, as well as during critical world events. How an organization reflects and interprets significant events in its history to those internal and external to the organization mirrors its identity and its central identity claims. For example, when a founder dies, how he or she is commemorated both in memorial services as well as anniversaries of the death (Bell & Taylor, 2016) reflect and can reinforce the organization's identity. These events are often portrayed in exhibits created for a corporate museum or visitor center. Castellani and Rossato (2012) referred to the importance of the communication potential of corporate museums and archives as one example—with communication to both employees and external customers and stakeholders.

Second, from a learning perspective, the relationship between organizational identity and memory is influential in determining what events are reflected upon and how new knowledge or learning about the organization's identity and history is created through this reflection. For example, corporate histories as displayed in these museums are a way to remember and reflect upon past successes and failures—to learn from the past and to engage with and protect the future of the organization. These exhibitions also engage with employees to help them articulate how staff and founders who came before them created and grew the organization. Formal history programs in organizations "are a reminder of roots, a testament to the people and events that got the entity where it is today and an inspiration to present and future generations" (Wizniuk, 2001, p. 13).

This chapter discusses the relationship between organizational memory and identity in the context of five practice examples related to the communications and learning perspectives: (1) corporate museums and visitor centers, (2) archives, (3) anniversaries and memorial services; (4) websites; and (5) major transitions in organizations, including mergers and acquisitions. Throughout, this chapter explores some of the key factors that influence this relationship, such as the role of physical space, power, and social interaction.

Corporate Museums

Corporate museums and visitor centers are valuable settings in which to explore the relationship of organizational memory and identity. Critical facets of this relationship as well as the factors that influence it are resident in these exhibitions—whether it is a display case highlighting the birth of the organization and the founder's life in the corporation's lobby or executive offices or a large, state-of-the art high-tech/high-touch museum and visitor center, such as the World of Coca-Cola in Atlanta, Georgia, Guinness Storehouse in Dublin, Ireland, or Harley-Davidson Museum in Milwaukee, Wisconsin. Factors include physical space, such as how the physical space is created and used; time as operationalized in displays of past, present, and future products or the past and future organizational strategies; commemoration, i.e., commemorating significant people and events in the organization and their community through stories, both the organization's and consumers'; emotion, i.e., what emotions are expressed in the stories; and power, as it influences which stories are told and how they are told as well as the stories that are never told.

Castellani and Rossato (2012) referred to the communication potential of corporate museums—including both internal communication with employees and executive teams and external communication with current and future customers and shareholders. Bonti (2014) noted that a corporate museum resides at "the intersection of the cultural realm of public museums and the world of business, and is characterized by a managerial vision" (p. 141). There is limited empirical work on corporate museums (Bonti, 2014). They are mainly studied in the corporate communications literature and, to a lesser degree, in organizational studies. In organizational studies, they have been studied particularly in reference to how they represent organizational memory and identity and the relationship between these concepts (Bonti, 2014; Casey, Byington, & Nissley, 2003; Nissley & Casey, 2002; Stigliani & Ravasi, 2007).

There are many definitions of corporate museums (Castellani & Rossato, 2012). Danilov (1991), one of the earliest and leading scholars of corporate museums, provided a definition in his directory of corporate museums: "a corporate facility with tangible objects and/or exhibits, displayed in a museum-like setting, that communicates the history, operations, and/or interests of the company to employees, guests, customers, and/or public" (p. 2). Similarly, Bonti (2014, p. 141) described the museums as "physical structures in which the history and the memory of a company are told" and "as a tool for public relations and marketing, that is, for corporate communication" (p. 141). Bonti (2014) added that they offer the opportunity for a visitor to "retrace both the past and the present of the business from different points of view, such as strategic, techno-productive, and social" (p. 141). Other definitions of corporate museums have included historical accounts of the organization's past that are displayed in a small case, a group of pictures on the wall, or in or on the buildings on a corporate campus. At other times, exhibition of the organization's history may be woven into retail spaces, such as has occurred with Nike. This wide range of definitions has constrained the research on these structures, how they are used, and their influence on the organization.

While the newer museums are open to the public and may be combined with a visitor center, many of the early museums were created primarily for internal purposes, such as new employee orientation and training, anniversary celebrations of significant events in the organization's history, and engagement with current and possible important customers or clients at sales meetings. In such settings, the public was not allowed to access the museum except by invitation or when community events were hosted there.

Harris (1995) explained that these museums are built "upon popular awareness of their product advertising to represent entire periods, cultures, and industries through their commodities. Like museums of art and natural history, corporate museums are selective and argumentative, but their aspirations are not necessarily more limited" (p. 154). Others have emphasized that these museums "may follow very different agendas and operating standards than publicly funded and professionally accredited ones" (Livingstone, 2011, p. 16) because they are not required to be concerned with the authenticity or "cultural sensitivity" (p. 16) of the contents. Corporate museums exist to serve the organization's stakeholders. From early to present-day corporate museums, their purposes have grown from displaying the past and product developments to marketing and influencing the strategy of the organization (Bonti, 2014). They are a "means for reaffirming, both inside and outside the company, the collective identity and the organizational core values" (Bonti, 2014, p. 143).

History of Corporate Museums

Corporate museums were introduced in the United States in the late 1800s and then rapidly spread to Europe, including the United Kingdom, Germany, Italy, and Ireland (Castellani & Rossato, 2012; Danilov, 1991). Their efforts to imagine the past and the future of a firm were part of the momentum of the World's Fair, which concentrated largely on the future. One of the earliest collections was children's penny banks created by Seamen's Bank for Savings in New York City (Danilov, 1991). This collection was for internal purposes but was on display in 1938. The Baltimore and Ohio Railroad is credited as having the first museum created for public display as part of the exhibition at the World's Columbia Exposition in Chicago in 1893 (Danilov, 1991). Most corporate museums were developed after World War II, and approximately half were developed during the 1970s and 1980s, representing industries ranging from automobiles to food and beverage (Bonti, 2014) to banking. The worldwide development of corporate museums primarily occurred in the second half of the 20th century. The goals of these new museums were to display and "preserve a tangible record of the development of their industries and to illustrate the business or their entrepreneurial history" (Bonti, 2014, p. 143). There are now hundreds of corporate museums throughout the world (McKay, 2007), and most are very successful. Some of the most prominent corporate museums are those of Porsche, Levi Strauss & Co., McDonalds, Intel, and Wells Fargo.

Italy has a large number of corporate museums, and a few empirical studies have been conducted on these museums (Bonti, 2014). These museums were founded by companies that have long histories and well-established traditions. They are "strongly rooted in the territory and have developed a strong identity with the local area in which they are located" (Bonti, 2014, p. 142).

Some museums and visitor centers developed from factory tours of manufacturing facilities. A classic example is Hershey Corporation. The company had factory tours in the town of Hershey for many years. In Casey et al.'s (2003) study of corporate museums, the representative from Chocolate World noted that Milton Hershey probably began factory tours because he knew he had a good product and wanted people to experience it and see how it was made. This was very innovative in the 1920s. Actual tours of the factory were discontinued in 1973 when the company decided to build Chocolate World and include a simulated tour in that experience. Like the original tours, Chocolate World is a way for people to experience the brand.

Although many plant tours were closed because of government health and safety regulations (McKay, 2007), some firms continue to conduct factory tours, such as Harley-Davidson in Pennsylvania. These factory tours invite customers and the community to see how their favorite products are made. Museums often become top tourist destinations in small towns, such as the Crayola Factory in Easton, Pennsylvania, as well as in large cities such as Dublin, Ireland, and Atlanta, Georgia. The Harley-Davidson Museum is an example of a museum that had its origins in factory tours.

In 2008, Harley-Davidson, Inc., spent more than $75 million to develop and open its museum and visitor center in its hometown of Milwaukee, filling this visitor center with classic motorcycles, consumer photos, memories, stories, and weekly events such as blues concerts. The museum's website depicts the museum as a place where "history roars to life" and describes it as "the best of American design and culture— seasoned with freedom and rebellion, showcased in a landmark building." The company's organizational identity surfaces in its roaring (noise and speed), identifying Harley as an American company with the culture and trademark of "freedom and rebellion." The archives section of the website is titled "History with all the dust blown off," with the tag line "Traveling into the past is a thrill when you ride with Harley-Davidson" (www.harley-davidson.com/content/h-d/en_US/home/museum/explore/ archives.html).

The idea for The Crayola Factory began in 1992 after manufacturing plant tours were discontinued because of overwhelming demand. The plant tours often had a 2½-year wait for group reservations. Realizing that the downtown area of Easton needed assistance, the company opened its museum and visitor center near its home factory. The Crayola Factory has since expanded to Minneapolis, Minnesota, and Orlando, Florida. The identity of Crayola is on display in the factory, as it fosters creativity, and its history is on display through a timeline of the organization, including its acquisition by Hallmark Corporation.

The Guinness Storehouse Museum is another example of a corporate museum that is also a major visitor center. Open 363 days a year, it is one of Ireland's most popular tourist attractions. Inside, the journey begins at the "bottom of the world's largest pint glass and continues through several floors filled with interactive experiences that fuse our long brewing heritage with Ireland's rich history. At the top, you'll be rewarded with a pint of perfection in our world-famous rooftop Gravity Bar. Now that's our kind of higher education" (www.guinness-storehouse.com/en/

about-us). Perfection in brewing, its corporate history, and its connection with the country and community are part of Guinness's identity and history and are displayed throughout the museum. The museum also reflects what the organization has learned through the years about the impact of drinking and the educational programs it has developed and offered to the community.

Corporate museums frequently reside in the city where the headquarters is located and/or the city in which the corporation was founded, i.e., their home. For example, the McDonald's Store Museum was opened in 1984 in the original red and white tile building that served as the first restaurant created by founder Ray Kroc in Des Plaines, Illinois, in 1955 (Wizniuk, 2001). This store museum was later supplemented by the opening of The Ray A. Kroc Museum at McDonald's Plaza in nearby Oak Brook, Illinois, in 1987 following the death of Mr. Kroc. The latter museum holds examples of commemoration of a founder's death. This museum intertwines the life and history of the founder, the nation, and the corporation with interactive exhibits. A third McDonald's museum that opened in 1999 features the evolution of the official Kroc offices over time. This was followed by the Big Mac Museum in 2007. The latter is located near Hamburger University on the corporate campus in Illinois.

Finally, as another example, Intel, founded in a small structure in Mountain Brook, California, grew its museum from the early collections of a staff person. The museum was opened in 1992 in nearby Santa Clara, California, and expanded in 1999. The museum is open to the public and presents the history of Intel and the computer chip industry. Its education programs concentrate on technology literacy and the technology and science behind the computer chip. This museum is also accessed via its popular interactive website (Wizniuk, 2001).

Social Interaction and Interaction Between Consumers and the Product

From sitting on a Harley to drinking Guinness or Coke at the corporate museums, consumers interact with the product, the company, their own personal memories, and each other. Corporate museums have followed the trend toward interaction as a way to engage the customer. They want the customer to engage with their past, present, and future and interact with their products. These museums also frequently tell the story of the brand in relationship to their community (Seligson, 2010) or their customer in the permanent and rotating collections (p. 36). They preserve, store, and display artifacts from the organization, with great care in preserving its history. Their exhibits may tell part of the history of an industry or a community, but the focus is more on the organization's or the brand's contribution to that history.

Whether the museums are open to the public or only engage with certain invited stakeholders or potential customers, these structures may attract thousands to millions of visitors a year. The museums promote the brand and also tell stories about or portray the history of events related to industries or communities. They are often uniquely personal, connecting the story of the brand with the customer and his or her story, as well as nationalistic, such as narrating the story of a brand's or product's contribution to a war. A company's unique history and story of its founder can differentiate it from others like it, particularly if it builds on its own unique organizational identity as well as its history.

Corporate museums are vehicles for connecting with stakeholders, both internal and external (Castellani & Rossato, 2012). At times they bring the history of the stakeholders and the organization together. Museums also reinforce and build an organization's culture by disseminating its historic values through visual and, often, interactive media (Castellani & Rossato, 2012). In addition, corporate museums have also become virtual; their interactive displays are available through websites, and both internal customers such as new employees and external stakeholders can interact with the displays and the museum staff online through virtual tours (Castellani & Rossato, 2012) and virtual access to the organization's products and archives.

In an empirical study of 52 corporate museums in Italy, Castellani and Rossato (2012) found that museum staff stressed the importance of these venues for expressing their organizational identity and their history and indicated that this relationship impacted their image, reputation, and connections with the community. Based on their study, Castellani and Rossato (2012) recommended that organizations should use corporate museums and archives to strengthen their identity and could do this through making museums more interactive and have the museums demonstrate through their exhibits the passion for the vision of the organization or the products and convey their "future-oriented memory" (p. 240).

Time—Past, Present, and Future—and Emotion

Castellani and Rossato (2012) found that corporate museums reflect an organization's interest in all aspects of time—from preserving its history to influencing its current environment to building and strategizing for the future. They found that the museum staff they interviewed thought the museums influenced the "life of the company, including its image, its reputation, its placement, its loyalty-inducing potential, its market share, and the reciprocal sense of belonging for the company and the community" (p. 249). These museums highlighted "decisive passages in the history of the organization" (Castellani & Rossato, 2012, p. 243) and its identity. These museums recognized the "value of dialogue and engaging with internal and external members about these events because it strengthened the meaning at an affective level" (p. 243) and strengthened their "sense of belonging" in the organizations (Castellani & Rossato, 2012, p. 246).

Stories and Narratives of the Past

Stories or narratives of a past are increasingly important in organizational life and are an essential part of the organizational culture. They have been researched regarding their uniqueness across industries and organizations (Martin, Feldman, Hatch, & Sitkin, 1983), their significance in constructing the organization's present (Casey, 1997), and their communication of the heritage and legacy of a family business (Hitch, 2016; Tompkins & Casey, 2012). Organizational members tell stories of the history of the organization to support or refute current decisions and to aid in strategic planning. Which stories and events are chosen to be highlighted in a narrative reflect facets of the organization's identity. Research suggests that leaders and managers should carefully consider how to select and frame the stories of its organizational history and when it's appropriate or useful to tell them. What does the story say about the organization and whose past is being used for what purposes? Does the story reflect organizational identity claims and the meaning of these claims? Are some claims more frequently represented while others are neglected?

Organizational stories are a critical component of the museum displays. The events selected, why they are considered significant, and how the stories of the events are constructed often highlight organizational identity claims. Allen and Brown's (2016) work encourages practitioners to note the stories that are told in relationship to material objects, perhaps in a lobby or visitor center, and to be aware of and seek out conflicting views or stories. It is critical for leaders to be aware of and consider which voices are not being heard and what stories are not being told in the visitor centers and why. Other work (Berliner, 2005; Haukanes & Trnka, 2013; Nissley & Casey, 2002) suggests the importance of acknowledging multiple voices and the related meanings attributed to stories. This acknowledgment can inform the organization of the views of different stakeholders, internal and external, and help build connections across these groups. It can also inform leaders regarding the potential evolution of organizational identity claims as these claims surface in stories. Such an effort is particularly critical in multinational organizations and organizations whose products are marketed and consumed around the world (Rajan & Casey, 2015). The stories on websites are viewed and socially constructed through interactions of time (present, past, and future), individuals, and national cultures.

Problematizing Corporate Museums

Harris (1995) and others have problematized the relationship between the organization, its identity, its consumer or employee, and the organization's history. In reviewing the World of Coca-Cola, Harris noted that the organization objectifies "Coca-Cola as a worldwide power unifying the peoples of the earth in what may be the best-known commercial symbol" (p. 154); the firm concentrates on the narrative in a way that does not overwhelm visitors but engages them through selected short stories or components of their history. The company wants to ensure that the organization is seen as a major player in the world's top events and its photos are seen in every part of the world. Harris asserted that such a stance represents power and dominance in the social construction of the past versus free engagement with the past.

Selective recall of an organization's history and ways to tell the story about the chosen events are ongoing concerns of corporate museums. Research has demonstrated that an organization's identity guides what is displayed and how, when, and where it is displayed. For example, the Coos Bay Gallery is an essential part of the welcome for visitors at the Nike headquarters campus in Beaverton, Oregon. This gallery is a display of pictures of the founding—Nike's founders and the story of the founding—along with stories of significant events and exhibits related to current successes (Casey & Byington, 2013). Visitors are greeted and checked in through this gallery. The events selected and the constructed stories are chosen by organizational members to best represent the organization and its history, rather than portraying the breadth and diversity of stories that stakeholders might see as significant to the organization and its history.

Frequently the archivist or a public relations director chooses what events are displayed and how. For example, in 1999, DeSyon noted that at the Zeppelin Museum, the museum's historical record of the Zeppelin Company during 1933 to 1945 was very selective, and "there are clearly limits to propaganda flights carried out for the [nondemocratic] elections of March 1936, but it ignores the numerous other uses of the airship by Nazis and Zeppelin director, Hugo Eckener's, attempts to resist Nazi directives" (p. 118). As De Syon (1999) stated: "Zeppelin Museum certainly informs its visitors, but it does not challenge them. This, of course, raises the issue of whether a museum should be a temple to the past or a forum for discussion and debate" (p. 119).

Archives

Originally archives were developed to save memorabilia or products that showed how a product was made to assist with future product development. They were also focused more internally rather than on what should be saved to provide a connection with the external community. Now archives are created and saved to provide products or other artifacts that might provide a potential connection between the organization and its external community and stakeholders (Castellani & Rossato, 2012). Archives have become key components of marketing and public relations departments (Nissley & Casey, 2002). Dahlstrom (2005), in his role as reference archivist at the Deere and Company archives (created in 1976), noted one dilemma that surfaces in some archives. As Dahlstrom stated, the mission of the archives in 2005 was to "collect, preserve, and promote the heritage of Deere & Company," but the company also added a "statement of purpose—to leverage the heritage of Deere & Company" (p. 13). The Deere and Company archives were not open to the public at that time, with few exceptions.

In the study of Casey et al. (2003) of the collective memory and identity at corporate museums and archives, an employee noted that the archives "collect, preserve, and make available historical resources for external and internal clients. Human resources may ask for . . . memorabilia for new employee orientations; external clients may ask for memorabilia to support TV commercials or programs." He also noted that the archives can help protect the organization because they can document when and how company logos have been used as well as how products have been developed. Archives have also been used for defending company trademarks, for employee publications, and for answering consumer queries. Company archives are often intermingled with the community archives and the records for other companies. An important factor influencing the archives is frequently the longevity of employees. They are an important source of organizational memory, as long-term employees keep track of products and other memorabilia before the company hires its first archivist (Casey et al., 2003). Archivists note that "history is . . . something that sets them apart"—similar to organizational identity, which differentiates an organization in its industry.

Often archives are created by one or two individuals who see the need to preserve artifacts and documents related to the organization's history. For example, the Golden Archives was formed in 1987 with a one-person staff in the McDonald's Home Office headquarters in Illinois (Wizniuk, 2001). At Intel, the birth of the archives began when secretary Jean Jones began collecting products and documents in the 1970s. This grew to become the Intel Museum and archives, with more than 55,000 records and artifacts (Wizniuk, 2001). Both archives and related museums use the contents of the archives for marketing as well as product development.

One issue related to archives is limited space, which requires decisions about which artifacts are preserved and how they are used. Are items kept to support the development of the community or to support the corporate profits of the firm? The Guinness archive "collects, preserves and makes accessible records and artefacts from the formation of the company in 1759 to the present day" (www.guinness-storehouse.com/en/archives). The company notes on its website that "the Archive is a treasure chest of Guinness history, used by Guinness marketing communities around the world, economic and brewing historians, collectors, family history researchers and anyone with an interest in the Guinness Company and brand" (www.guinness-storehouse.com/en/archives). The archive was established in 1998 when the "company employed its first professional archivist to curate the company's history" (www.guinness-storehouse.com/en/archives).

Archives are the foundation of most corporate museums and visitor centers. The relationship between organizational identity and memory in the context of archives has not been researched. The relationship appears to be critical in making decisions about the process of how and what is collected or destroyed, similar to the research on corporate museums—i.e., what, why, and how memory is displayed or constructed is often based on organizational identity. Taking a critical approach to archives research, this relationship could also be explored from theories of power, dominance, and oppression (Nissley & Casey, 2002).

Anniversaries and Memorial Services

Anniversary celebrations and memorials are two events in organizations that also display the relationship between organizational identity and memory. Organizations are known to celebrate anniversaries such as the 50th or 100th year of their founding, a type of commemoration or remembering the past together. What events are commemorated, how they are related to the organization's founding, and how the story is told are key to the evolution of organizational identity from the perspective of both the labels for identity claims and their associated meanings. Some companies have two individuals who are considered founders, such as Bill Bowerman and Phil Knight at Nike. Their stories are told in the Coos Bay Gallery (Casey & Byington, 2013). The organizational identity claims such as athletes, innovation, relationships, and integrity are present in the events selected and the construction of the story.

Frequently for anniversary celebrations, organizations create books on their history. Some companies rely on public relations or marketing firms to create the text for the books or videos; other companies have a stronger focus on the discipline of history and incorporate principles and processes from that discipline. Once again, selecting which individuals and what events to highlight in these books is linked to the influence of organizational identity, i.e., who the organization was at various points in time and how that is related to who it is now.

These texts and other commemorative activities frequently relive the founding of the organization. In Casey and Byington's (2013) study, the organizational identity claims emerged in the stories of critical events in the organization, in particular the founding. These claims were key to which facts of the story were emphasized in addition to why they were recalled. The identity claims and their related meanings helped the organization sustain a sense of "who they are as an organization," in part because it commemorated events like the founding in anniversary celebrations and the routine day-to-day life in the organization. Its identity claims provided a broad, stable, yet flexible meaning foundation from which the organization grew, adapted, and prospered in a complex, changing diverse global environment. Whetten (2006) noted that founding events often serve as "institutional reminders of significant organizing choices" and "binding commitments" or "morals embedded in well-told stories of the defining moments of an organization's history" (p. 221).

Studies of Cadbury Corporation (Rowlinson, 2002; Rowlinson & Hassard, 1993) found that selected events of Cadbury's history were constructed to "create an identity aligned with their Quaker roots and values" (p. 92). This influence is also reciprocal, in that organizational commemoration and forgetting processes have the potential to shape the organizational identity (Rodgers, Petersen, & Sanderson, 2016). Schwartz (2005) asserted that the tension between historical facts and what is commemorated (such as in books created for an organization's anniversary) is important to the future identity and strategic actions of the organization. Schwartz and Schuman (2000) proposed that history and commemoration are interdependent in that "commemorative symbols mark the morally relevant zones of history—events reflecting our values and ideals most vividly—while historical accounts ground commemoration factually" (p. 2).

To help resolve this tension, organizations need to realize that commemoration can be sufficiently abstract (Wagner-Pacifici & Schwartz, 1991) so that groups with differing views in an organization or different stakeholders in an organization can "share the same commemorative space" (Rivera, 2008, p. 614). Schwartz (2000) noted that people not only recall the past but they identify with it; they become part of the past in creating the present and the future (Casey, 2010). These evolving interpretations of the past and the identity of the organization can serve as a foundation for organizational change at times and organizational stability at others (Casey, 2010).

Memorial services for key organizational members are also important in surfacing the relationship between identity and memory. Upon the death of founders and other key figures in organizations, Bell and Taylor (2016) suggested that organizational leaders be aware of how these individuals are memorialized in formal services as well as online; this type of commemoration and memorializing is controlled by power dynamics, often with the intention of preserving the identity of the brand and organization for the future. It is important for organizations to be cognizant of the relationship between organizational identity and memory and its impact on the memorializing and commemorative processes and to be mindful in their actions of including the perspectives of different subcultures or groups in the organization and incorporating them into the memorializing process. This connection has the potential to build organizational identification and commitment in the organization across groups.

Websites

Most organizational websites emphasize aspects of the organization's identity as well as its history. The organizational identity surfaces when the firm describes its essence or its values and what is most important to it as a social actor in society. Usually this description is under "about us" and is connected to a timeline or a link to the organization's history. Other identity features are on the front page of the website, where images or pictures represent what is most important to the organization.

There is no research on the relationship between organizational identity and memory in connection with websites or social media. Just as with corporate museums and commemorations, the organization needs to take into account critical events in its history and how the retelling or highlighting of these events can signify what is most key to the organization—i.e., its identity. For example, the Nike website in 2016 showed that the athletic shoe predominates and the organization is about innovation, performance, the athlete, and the community or relationships. The company's mission was also highlighted: to "bring inspiration and innovation to every athlete in the world—if you have a body, you are an athlete" (http://about.nike.com). This mission statement included several Nike identity claims—sports, athlete, innovation, and relationships—and it spotlighted a key piece of the company history, i.e., Coach Bowerman's iconic statement, "If you have a body, you are an athlete." Another tab from their "About Us" section was the company profile statement: "NIKE, Inc. fosters a culture of invention. We create products, services and experiences for today's athlete while solving problems for the next generation." The identity claims of the organization focused on athletes/sport, innovation, and connecting through solving problems for the next generation of athletes. On its website at one time, Nike also had a link for the history and identity of one of its few acquisitions, Converse.

Major Transitions in Organizations

The relationship between organizational identity and memory is key during major organizational changes or initiatives such as an acquisition of or merger with another organization. This relationship may surface when employees are told about critical events in the history of the organization that is acquiring them and then use this information to help make sense of the organizational identity of that organization.

In museums and visitor centers, it's important to remain sensitive to the multiple versions of the acquisition story and the meanings attributed to the acquisition by organizational members of both the acquiree and the acquired. In addition, organizations need to decide which organization's history will be preserved and how it will be displayed. How will events from the past be commemorated in both organizations? Will the organizational identity of the acquired organization be sustained, and will it influence the stories that are told and how they are retold? Will these stories of the past emphasize elements of the organizational identity claims of the acquiring organization to make sense of the past?

As the literature has noted, there are debates about the nature of this multivocal relationship between memory and identity (Gabel, 2013; Haas & Levasseur, 2013). Managers and those who create commemorative spaces in organizations need to be aware of the multiple voices with different perspectives and offer space and time for the voices with multiple stories to be told. What physical space will these stories occupy in relationship to each other in a display, and what affect or emotions will be emphasized?

The connection between organizational identity and memory needs to be considered in relationships with internal stakeholders as well as external stakeholders. Today, employees experience frequent job transitions into and throughout the organization, and differences exist among employees from different generations or age cohorts. Where before there may have been large cohorts of employees hired at the same time with a common recollection and interpretation of a critical past event, now it's possible that the events were experienced by only a small number of existing employees. Hewer and Roberts's (2012) work noted generational differences in how events are perceived and the potential relationships of these events to them as individuals. Linde's (2000) work on the nonparticipant narrative indicates the critical importance of individuals assuming the organizational story as their own even if they didn't experience the events.

In all cases, providing opportunities for interaction of different employee groups in organizations during these events or in the recollection of these events is important so as to surface and incorporate the multivocal meanings. Meaning creation is a social process (Melchior & Visser, 2011). Linde proposed that the process of narrative induction is how collective memory emerges and evolves over time through the interaction of individuals. She suggested that nonparticipant narratives or stories told by individuals who were not part of an event are used to "reproduce collective memory and induct new participants into this memory" (Linde, 2000, p. 608).

References

Allen, M., & Brown, S. D. (2016). Memorial meshwork: The making of the commemorative space of the Hyde Park 7/7 Memorial. *Organization, 23*(1), 10–28. https://doi.org/10.1177/1350508415605103.

Bell, E., & Taylor, S. (2016). Vernacular mourning and corporate memorialization in framing the death of Steve Jobs. *Organization, 23*(1), 114–132. https://doi.org/10.1177/1350508415605109.

Berliner, D. (2005). The abuses of memory: Reflections on the memory boom in anthropology. *Anthropological Quarterly, 78*(1), 197–211. https://doi.org/10.1353/anq.2005.0001.

Bonti, M. (2014). The corporate museums and their social function: Some evidence from Italy. *European Scientific Journal, 1*, 141–150.

Casey, A. (1997). Collective memory in organizations. In P. Shrivastava, A. Huff, & J. Dutton (Series Eds.), J. Walsh & A. Huff (Vol. Eds.), *Organizational learning and strategic management* (Advances in Strategic Management, Vol. 14, pp. 111–151). Greenwich, CT: JAI Press.

Casey, A. (2010). *The role of collective memory in organizational identity*. Presented at the annual conference of the Academy of Management, Montreal, Quebec, Canada.

Casey, A., & Byington, L. (2013). *Nike: A case study of identity claims in a complex global world*. Presented at the annual conference of the Academy of Management, Lake Buena Vista, FL. https://doi.org/10.5465/ambpp.2013.12456abstract.

Casey, A., Byington, L., & Nissley, N. (2003). *Corporate museums: The politics of exhibiting organizational memory, identity and image*. Presentation at the annual meeting of the Academy of Management, Seattle, WA.

Castellani, P., & Rossato, C. (2012). On the communication value of the company museum and archives. *Journal of Communication Management, 18*(3), 240–253. https://doi.org/10.1108/JCOM-02-2012-0018.

Dahlstrom, N. (2005). Perceptions and realities: Dilemmas of a corporate historian. *Historical News, 60*(4), 12–15.

Danilov, V. J. (1991). *Corporate museums, galleries and visitor centers: A directory*. Westport, CT: Greenwood.

De Syon, G. (1999). The Zeppelin Museum in Friedrichshafen. *Technology and Culture, 40*(1), 114–119. https://doi.org/10.1353/tech.1999.0052.

Gabel, I. (2013). Historical memory and collective identity: West Bank settlers reconstruct the past. Engaging in illegal acts is accepted. *Media Culture & Society, 35*(2), 250–259. https://doi.org/10.1177/0163443712467592.

Haas, V., & Levasseur, E. (2013). Rumour as a symptom of collective forgetfulness. *Culture and Psychology, 19*(1), 60–75. https://doi.org/10.1177/1354067X12464986.

Harris, N. (1995). The World of Coca-Cola. *The Journal of American History, 82*(1), 154–158. https://doi.org/10.2307/2081923.

Haukanes, H., & Trnka, S. (2013). Memory, imagination, and belonging across generations: Perspectives from postsocialist Europe and beyond. *Focaal—Journal of Global and Historical Anthropology, 66*, 3–13.

Hewer, C. J., & Roberts, R. (2012). History, culture and cognition: Towards a dynamic model of social memory. *Culture and Psychology, 18*(2), 167–183. https://doi.org/10.1177/1354067X11434836.

Hitch, S. A. (2016). *Once upon a time: A case study identifying and analyzing the stories shared in the collective memory of a family-owned business.* Unpublished dissertation, The George Washington University, Washington, DC.

Linde, C. (2000). The acquisition of a speaker by a story: How history becomes memory and identity. *Ethos (Berkeley, Calif.), 28*(4), 608–632. https://doi.org/10.1525/eth.2000.28.4.608.

Livingstone, P. (2011, Spring). Is it a museum experience? Corporate exhibitions for cultural tourists. *Exhibitionist,* 16–21. Retrieved from https://static1.squarespace.com/static/58fa260a725e25c4f30020f3/t/594ba04317bffc5292a023a2/1498128504903/6+EXH_spg11_Is+It+a+Museum+Experience_Corporate+Exhibitions+for+Cultural+Tourists_Livingstone.pdf

Martin, J., Feldman, M. S., Hatch, M. J., & Sitkin, S. B. (1983). The uniqueness paradox in organizational stories. *Administrative Science Quarterly, 28*(3), 438–453. https://doi.org/10.2307/2392251.

McKay, B. (2007, May 21). More pop for corporate museums. Coke's exhibit leads to trend of bigger, flashier, costlier. *Wall Street Journal.* Retrieved from www.wsj.com/articles/SB117970733999609067

Melchior, I., & Visser, O. (2011). Voicing past and present uncertainties: The relocation of a Soviet World War II memorial and the politics of memory in Estonia. *Journal of Global and Historical Anthropology, 59,* 33–50.

Nissley, N., & Casey, A. (2002). The politics of the exhibition: Viewing corporate museums through the paradigmatic lens of organizational memory. *British Journal of Management, 13*(S2), S35–S44. https://doi.org/10.1111/1467-8551.13.s2.4.

Rajan, H. C., & Casey, A. (2015). "Who are we as an organization?" Organizational identity in a multinational company's subsidiary. *Academy of Management Annual Meeting Proceedings, 2015*(1), 15502–15502.

Rivera, L. A. (2008). Managing spoiled national identity: War, tourism, and memory in Croatia. *American Sociological Review, 73*(4), 613–634. https://doi.org/10.1177/000312240807300405.

Rodgers, D. M., Petersen, J., & Sanderson, J. (2016). Commemorating alternative organizations and marginalized spaces: The case of forgotten Finntowns. *Organizations, 23*(1), 90–113. doi: 10.1177/1350508415605110.

Rowlinson, M. (2002). Public history review essay: Cadbury World. *Labour Review, 67*(1), 101–119.

Rowlinson, M., & Hassard, J. (1993). The invention of corporate culture: A history of the histories of Cadbury. *Human Relations, 46,* 299–326.

Schwartz, B. (2000). *Abraham Lincoln and the forge of national memory.* Chicago, IL: University of Chicago Press.

Schwartz, B. (2005). The new Gettysburg Address: Fusing history and memory. *Poetics, 33*(1), 63–79. https://doi.org/10.1016/j.poetic.2005.01.003.

Schwartz, B., & Schuman, H. (2000). The meanings of collective memory. *Newsletter of the Sociology of Culture Section, American Sociological Association, 14,* 1–3.

Seligson, J. (2010, November-December). Corporate culture? One part education, one part sales: This is the corporate museum. *Museum,* 34–41. Retrieved from www.wiu.edu/cas/history/pdf/Corporate-Museums.pdf

Stigliani, I., & Ravasi, D. (2007). Organizational artefacts and the expression of identity in corporate museums at Alfa-Romeo, Kartell, and Piaggio. In L. Lerpold, D. Ravsi, J. van Rekom, & G. Soenen (Eds.), *Organizational identity in practice* (Chap. 11). London, UK: Routledge.

Tompkins, R., & Casey, A. (2012). *Family ownership: 'Governor' of the hybrid organization's identity*. Presented at the annual meeting of the Academy of Management, Boston, MA.

Wagner-Pacifici, R., & Schwartz, B. (1991). The Vietnam Veterans Memorial: Commemorating a difficult past. *American Journal of Sociology, 97*, 376–420.

Whetten, D. A. (2006). Albert and Whetten revisited: Strengthening the concept of organizational identity. *Journal of Management Inquiry, 15*(3), 219–234. https://doi.org/10.1177/1056492606291200.

Wizniuk, A. (2001, Winter). Documenting corporate history: Thriving or barely surviving. *Historical News, 56*(1), 13–18.

Index

For Product Safety Concerns and Information please contact our EU
representative GPSR@taylorandfrancis.com Taylor & Francis Verlag GmbH,
Kaufingerstraße 24, 80331 München, Germany

Printed and bound by CPI Group (UK) Ltd, Croydon, CR0 4YY

01/05/2025

01858422-0003